早期儿童英语
游戏、理念和活动

【英】吉尔·科尔森
【英】琳恩·考辛斯◎著
Gill Coulson
Lynn Cousins

陈东岚◎译

Games, Ideas and Activities
for Early Years Literacy

华东师范大学出版社
·上海·

Pearson

图书在版编目(CIP)数据

早期儿童英语游戏、理念和活动/(英)吉尔·科尔森,(英)琳恩·考辛斯著;陈东岚译.—上海:华东师范大学出版社,2021

ISBN 978 - 7 - 5760 - 2215 - 5

Ⅰ.①早… Ⅱ.①吉…②琳…③陈… Ⅲ.①英语课-教学研究-学前教育 Ⅳ.①G613.2

中国版本图书馆 CIP 数据核字(2021)第 217400 号

Classroom Gems:*Games*,*Ideas and Activities for Early Years Literacy*
by Lynn Cousins & Gill Coulson
© Pearson Education Limited 2011

This Bilingual Edition of **Classroom Gems**:**Games**,**Ideas and Activities for Early Years Literacy**, published by arrangement with Pearson Education Limited, copyright © East China Normal University Press Ltd.,2021

本书译自 Pearson Education Limited 2011 年出版的 *Classroom Gems*:*Games*,*Ideas and Activities for Early Years Literacy* by Lynn Cousins & Gill Coulson。

双语版 © 华东师范大学出版社有限公司,2021。

上海市版权局著作权合同登记 图字:09 - 2019 - 473 号

早期儿童英语游戏、理念和活动

著　　者　吉尔·科尔森　琳恩·考辛斯
译　　者　陈东岚
责任编辑　蒋　将
责任校对　时东明
装帧设计　卢晓红

出版发行　**华东师范大学出版社**
社　　址　上海市中山北路3663号　邮编 200062
网　　址　www.ecnupress.com.cn
电　　话　021 - 60821666　行政传真 021 - 62572105
客服电话　021 - 62865537　门市(邮购)电话 021 - 62869887
地　　址　上海市中山北路 3663 号华东师范大学校内先锋路口
网　　店　http://hdsdcbs.tmall.com

印 刷 者　上海雅昌艺术印刷有限公司
开　　本　787×1092　16 开
印　　张　42.25
字　　数　919 千字
版　　次　2021 年 12 月第 1 版
印　　次　2021 年 12 月第 1 次
书　　号　ISBN 978 - 7 - 5760 - 2215 - 5
定　　价　125.00 元

出 版 人　王　焰

关于作者

　　吉尔·科尔森和琳恩·考辛斯是两位有着丰富教学经验的小学老师，主要集中在早期教育阶段和基础阶段一（即英国小学一、二年级）。吉尔和琳恩曾在一所媲美英国"灯塔奖"*地位的幼儿园分别担任副园长和园长职位。

　　她们在自己的教学职业生涯中继续深耕：吉尔获得了哲学硕士学位，主修阅读教学；琳恩获得了教育硕士学位，主修幼儿早期教育。

　　毕业离开深造的大学后，琳恩成为了一家教育出版社的编辑，同时是教育专题的自由撰稿人。她已出版了许多专著，并且参与编写英国菲尔德教育集团的国际小学课程教材。

　　吉尔在教育生涯中始终保持对儿童文学研究的极大热情，用儿童文学作品激发课堂教学，帮助儿童学会阅读和撰写自己的作品。她目前在英国白金汉郡米尔顿·凯恩斯多所学校开展写作教学。

　　早前，吉尔和琳恩已合著出版了课堂宝典系列丛书中的《幼儿自然拼读》，而且琳恩已完成基础指导系列丛书中的《早期儿童行为塑造》一书。

※　英国教育界三大荣誉奖项之一的英国政府"灯塔奖"（Beacon Awards）。——译者注。

编写说明

    2021 年 3 月，新版《早期教育阶段实施框架》（Statutory Framework for the Early Years Foundation Stage，以下简称新版 EYFS 框架）首次推出，随后作为落地配套的指导性文件《发展很重要》（Development Matter）也是历经几稿后于 2021 年 7 月正式执行。 2021 年 9 月，新版 EYFS 框架在英国正式生效。是否新版本发布后，旧版本就失效了呢？ 新旧版本的关系是怎样的？

    英国早期教育这次对于 EYFS 框架的修订完全是基于 EYFS 在全球逐渐普及发展的需求，旨在让 EYFS 教育体系在实践中能更多适用全球非英语体系国家的幼儿。因此，针对母语非英语的儿童，无论是新版 EYFS 框架还是新版《发展很重要》，最大的变化都是在支持英语作为第二语言的学习方面将提供更为详尽的指导。身体发展 (Physical Development)，个性、社会性与情感发展（Personal, Social and Emotional Development），交流与语言发展（Communication and Language），数学（Mathematics），读写能力 (Literacy) 等仍是新版 EYFS 框架的基础领域和核心领域，新旧版本在早期儿童学习发展领域上的底层逻辑是保持延续性的。因此，反倒是一直在一线打磨这两个领域教学策略的本书显得更为弥足珍贵。老师家长们可以更好地利用本书进行两个版本的新旧对比，并将新版的内容融合，将有助于探索非母语孩子的英语语言学习的发展。基于上述思考和认识，我们基于新版的改革趋势和理念重新审视了全书内容，并争取到了双语版的授权，希望读者们在汉英对照的语境中，原汁原味地收获 EYFS 的教育真谛。

引言

本书将提供丰富的资源来促进教师在早期教育体系（Early Years Foundation Stage，以下简称 EYFS）中关于"沟通、语言和读写"（Communication, Language and Literacy，以下简称 CLL）领域能力的教学。

结合不同领域的学习被认为是幼儿早期教学的一个良好手段。这种关联教学可以帮助儿童去感知他们的世界和他们的学习，同时提供机会去强化他们的技能。因此，虽然我们已经把这些读写活动分为三个单独的部分——说、读和写，但是很明显在任何一个读写活动中都融入了这三种读写能力的要素。举例来说，无论何时儿童在写的时候，也需要去读懂他们所写的内容，同时一个孩子无论何时在对另一个人讲话的时候，也是在倾听。读写能力的相互依存性是永远存在的，你可以把每一个活动中的某一个部分（说、读和写）放大地来看，也可以改进并侧重读写能力的其他方面。

这本书以 CLL 领域的学习——说、读和写依次分三个部分展开，且每个部分细分三个板块组成，具体如下：

说

包括用来交流的语言和用来思考的语言。

• **分享观点**：鼓励儿童参与对话，边听别人的话边参与讨论，按照一定的秩序，同时尊重别人的观点。

• **说出我的意思**：帮助儿童通过发展他们的沟通词汇，运用更精准的语言，来表达他们的思考和想法。

• **记忆、反思和复述**：在儿童认真聆听的时候，帮助他们记住事件的细节和顺序，思考他们听到的内容，反思一些重要细节。

读

以阅读为主。

在我们《课堂经典系列：早期教育语音教学》一书中，你还可以找到 250 多个*链接声音和字母*的活动。

• **书的世界**：向儿童介绍书的作用，引入一些想法去建构儿童阅读区，以一种具有想象力的方式去营造吸引人和受欢迎的环境。

- **发现**：引导孩子去关注打印的文字，如周围的海报和标语和一些非小说类书籍，如说明书或者菜谱，同时学习去识别一些常用的词汇。

- **欣赏故事和童谣**：帮助儿童识别一个好故事的要素，通过活动当分享一些出版的经典文学作品，这些作品基本都是耳熟能详的故事和童谣。

写

包括写作和书写。

- **手指游戏**：找到有趣的方式去锻炼精细动作，为书写做准备，同时提供接触字母形状的机会。

- **把它写下来**：这些活动贯穿于整个课程体系的所有领域，这将帮助儿童了解记录信息的重要性。

- **制作一本书**：写下你的想法——事实性的或创造性的——以有序的方式去制作任一形状和大小的书籍供大家阅读。

"读写能力应当是课程计划的核心。"

——英国皇冠出版社 2006 年版，《小学读写与数学概论》（国家小学教育战略），第 20 页。

这些精心设计的活动，融入幼儿生活环境中的每一天，所以这些活动很自然地含在课程计划中。课程计划中的想法有：使用角色扮演区，拓展这个世界，创造艺术作品和展板以及学习如何去交朋友。活动特别强调的是实践参与性，而且许多活动会把孩子带到室外，这符合早期教育体系（EYFS）推荐的方法。还有一些想法是创造有趣的场景来对话，还有许多活动是提供机会做出评估。

在每一个部分，我们会建议使用故事书、诗歌或者童谣去激发儿童自己阅读、写作和谈话。给孩子们大声朗读故事本身就是一种很有价值的体验，不仅分享了朗读的乐趣，而且展示了童谣中规范语言的结构，拓展儿童的词汇量。

每一个活动本身是独立的，所以你可以根据自己教学计划的需要进行选择。虽然我们建议其他的课程领域可以与此活动建立关联，但是这些想法都是灵活的，你可以根据自己的计划将其改用到其他主题中。这些活动可以运用在不同能力的培养上。你也会发现许多活动适合个别化学习，因此理想状态下，这些活动的使用可以帮助那些需要额外练习的孩子，或有机会拓展自己的孩子。

每一个活动的页面有清晰的标题，体例的设计方便读者使用。

标题：有许多活动围绕一个主题或者基于同一本绘本，我们将这些活动标上（1）这样的数字，这样可以根据你的需要结合使用这些活动。

一个"蓝色底纹框"加左上角"心形"标志*：在每个活动的标题下方，我们简要地介绍和

---

* 此处本书按中文版的版式标注。英文原版版式为"回形针"标志，如第 317 页所提 "paper-clipped note"

解释了这个活动，这样可以帮助你找到符合你要求的活动。

目标：活动的目标直接来自早期教育体系（EYFS）"沟通、语言和读写"领域的要求。这是基于四个大类的任何一项（发展中的问题，看、听和记，有效的练习，或是制定计划和资源）。因此这些活动可以便捷地运用在你的教学计划中。

教学资源：我们罗列了所有需要的资源。

教学准备：所有你需要提前准备的事情，我们都会在这里指出。

怎么做：我们将一步一步地指导这些活动，包括提供一些想法和例子来帮助忙碌的参与者。

词汇：通过这些活动，我们将清晰地解释新的或不熟悉的词汇。

小贴士：一份便捷小贴士会提供额外的建设性建议，来确保顺利地开展这个活动，或建议这个活动可以拓展或改动的方法。

跨领域链接：这部分提醒参与者，这个活动与早期教育体系（EYFS）中六个学习领域能力相匹配的一方面，从而最大程度上被运用于你的教学准备。

儿童在沟通、听说、被动阅读和主动阅读以及写这些方面的学习和能力必须得到支持和拓展。我们应当给予儿童机会和鼓励儿童在不同的环境和目的下去运用他们的技能，提高儿童的自信心和主动性。

——英国皇冠出版社 2008 年版《幼儿早期教育体系的实践指导》，第 41 页。

幼儿在玩中学，而且他们喜欢正在做的事情而且明白学习的目的是非常重要的。在这本书中，你会发现很多基于玩中学的活动会促进幼儿发展沟通和读写能力。

译者序

幼儿教育，一项任重而道远的工作，欣然已逐步得到了社会、学校和家庭越来越多的关注。但是，到底怎样的幼儿教育才是最好的？幼儿是否越早学习语数外越好呢？如何让幼儿高效地接受学习呢？这也许是学校、教师和家长共同面临的话题。幼儿教学表面看似简单，和孩子玩玩闹闹，实则远没有我们想象的那么简单。

本书是英国著名的培生出版社的"课堂宝典"系列丛书之一，以英国早期教育体系（EYFS）为大纲，立足"沟通、交流和读写"领域能力①的培养，由幼教经验丰富的作者执笔，共设计了 153 个实用教案。译者从一个语言教学工作者的角度，边译边学，感触颇深，特此与大家分享：

1. 全部活动目标明确：以早期教育体系中"沟通、语言和读写"学习领域能力为目标；布局清楚：3 大板块，9 个主题，每个活动链接学习领域的 6 个方面；层层递进：从说—读—写依次展开，这三个幼儿读写能力的发展中各领域既相互独立又相互依存，最终实现较为完整的幼儿早期读写能力培养计划，专业可信。

2. 每个活动从宏观目标的实现到微观材料的准备，步骤讲解细致，注意事项考虑周到，并提出或拓展或削减等各项因材施教的贴心提示。无论是教师还是家长，无论在课堂还是家庭，几乎都可以保证顺利地将活动开展起来，实属不易。

3. 绘本是贯穿本书大部分活动的一个重要资源，作者也将绘本教学的优势充分发挥，从不同角度多次开发，实现不同的教学目标。即便书中的教育对象为英语母语使用者，但笔者认为，推荐的活动可用于外语学习者和汉语母语的使用者同时借鉴，值得考量。

4. 以"玩中学"的理念出发，全书 153 个活动充满了奇思妙想和大胆尝试，作为成人的译者本人有时也觉得大开眼界，受益无穷。活动以游戏为载体，以语言能力的获得为目的，但儿童在活动过程中的收获不限于此，还有社交、对世界和自我的认知、身体发展、计算、艺术和创造力等各个领域的发展，意义深远。

5. 授之以渔，而非鱼。诚然，本书既是一本教案汇总，又是一本很好的教研型参考书。读者可以仔细品味作者通过一个个绘本展开的一系列教学设计，一定能学习到许多经验和独到之处，自然能带给自己的绘本教学方案以崭新的开拓和指导。

---

① 本书中关于英国早期教育体系（EYFS）中的领域教育目标等等的译法，均参考中国民办教育协会 2018 年在其官网上发布的《英国早期教育体系 EYFS 介绍》。

不可否认，这是一本优秀的促进幼儿读写能力教育的指导宝典，但译者还有几点提醒读者使用的注意事项：

　　1. 最好的教育方式还是应该因材施教，读者根据实际情况，有选择性使用和改进，这样也许能有很有效的收获。

　　2. 书中提到的所有绘本，因为翻译版权问题，使用中文表述，请读者在搜索英语绘本时，务必仔细核查。

　　最后，译者在此向华东师范大学出版社对我的信任和帮助表达衷心的感谢。本人翻译不当和研究不准确之处，还请各位专家、学者以及广大读者不吝指出，共同探讨，不胜感激！

陈东岚

2020 年春

目录

第一部分：说

第二部分：读

第三部分：写

Contents

Part 3　Writing

第一部分

说

听说能力对儿童的学习和语言全面发展具有重要意义，因此，非常有必要在课堂讲授听说技能的基础上分配时间让儿童去复习、使用并扩展这些技能。

——英国皇冠出版社 2006 年版《小学读写与数学概论》，第 17 页。

随着儿童不断发展自己的听说能力，他们也在为识字、视觉与语言符号理解并最终为读写能力打下基础。

——英国皇冠出版社 2008 年版《早期基础阶段实践导引》，第 41 页。

第一章

分享想法

介绍"圆圈时间"

 · 鼓励孩子们提出想法实现"圆圈时间"的成功。

教学目标
- 帮助孩子们在群体中展示恰当的日常规范。

教学资源
一件小物品，例如一个发亮且光滑的贝壳或一块小石头。这些物品的大小以孩子们可以用手握住为宜。

教学准备
- 安静地坐在一起。

怎么做
- 向孩子们解释，大家将要在一起分享自己的想法。要求每一个人应当能够看到和听到别人说话。让孩子们决定最好的围坐方式以便于他们都可以做到。让孩子们提出他们自己的建议。
- 当围坐的建议被采纳后，要求孩子们安静地移动，直到每个人都这样坐好。询问他们："大家都能看到别人吗？"然后告知他们，当我们以这样的方式坐在一起的时候就叫做"圆圈时间"。
- 向孩子们解释，他们在"圆圈时间"时，必须遵守一些规则，这样每个人有机会发言，每个人应当认真聆听。鼓励孩子们提出一些规则。
- 当孩子们提出建议时，你应当用积极肯定的方式再强调一遍。例如：如果一个孩子说："我们不许大叫。"你可以说："那么我们应该怎么做呢？""我们必须小声地但清楚地发言，要让大家都能听见。"
- 把建议整合一下，例如：每次发言讲一件事情，互相聆听，礼貌待人，等等。
- 把你准备好的小物品展示给孩子们看，然后告诉他们，这将是一个帮助他们记住一次讲一件事情的规则的方法。拿着这个物品的人是唯一一个可以发言的人。他们必须依次把物品传递下去。
- 练习使用这个小物品。你开个头，说"我的名字是……"然后把物品传给圆圈里的下一个孩子。当这个物品又传回到你手里，你可以开始讲一个新的句型。
- 这样你可以组织孩子们开展其他的"圆圈时间"的活动了。

词汇

听、依次、清楚地讲、有礼貌的。

小贴士

一些常用的开头句型:

当……时,我喜欢它。

当……时,我很伤心。

我最喜欢的食物是……

我的朋友×××很特别,是因为……

跨领域链接

个人、社会和情感的发展:气质和态度。

花园中心（1）

• 计划和制作一些模型植物在你的花园中心出售。

教学目标
• 让孩子们思考他们将如何完成一项任务，讨论各个阶段的流程。

教学资源
1）选择生长不同阶段的幼苗或植物； 2）用橡皮泥或面团（做泥土）填充的小花盆；3）若干绿色的吸管和绿色的纸（做茎和叶）； 4）若干彩色纸（做花朵）； 5）若干可食种子（做花的种子）。

教学准备
• 孩子们在数周内种植和照料种子，这样他们能够意识到植物生长的各个阶段。

怎么做
• 讨论孩子们种植植物的生长模式。他们还记得各个阶段的顺序吗？例如：

一盆埋着种子的土；

一个小嫩芽从土里冒出来；

一棵有叶子的幼苗；

一棵有花苞的植物；

一棵有种子形成的植物。

• 向孩子们解释，他们要制作一些植物模型在他们的商店出售。谈一谈每个孩子想做哪个阶段的植物模型。是幼苗还是有花苞的模型呢？
• 向孩子们展示你收集到的所有制作材料。识别这些材料，问问他们每一种材料的用途。
• 让孩子们告诉你，他们可能会用什么来制造自己的一组植物吗？他们先做什么吗？
• 让孩子们制作自己的植物。在他们制作过程中，问问他们正在做什么，为什么要做以及他们下一步要做什么。

词汇
首先、下一步、之后、接着、最后。

小贴士　　　如果可能的话，根据植物生长的不同阶段，提供一些真实的植物，可以提醒孩子们植物发生了什么变化。

跨领域链接

认识与理解世界：探索与观察。

跟着领队走

• 孩子们组织他们自己的游行，决定服装和器械，并规划每个人的位置。

教学目标

• 帮助孩子们讨论和规划他们的角色。

教学资源

1）装扮的衣服，包括帽子、珠子和围巾等； 2）乐器，例如：沙锤和铃鼓。

教学准备

• 练习跟着领队走——不穿演出服。

• 确保所有的孩子都知道该做什么，鼓励他们注意领队，并且模仿他们所做的，包括音效和不同的动作。

• 孩子们可以轮流做一会儿领队。

怎么做

• 把装有衣服、配饰和乐器的箱子放在外面，这样孩子们就可以自己穿上演出服，选择一种乐器。

• 选一个孩子做游行的领队，然后确定排在后面的成员顺序。

  – 观察一下孩子们的着装。你希望所有的公主都排列在一起吗？

  – 孩子们可以决定是否使用乐器，他们是否唱歌，或者是不是一场非常安静的游行。

  – 乐器是否引导游行？

• 带着你的游行队伍在整个场地上走走。

• 保留好教学资源，以备孩子们之后使用。

词汇

首先、在前面、在后面、旁边。

小贴士　　你可能需要限制游行占用的空间，以便其他孩子可以安全地使用其他设备。

跨领域链接

身体的发展：运动和空间。

在诊所

· 思考在医生的诊室中适当地谈话。

教学目标

· 鼓励孩子们依次排序，倾听他人的意见，并使用适当的符合惯例的表达方式。

教学资源

角色扮演区设置为外科医生的诊室。

怎么做

· 与一小群孩子谈论他们将在本课程中扮演的角色——患者、接待员、护士和医生。帮助孩子们穿上适合各个角色的衣服。

· 解释病人的腿受伤了，需要去看医生。让他们想想：

病人的腿是如何受伤的？

医生需要问病人什么？

接待员可能会对病人说些什么？

护士将如何帮助医生？

给孩子们时间去计划他们会说些什么，并且如何说。

· 在一个腿受伤的病人来到诊所后，孩子们要演出这个情节，例如：

接待员问候病人并让他坐下，然后告诉医生，病人已经到了。

护士帮助病人走到医生跟前，医生询问病人腿是怎么受伤的。

病人解释受伤原因，然后医生检查腿部，并询问问题，从而找到疼痛的地方。

医生让护士传递治疗所需的物品，然后告诉病人什么时候需要复诊。

在病人离开之前，接待员做了一个新的预约。

词汇

请，谢谢，我可以做……吗？你怎么会……呢？在哪里……？

小贴士　　　当孩子们第一次参与这个活动时，大人不妨选择其中的一个角色来做个对话的样板。

跨领域链接

创造力的发展：想象力和想象性游戏。

玛格丽特 · 梅奥 《紧急情况!》（1）

· 欣赏一本有很多令人兴奋和有趣的描述性语言的书。

教学目标

· 拓展孩子们的词汇量。

教学资源

1）《紧急情况！》（玛格丽特 · 梅奥. 伦敦：果园出版社，2003.）；2）书中提到的一些急救车辆。

教学准备

· 和孩子们阅读这本书。

怎么做

· 围坐在一起，把各种急救车辆放在中间。当你阅读这本书的每一页时，选择一个孩子指向那一页上提到的车辆。当这个孩子回到他在圈里的位置时，每个人都可以重复这句话："救援来了，就在路上。"

· 当你读完这本书时，所有的车辆都被确认了，告诉孩子们，这次你只读出描述紧急情况的文字，孩子们必须记住哪种车辆来帮忙，例如："紧急情况！高速公路上的交通量增加了，谁能帮忙？"

· 选择一个知道答案的孩子来挑选车辆，当你读到车辆移动的描述时，例如：
"呜——！警用摩托车快速移动，小轿车开路。"

· 孩子把这些车辆放回到圈内前，他可以重复这句话："救援来了，就在路上。"

· 最后，告诉孩子们这次你将描述这种车辆正在做什么，然后请孩子们猜一猜，这是什么车。读一读书中描写急救车辆声音和动作的语句。例如：
"在路上急速开来，猛冲，猛冲，猛冲过来，接着抽水。"
大家可以猜到什么车吗？

· 当你再次阅读相关页面的时候，正确识别出车辆的孩子可以将这些车辆移动到内圈。

· 把这些玩具车辆放在游戏垫上，这样孩子们在自由活动时间可以演出这些紧急场景。

词汇

警车、抢修车、救护车、直升机、铲雪车、救生艇、充气艇、警用摩托车、消防飞机、消防车、吊车。

小贴士　　　孩子们可能喜欢在室外想象各种紧急情况，演出救援场景。你可以大声叫出紧急情况，孩子们假装开着或驾驶着交通工具来救援。

跨领域链接

个人、社会和情感的发展：团队意识。

婚礼（1）

· 为你的泰迪熊组织一场婚礼，鼓励孩子们解释他们的选择。

教学目标

· 帮助孩子们扩展他们所说的内容。

教学资源

1）一些婚礼上的照片；2）一些泰迪熊和娃娃；3）娃娃的衣服和其他物品，例如照相机、鲜花、面纱和书。

怎么做

· 有孩子参加过婚礼吗？鼓励他们谈谈自己的经历。

· 观察一些照片，辨认新娘等人。谈论其他参与的人，例如登记员（或其他人员），摄影师。

· 分享经历，直到每个人都对发生的事情有一个简单的了解。

· 让孩子们选择一对将要结婚的泰迪熊，选择将扮演其他角色的玩偶。让孩子们解释他们的选择。

· 给孩子们展示可供选择的衣服。让孩子们选择每个泰迪玩具应该穿什么，鼓励他们商讨。让他们为婚礼准备好玩具。

· 腾出一个可以举行婚礼的地方，然后把场景表演出来。

词汇

新娘、新郎、伴娘、客人、登记员、摄影师、衣服、夹克、领带、面纱、鲜花、照相机。

小贴士　　对不同文化体验要敏感。

跨领域链接

个人、社会和情感的发展：团队意识。

选择和分类

• 孩子们喜欢把物品和可能性的描述匹配起来。

教学目标
• 通过分组和命名来扩展孩子们的词汇量。

教学资源
1）一些大号纸盘子； 2）房间里摆放一些孩子们可以拿到的小物品； 3）几个圆环；
4）一些可以做标签的纸张。

教学准备
• 制作一组标签，每个标签都带有一个描述性的词，例如：闪亮的、光滑的、坚硬的。
• 给每个孩子一个纸盘，让他们从房间里收集十件小物件。它们的大小都应该适合放在纸盘上。

怎么做
• 当孩子们有十件物品时，他们应该坐成一个圆圈，纸盘子就放在他们前面的地板上。
• 在围坐的圆圈中间放一个圆环。把手伸进你的标签堆里，随机挑选一个。可以让每一个孩子把手伸进装满做好标签的容器里（去挑选）。
• 把挑出的标签放在圆环里，告诉孩子你正在找……样的东西，比如闪亮的。
• 绕着圆圈依次问每个孩子："你有什么闪亮的东西可以放在圆环里吗？"
• 每个孩子依次查看自己拿到的物品，进行选择。
• 随着游戏进行，孩子们可能开始希望自己已经保留了红色易碎的玩具，可以符合"易碎的"这个词的选择，他们也希望有几个红色的物品，可以选择来符合"红色"这个词。但没人知道标签上会是什么词。
• 如果你在第二天再玩这个游戏，孩子们将选择更多的物品吗？

词汇
任何描述性词汇，例如：闪亮的、光滑的、坚硬的、柔软的、圆的、红的（其他颜色）、长的、瘦的、胖的、易碎的、坚固的、重的。

小贴士

如果再次玩这个游戏，可加入另外一些标签，这样孩子们就不能预料到后续内容。

跨领域链接

认识与理解世界：探索与观察。

伯特的一天

 · 用每个人不同的想法来创作关于一个人物的故事，讲述他一天中发生的事情。

教学目标
- 鼓励孩子们创作自己的故事。

教学资源
1）游戏垫； 2）建筑模型； 3）玩具货车。

教学准备
- 用一系列的建筑来布置你的游戏垫。例如车库、商店、农场、房屋。
- 在晴朗的日子把游戏垫摆在室外。

怎么做
- 为你的主要角色选择一个名字，比如：伯特。向孩子们解释，这些材料将帮助你讲述伯特一天发生的故事。
- 选择一个孩子，扮演伯特，他将在故事中驾驶他的货车。
- 告诉这个孩子，伯特从他的货车上下车，去车库取一些油。这个孩子将沿着垫子上的马路"驾驶"这辆货车。
- 他看到一些正在出售的花束。他为他的妈妈买了一些。
- 他开着货车去他妈妈的家。要决定哪幢房子是他妈妈的房子和他要开的路。当他开到那里时，把花给了妈妈。妈妈很喜欢这些花。
- 妈妈让伯特带一罐刚做好的果酱给老汤姆叔叔。
- 这个故事以这样的方式继续着。每次伯特送东西的时候，别人都要求他去别的地方再送东西。
- 故事会怎样结束？

词汇

你可以在故事中加入任何重复性短语。

 小贴士　　　随着你为你的小组中尽可能多的孩子创作故事情节，这个故事创作可以成为一个戏剧活动。

跨领域链接

创造力的发展：想象力和想象性游戏。

看不见的墨水

 • 在孩子们发现防蜡的魔力时，他们要分享关于为什么会发生这种情况的想法。

教学目标
• 鼓励孩子们专心倾听，并用相关的评论作出回应。

教学资源
1）白纸； 2）白色蜡笔； 3）稀薄呈水状的颜料。

教学准备
• 确保孩子们已经多次使用过蜡笔做记号。

怎么做
• 组织一组孩子围坐在美术桌旁。如果天气晴朗，可以在室外活动。告诉孩子们你要写一条秘密的信息。
• 在白纸上用白色蜡笔给一些粗体字上色。问孩子们：
　　"为什么你们看不清楚这条信息？"
　　"为什么白色蜡笔不适合使用？"
• 解释一下白色字是看不见的，然后你看起来很失望地说："哦，亲爱的孩子们，怎样才能看到这个信息呢？"询问是否有人有任何建议该怎么做。
• 给他们展示颜料，告诉他们你有办法看到这条看不见的信息。
• 轻轻地在纸上涂上颜料，看看这些粗体字如何通过颜料显现出来了。
• 孩子们能解释为什么会这样吗？听听他们的想法。
• 让孩子们去写一个看不见的信息，然后在它上面涂上颜料。

词汇
白色、看不见的、闪亮的、光滑的、防御的。

 小贴士　　　这些标记需要写得很粗很厚，如果这项活动要继续进行的话，颜料需要足够稀薄。

跨领域链接

创造力的发展：探索媒介与材料。

混合颜料（1）

• 鼓励孩子们预测把不同颜色颜料混合在一起后会发生的情况。

教学目标

• 给孩子们提供一个机会向别人表达想法。

教学资源

1）红色、黄色和蓝色的颜料； 2）纸、笔刷和水； 3）调色盘。

教学准备

• 孩子们之前有大量机会用颜料自由作画。

怎么做

• 和一组孩子在一起，讨论三个主要的颜色。
  – 他们能说出这三种颜色的名字吗？
  – 他们最喜欢哪一个？为什么？
• 告诉孩子们，他们要用这些来制造新的颜色。
• 让他们选择两种颜色，例如蓝色和黄色。
• 他们能猜出如果他们把这两种颜色混合在一起会是什么颜色吗？
• 让他们做实验，把两种颜色混合在一起制成新的颜色，例如：
  – 红色和蓝色混合成紫色。
  – 蓝色和黄色混合成绿色。
  – 红色和黄色混合成橙色。
• 说说他们所制造的新颜色，以及他们是如何制造的。他们从什么颜色开始，然后他们制成了什么？
• 现在让他们向大家解释一下，他们是如何制造出了新的颜色。

词汇

红色、蓝色、黄色、绿色、橙色、紫色、混合。

小贴士　　　　鼓励孩子们用他们原有的颜色颜料和他们创造的颜色颜料画色块，创作一个展板可以记录他们的实验发现。

跨领域链接

创造力的发展：探索媒介与材料。

混合颜料(2)

· 孩子们有机会描述用颜色做实验时发生的事情。

教学目标
· 为孩子们提供有意义的演讲和聆听活动。

教学资源
1）红色、蓝色、黑色和白色的颜料； 2）调色盘、笔刷和水。

教学准备
· 你们需要在这个分类活动的前一天完成绘画。

怎么做
· 和一组孩子在一起活动，告诉他们要改变蓝色和红色。
· 让每个孩子选择一种颜色，并取一些放在调色盘上。然后他们在纸上用这个颜色画一个色块。
· 现在让他们在调色盘上加入少量的黑色颜料，然后画出另一个色块。鼓励他们将较深的颜色与原来的颜色进行比较，并描述发生了什么变化。
· 要求他们预测添加更多的黑色颜料后会发生什么。让孩子添加更多的黑色颜料，并调制出比原色更深的颜色。
· 与另一个小组合作，重复活动，但这次提问孩子们，如果他们在自己的颜料中加上白色颜料，会发生什么？
· 鼓励他们画出加了白色颜料后的色块，并记录下这个较浅的颜色。
· 把这些色块都放在一边，隔夜晾干。
· **第二天**：把色块剪下来，这样你就可以制作出六个不同深浅颜色的几个组合。给制作出这些颜色的孩子们留出时间解释他们是如何制作出来这些颜色的。
· 现在给两个一组的孩子一套六种色块，让他们按照从浅到深的顺序把色块排序。鼓励他们在排列色块时进行交谈和协商。

词汇
红色、蓝色、黑色、白色、混合、深色、更深色、浅色、更浅色、深浅浓淡各种颜色。

小贴士　　　建立一个展示板呈现孩子们用色块做实验的过程、扩充的词汇和孩子们实验过程中的照片。

跨领域链接

创造力的发展：探索媒介与材料。

小型动物（1）

• 建立一个角色扮演的场地，帮助孩子们从别人的角度想象生活。

教学目标
• 鼓励孩子们想象并重新创作角色。

教学资源
各种单色简单图案的大号 T 恤衫。

教学准备
• 建立一个像花园一样的角色扮演区域：
用纸制作超大的树叶、草和花。从地面高度开始，将它们固定在墙壁展示板上。这应该像是一个巨大的花园。将其作为一个单独的活动，和孩子们一起完成。
• 把 T 恤衫放在附近的箱子或筐子里。

怎么做
• 组织孩子们一起坐在他们所做的"花园"附近。所有人都坐在地板上，让"草"等植物比他们高。
• 谈论"草"等植物的高度，与他们自己的高度比一比。
"这里一个蜘蛛或甲虫来说是个花园。"
• 让孩子们想象自己成为一只花园里的昆虫。他们能想到花园里的其他东西吗？这些东西对于蜘蛛来说看起来很大，但对我们来说却不是，比如：
一只脚；一个球；一只鸟。
• 鼓励孩子们在他们制作的花园里玩耍，穿上一件 T 恤，打扮成他们要成为的小型动物。老师可以穿上黑色扮演甲虫，穿上红色扮演瓢虫，等等。

词汇
巨大的、微小的。

小贴士
写下一些关于小动物的童谣，把童谣贴在"花园"附近一起读。例如：
小玛菲丁小姐
小蜘蛛

小瓢虫，飞回家吧

跨领域链接

创造力的发展：想象力和想象性游戏。

押韵指导

> • **在准备上体育课时，孩子们快乐地吟诵着有韵律的童谣。**

教学目标

• 鼓励孩子们乐于使用押韵的词汇。

教学资源

1）体育用品；　2）成人帮手。

教学准备

• 准备一个适合教学环境的简单童谣（见下面的例子）。

怎么做

• 让孩子们准备好他们的包，包里放有他们准备上体育课的服装。

• 告诉孩子们，你编了一首特别的短小的童谣来提醒他们该怎么做。在你说这首童谣时，要求孩子们仔细听押韵的单词。

　　谁可以猜到结尾吗？

　　把书包放在桌上。

　　把衣服放在椅子上。

　　把鞋子放在地板上。

　　然后把短袜放到那儿！

• 在他们准备上体育课的时候不断重复这首童谣。鼓励孩子们一起念。下次有人会记得吗？

• 孩子们能帮忙创作一些其他的童谣吗？例如：果汁时间/午饭时间/准备回家的时候。

词汇

几组押韵的词汇*。

小贴士　　　　更多关于用童谣组织活动的想法和更多童谣，可以在课堂宝典系列丛书中的《幼儿自然拼读教学游戏、想法和活动》一书找到。

---

*　此处略，不作翻译，因是针对英语语言中的押韵词汇，可具体见此书原文。

跨领域链接

个人、社会和情感的发展：自理能力。

我们今天应该画画吗？

• 孩子们营造不同的天气条件，谈论天气如何影响他们的绘画。

教学目标

• 帮助孩子们通过联系因果关系来解释他们的选择。

教学资源

1）颜料、纸张和画架； 2）吸管、水罐和报纸； 3）纸围裙和防水罩。

教学准备

• 选择一个晴朗无风的天气，在室外支好四个画架。这是一个比较忙乱的活动，所以最好安排在一个远离墙壁、避开其他活动场地或有门的地方。

怎么做

• 向孩子们解释他们将要考虑去室外画画。有时我们可以这样做，有时我们不能。

• 一个原因可能是天气。为什么？听听孩子们的想法，然后谈论一下。

"如果风很小或很大，会有什么区别？"

"如果遇到阵雨或是强暴风雨天气，该怎么办？"

• 告诉孩子们，他们今天要营造四种不同的天气，这样他们就能知道在这些不同的天气情况下他们的画会发生什么状况。鼓励孩子们提出一些想法来营造不同天气，例如：

活动 1：一个微风天

画完你的画。当它还没有干的时候，

— 向画吹气。

— 用吸管向画吹气。

活动 2：一个大风天

画完你的画。当它还没有干的时候，

— 在旁边用报纸快速扇动。

— 把画从画架上取下，在四周挥舞。

活动 3：一个阵雨天

画完你的画。当它还没有干的时候，

— 用你的手指把水溅到上面。

— 用一个滴管把整个画面滴满水。

活动 4：一个潮湿天

　－ 在你画画之前先把纸弄湿。

　－ 在你完成你的画之后，用一个水罐把纸浸泡一下。

- 在这四个活动中，每一组都有两个孩子。首先让孩子们讨论在他们一组的天气情况下，会发生什么情况。

- 在他们进行活动时观察他们。当他们完成任务后，问他们

　"发生了什么？"

　"为什么？"

　"哪些方面你们的做法是正确的？"

　"今天是个适合画画的好天气吗？"

词汇

原因、影响、决定。

小贴士　　　　孩子们可以在不同的活动中两两结队，然后作为一个小组一起报告他们的发现。

跨领域链接

认识与理解世界：探索与观察。

真是胡说八道！

 · 编造一些搞笑的词来改写一首著名的童谣。

教学目标

· 鼓励孩子们使用词汇和声音进行实验。

教学资源

"手指喜欢摇摆摇摆"，马特森改编（《这只小海雀》，企鹅出版社 1991 年出版）

教学准备

· 和孩子们一起欢快地唱这首手指童谣。

怎么做

· 当孩子们唱这首童谣时，让他们展示手指是如何摆动的。

· 告诉他们下次你们唱这首童谣的时候，尝试用一些新的词汇。

· 你用手指打节拍，开始唱新的童谣。

· 让孩子们为这个动作编造一些单词，例如，

　提皮　塔皮

　唱出童谣第一行。

· 告诉孩子们，当他们用手指打节拍的时候，他们可以说出任何搞笑的单词。

· 问问孩子们的想法，例如：

　宾吉　邦吉

　叮比　铛比

　随着创作的词汇越来越搞笑，大家享受这份随意带来的快乐。

· 选择一些既搞笑又有用的词汇。然后告诉孩子哪些词用在四行诗句中的哪一行。鼓励他们在说这些话的时候移动手指。

词汇

任何有相同字母开头的两音节无意义单词。

 小贴士　你可能想用这个活动来关注头韵词，通过选择两个以相同声音开头的单词，或者用拍手来展示 Wiggle and Waggle 故事中的两音节词的节奏。

跨领域链接

创造力的发展：音乐和舞蹈。

问问题

· 设计一组孩子们可以询问客人的问题。

教学目标

· 帮助孩子们准备一些适合询问客人的问题。

教学资源

疑问词事先写在卡片上或者是互动白板上，例如：什么、何时、在哪里、怎样、谁。

教学准备

· 安排一位来访客人和孩子们谈谈他们的职业，例如：图书管理员、护士或警察。

怎么做

· 告诉孩子们有一位客人将来访并且指明他的身份。问问孩子们关于这个人的工作，他们想知道什么。

· 告诉孩子们你想准备一些问题问一下这位客人。

  – 他们想要了解什么呢？

· 给孩子们展示这些疑问词。依次朗读每一个单词。

· 举例说明如何使用其中一个单词设计一个问题，例如：

  "你最喜欢你的工作中的哪部分？"

  "你在哪里工作？"

  "你和谁一起工作？"

· 尽力提一些开放性问题，这样客人可以聊起来，不至于只回答"是"或"不"。

· 帮助孩子们想出更多的问题，例如：

  "你是什么时候决定要做一名护士的？"

  "你是怎么抓捕坏人的？"

· 写下他们的想法，然后让孩子们练习问客人们。

词汇

什么、何时、在哪里、怎样、谁。

小贴士　　记录下孩子们的问题，当客人来访时，可以提示并鼓励他们询问。

跨领域链接

个人、社会和情感的发展：团队意识。

解决问题（1）

> • 孩子们将如何相互合作按身高将他们自己排序。

教学目标

- 鼓励孩子们相互合作来设计方案。

教学准备

- 这个活动之前，孩子们已经学过比较大小。

怎么做

- 向孩子们解释你希望他们可以排好队，最高的孩子站在一头，最矮的孩子站在另一头。
- 为了做到这一点，孩子们将需要想办法找出整个队伍中最高的和第二高的，依次类推。他们需要一起合作找到答案。
- 给他们一些时间，并且观察他们是如何找出答案的。
  - 有没有一个孩子在组织整个队伍？
  - 他们允许其他人发表意见吗？
- 暂停一下活动，把他们聚集在一起。
  - 请他们告诉你，他们是如何解决问题的。
  - 给他们一些时间，谈一谈对于被人提出的建议，自己的想法或评论。
- 要求他们完成整个活动。提醒他们去用这样的问句提问，例如：

  "我可以……吗？"

  "我们应该……？"

  "你们对……有什么想法？"

词汇

更高、更矮。

小贴士　　　如果你们小组成员比较少或者活动很难开展，建议孩子们比较任何两个小朋友的身高，然后每次让较高的一个小朋友和另一个小朋友比较，一直到选出最高的一位。重复这个过程，直到依次确定好每一个小朋友的位置。

跨领域链接

问题解决、推理和计算能力：形状、空间与测量。

解决问题(2)

 · 当孩子们修建一个避暑地时，给他们一个机会去合作和协商。

教学目标
- 和其他孩子们一起协商计划和活动。

教学资源
1）大块的布料； 2）绳子。

教学准备
- 环顾你所在的室外区域。
- 在哪里修建避暑地呢？
- 有没有任何树或栏杆等可以利用呢？
- 如果没有，就留下一些椅子、盒子和长木条等在室外。

怎么做
- 向孩子们解释他们遇到海难了。确定他们所在的"岛屿"离他们的住所很远。他们必须待在这个"小岛"上，直到一艘船来接他们，所以他们需要建造一个避暑地来遮挡炎热的阳光。
- 给一组孩子提供一块布料和细绳。这是他们船上所有被冲下的东西！
- 向他们解释，他们必须一起努力找到一个地方来建造他们的避暑地，还要想出一个方法来建造它。在系绳子等方面你可以适时提供帮助，但鼓励孩子们自己想出解决问题的办法。
- 记录团队动态
  - 谁指挥？
  - 谁愿意把指挥权让给别人？
  - 谁在团队中努力工作？

词汇
避暑地、保护、安全的。

 小贴士　　　　选择炎热的日子建造避暑地，并把它当作真正的庇护所。

跨领域链接

个人、社会和情感的发展：自理能力。

解决问题（3）

• 孩子们一起帮助泰迪熊找到一种方法，把娃娃的鞋从水盘里取出来。

教学目标
• 鼓励孩子们与他人互动，制定和测试计划。

教学资源
1）水盘；2）泰迪熊；3）娃娃；4）娃娃的鞋。

教学准备
• 在孩子们到达之前，把娃娃的鞋放在水盘的中心。

怎么做
• 告诉孩子们，昨晚回家的时候，泰迪熊在捣乱。它把娃娃的鞋子扔进水里。娃娃非常伤心，因为她够不着鞋，无法把鞋子拿出来了。

• 问问他们是否能找到一种方法让泰迪熊把鞋子拿出来，确保他们明白，泰迪熊必须这样做——他们不能轻易地替泰迪熊把鞋子拿出来。

• 花时间讨论一下他们的想法。他们可能决定，例如：
  − 泰迪熊能拿着一个长长的东西把鞋子钩出来（可能是一个渔网，或是一样东西末端绑着一根棍子）。
  − 泰迪熊可以乘在某些漂浮在水面的东西上，用爪子把鞋子拿出来（一条小船，一块木头或任何他们可以找到的用来漂浮的东西）。

• 鼓励孩子们在正式测试他们的想法之前，认真思考一下这些想法，用"如果"和"可能"这类词汇讨论一下。

• 在活动的最后环节，每个小组依次将自己的计划向其他小组作出解释，看看是否可行。

词汇
一些鼓励讨论的问句句式：如果……会怎么样？……可能吗？我们能……吗？……是安全的吗？

小贴士　　　这是强调水安全规则的一个好机会。

跨领域链接

认识与理解世界：探索与观察。

第二章

表达想法

小餐馆（1）

· 讨论建立一个小餐馆需要准备些什么。鼓励孩子们认真考虑设备和组织筹备，同时成人负责记录他们的想法。

教学目标
· 组织一些活动让孩子们通过讨论来预测他们将要做的事情。

教学资源
给成人一张大纸和笔来记录孩子们的想法。

教学准备
· 鼓励孩子们分享他们去小餐馆吃饭的经历。可以问他们：

— 你喜欢吃什么，喝什么？

— 你和谁一起去？

— 你知道某个小餐馆的名字或在哪里？

— 你有没有因为一个特殊的日子去小餐馆用餐？

— 你在室外的小餐馆坐过吗？

怎么做
· 告诉孩子们，你们将去建造一个小餐馆。请他们思考需要些什么。通过画图片或写下一些简单的单词来记录孩子们的建议，例如盘子、餐具、杯子、桌子和椅子。

· 为了指导他们制定计划，引导他们思考以下问题：

— 顾客将如何付款？

— 他们如何知道自己可以选择什么？

— 他们如何点单？

· 孩子们可能会需要一个食品柜台、收银台，或者他们可能需要一些男服务员和女服务员。

· 几天后，你可以轻易将小餐馆从一种风格换成另一种风格，使其变化多样。在夏季，你可以试着建一个室外小餐馆，或者试着建一个冰激凌流动车！

词汇
蛋糕、三明治、汉堡、可乐、果汁、冰激凌、菜单、收银台、顾客。

小贴士　　　试着改变你的小餐馆，以方便提供不同类型的食物，例如印度式、中式或加勒比海盗式的。

跨领域链接

创造力的发展：想象力和想象性游戏。

寻找这本书

 · 使用对讲机来找到图书馆中的书。

教学目标
- 鼓励孩子们使用谈话来组织和澄清思考。

教学资源
1）简易的对讲机设备； 2）在室外或学习区域以外，可以访问的图书馆或书籍收藏处。

教学准备
- 检查可用的书籍，以便你了解活动中需要的资源。

怎么做
- 告知大家，两个孩子要去图书馆选一本书。
  他们需要记住书的样子和在哪里，然后他们回到教室。
- 另外两个孩子现在带着对讲机去图书馆。
- 教室里的两个孩子引导这两个孩子在图书馆里找到这本相同的书。
- 想一想：
  - 这本书是否在书架的最上层？
  - 这本书是否很大？
  - 书的封面上有什么图片？
  - 封面上的图片是什么颜色的？
- 教室里的两个孩子一直在提供线索，直到另外两个小朋友找到这本书为止。
  当他们带着这本书回来时，让室内的两个小朋友看看他们是否找到了正确的书。
- 交换角色继续活动。

小贴士　　　　　如果你有任何一本书的两个副本，就在每一个区域使用一本，便于能力较弱或年纪较小的孩子活动。

跨领域链接
认识与理解世界：信息通信技术（ICT）。

大灰狼！

· 当孩子们玩音乐剧《小红帽》游戏时，他们会仔细听指令。

教学目标
- 帮助孩子们聆听并做出相应的动作。

教学资源
舞蹈音乐。

教学准备
- 你需要一个很大的空间。
- 确定你的音乐。

怎么做
- 选择几个孩子扮成树，形成一个森林。如果你有额外的成人帮手，他们可以扮演这个角色。扮演"树"的人应该张开双臂就像树枝一样。
- 其他人跟着音乐，围着树跳舞。
- 当音乐停止时，你发出一个指令。孩子们可以选择如何按指令表演。可以尝试：
  - 为奶奶挑选一些花。
  - 在小道上一蹦一跳。
  - 检查你篮子里的蛋糕。
  - 你的帽子掉下来了。
  - 吃一块蛋糕。
- 但有时你会大声喊："大灰狼（来了）！！"。那么每个人都必须迅速躲到一棵树后。最后一个躲起来的人就被淘汰了，成为另一棵树，直到只有一个人留下来跳舞，那么游戏结束。

小贴士　　　　留意那些能迅速想到动作的孩子，也要观察是否有的孩子觉得很难完成。

跨领域链接
创造力的发展：想象力和想象性游戏。

我做，你也做

· 孩子们两两一组制作相同的模型。一个孩子解释，另一个孩子根据他的指令制作。

教学目标

· 让孩子们有机会能够使用位置性语言，清晰地解释说明。

教学资源

1）相连的方块或彩色砖块； 2）一个可以将桌子从中间隔开的隔断或屏风。

教学准备

· 每两个孩子有十个方块或彩色砖块。它们应该有相同的颜色。

· 让孩子坐下来，这样他们就看不到另一个人在做什么。他们应该是背靠背的，或者你可以在他们之间用一个屏障隔开。

怎么做

· 一个孩子用任意数量的方块制作一个简单的模型，甚至可以是一个简单的方块排列。

· 另一个孩子必须按照说明制作一个相同的模型。

· 一个孩子给出指令的同时，另一个孩子完成后示意再听下一个指令。

· 当另一个孩子完成后，他们会向彼此展示自己的模型。它们是一样的吗？

词汇

下一个、接着、在顶部、在底部、在中间、在一起。

小贴士　　　　你可能需要先演示一下，让两个孩子跟着你的指令完成一遍。

跨领域链接

问题解决、推理和计算能力：形状、空间和测量。

点亮一束光

· 孩子们使用手电筒，并且准确地描述他们可以看到什么。

教学目标

· 给孩子们提供一个机会，让其有意义地表达和聆听。

教学资源

1）一到两个迷你手电筒；2）一个黑暗的角落，一个橱柜或一个盒子；3）一些小玩具。

教学准备

· 设置你的黑暗区域，并在里面藏一些玩具。

· 教孩子们如何开关手电筒。

怎么做

· 告诉孩子们一些玩具被藏在橱柜或盒子里。每个人都会轮流使用手电筒去查看玩具。

· 他们打开手电筒后，必须选择一个玩具，然后描述给其他人听，例如，
我可以看到一个圆圆的、光滑的、小小的东西。
然后其他小朋友可以猜到吗？

· 如果这个玩具被孩子们猜到了，那么它将被从柜子里取出来。然后另一个孩子继续游戏。

词汇

大的、小的、柔软的、坚硬的、闪亮的、蓬松的、圆的、方的、长的、薄的……

小贴士　　低龄孩子可能需要玩具在被藏起来前先看一下玩具，然后讨论一下它们。

跨领域链接

认识与理解世界：信息通信技术（ICT）。

艾玛·加克莱《突突嘀嘀》（1）

· 帮助孩子们把书中的词汇分类成"快速的"和"慢速的"两组。

教学目标

• 增加孩子们的词汇量。

教学资源

1）艾玛·加克莱，圣·奥尔本斯的《突突嘀嘀》（博克思出版社 2009 年出版）；2）纸张若干；3）一些玩具车；4）两个圆圈，分别标有"快速的"和"慢速的"标签。

教学准备

• 通过再次阅读来提醒孩子们这个故事的内容。

怎么做

• 围坐成圆形，将两个有标签的圆圈放在中间。

• 观察书中第一辆车。它是如何移动的？
  "它急速前行。"

• 选择一个孩子去拿一辆车，然后显示急速前行的样子。

• 询问孩子们"急速前行"的意思是快还是慢？一旦每个人都同意后，就在一张纸上写下"急速前行"这个词，然后把它放在正确的圆圈中。

• 继续看书，找到一个词，用行动测试一下，然后决定这个词是否会加入"急速前行"表示快速的单词圈内，还是应该放在另一个表示慢速的单词圈内。

• 所有的单词归类后，朗读所有表示"快速"的单词，然后朗读所有表示"慢速"的单词。

• 每个人现在都可以开一辆车。你每次朗读单词库中的一个单词，孩子们每次都会用他们的车来演示一下——是快速还是慢速？

• 完成游戏后所有的汽车安静地停在停车场。

词汇

急速前行、加速、缓慢地移动、冲进、滑行、翻车、猛烈碰撞。

小贴士　　　　这个游戏可以作为你在车库角色扮演活动中的一部分。

跨领域链接

沟通、语言和读写能力的发展：角色扮演。

打电话订购商品

· 打电话是一种有趣的方式。孩子们使用形容词识别或描述一种水果或蔬菜。

教学目标

· 给孩子们提供一个机会参与有意义的表达和聆听。

教学资源

1）两个玩具手机或不使用的成人手机；2）一些孩子们熟悉的水果和蔬菜。

教学准备

· 确保大多数孩子都能说出物品的名称并描述它们的特点。

怎么做

· 围坐成圆形，一些水果和蔬菜放在中间。

· 说明你是打电话给蔬果店的顾客，但你不知道商店里所有东西的名字。一个孩子扮演接电话并提供帮助的店主。

成人：你有长得坚硬的、长长的、橙色蔬菜吗？

店主：是的，我们有，那是胡萝卜。你要多少个？

成人：请给我两个大的。

店主：好的，我给你留两个大的胡萝卜。

成人：非常感谢，再见。

· 让另一个孩子扮演店主的角色，接听你的下一个电话。

· 在孩子们对这个游戏有足够信心的时候，鼓励他们合作扮演两个角色——顾客和店主。

词汇

圆形的、长的、柔软的、坚硬的、光滑的、大的、小的、黄色的、绿色的、红色的、紫色的……

小贴士　　你也可以动物园或农场动物为主题玩相似的游戏，假装这个顾客正在建造一个新的动物园或农场。

跨领域链接

认识与理解世界：信息通信技术（ICT）。

穿上衣服

 • 一个生动的活动，可以帮助孩子们对于穿衣给出清晰又精确的指令。

教学目标

• 鼓励孩子们通过谈论来组织和排序事情。

教学资源

1）一件特大号套头毛衣；2）如果有可能，请另一个成人做你的模特。

怎么做

• 把一件套头毛衣放在地板上或附近的桌子上。

• 孩子们要告诉大人如何穿上这件套头毛衣。向孩子们解释，这位成年人将按照孩子们的建议做。

• 问孩子们："她应该先做什么？"

• 孩子们的建议可能是"把你的头从洞口钻出来"。大人应该这样做——不要把衣服拿起来，只能站在衣服原来放的地方穿。

把它演出来，让它成为一个喜剧表演。

• 大家一起玩得很开心，同时孩子们尽力去想他们错过的所有环节。

• 一些孩子可能喜欢走出来，试着穿上这件套头毛衣。

其他孩子会记起所有必要的指导步骤吗？

词汇

通过、在……下面、在……里面、在……外面、在……上方、拉。

小贴士　　　　　这个游戏也可以选择其他的场景，如穿上系紧鞋带的鞋子，或者在冬季需要穿上系紧的大衣。

跨领域链接

个人、社会和情感的发展：自理能力。

那是你吗？

· 孩子们通过对线索的反应来识别群体中的某个人。

教学目标

· 给孩子们机会正确使用各种各样的形容词。

教学资源

把群体中孩子们的一些名字分别写在一张张纸上。

怎么做

· 游戏开始时每个人都站起来。

· 你随机从你写出来的人名中挑选一个名字。不要让别人知道这个名字是谁。

· 告诉孩子们他们必须想办法找出这个孩子是谁，例如，

"我想找的那个人有一头长发。"

"所以，所有没有长发的人都坐下。"

"我想找的那个人穿着一双黑鞋。"

"所以，所有没穿黑鞋的人都坐下。"

· 一直继续下去，直到只有一个人站着。看看纸上的名称，你找到的就是那个孩子吗？

· 接着那个孩子走到前面，然后选择另一个名字重新开始游戏。

词汇

长的、短的、色彩词汇、高的、卷发的、直发的。

小贴士　你可能要帮助孩子们决定是坐着，还是选择站着，直到他们对游戏更加熟悉。

跨领域链接

个人、社会和情感的发展：团队意识。

小型动物(2)

• 在假装自己是小型动物之前，孩子们要想到一些词来描述小型动物是如何移动的。

教学目标

• 扩展孩子们的词汇量。

教学资源

1）鼓；2）铃鼓或沙锤。

怎么做

• 向孩子们解释他们要扮演住在花园里的小动物。让每个人都像蝴蝶一样来回移动。然后鼓励孩子们像蜘蛛一样移动。用模仿其他小型动物来继续这样的活动，例如：毛毛虫、蜜蜂或是蜗牛。

• 大家坐在一起，用一些词来描述不同的动物是如何移动的。一次举一只小型动物为例，然后收集一些单词，例如：

毛毛虫——匍匐爬行，无声缓慢前行

蝴蝶——飘浮，飞行，振翅而飞

蜘蛛——疾走，迅速逃走

蜜蜂——嗡嗡叫，悬停

甲虫——疾走

准备好添加一些单词以便孩子们可以增加他们的词汇知识。

• 现在每个人都站在一个准备玩游戏的空间里。

• 告诉孩子们他们将成为勇敢的探险家，在花园里寻找生物：安静地移动，不要惊动生物们。

• 当孩子们在花园中悄悄地移动时，你击鼓。

• 你停止击鼓，开始摇动铃鼓或其沙锤。同时，说出你想象中的一个动作，例如：

－ 像蝴蝶一样在空中飘浮。

－ 像蜘蛛一样迅速逃跑。

－ 像蜜蜂一样悬停，等等。

在你再次敲鼓之前，孩子们必须遵循指令做动作。

词汇

飘浮、飞行、振翅而飞、迅速逃走、疾走、嗡嗡叫、悬停、疾走、匍匐爬行、无声缓慢前行。

小贴士　　　　也可以在室外玩这个游戏。

跨领域链接

身体的发展：运动与空间。

挖掘机跳舞吗？

• 孩子们按照你的指示，两两组队扮演司机和起重机。

教学目标

• 鼓励孩子们使用谈话给出或遵循指令。

教学准备

• 观察现实生活中的起重机。

• 观看一段起重机工作的视频短片。

怎么做

• 要求孩子们找到一个足够大的空间，让他们可以在不触碰任何东西或人的情况下，向四面八方伸出手臂。

• 孩子们可以练习像起重机一样移动，例如：

  伸直你的手臂，然后双手紧握，看起来像挖掘机或起重机的手臂一样。

  保持你的脚不动，尽可能地移动你的起重机。

  练习在你移动起重机的时候来回移动你的脚——但是不要离开你的空间。

• 一旦他们能充当起重机的一部分，给孩子们发出口头的指示，就好像你是司机一样：

  把你的起重机移到高处。

  把你的起重机转向门口。

  把你的起重机弯到地上。

  等着有人把大箱子绑在你的钩子上。

  现在慢慢地把起重举起来。不要扔下板条箱。

  转向前方……。

• 现在孩子们可以两两组队依次扮演起重机和司机，给出或听从指令。

词汇

向上、向下、四周的、向左、向右。

小贴士　　　孩子们当司机时可以戴上"安全帽"。

跨领域链接

创造力的发展：想象力和想象性的游戏。

里面是什么？

· 孩子们可以通过调查和拍摄水果来制作一本立体翻翻书或是一个展示。

教学目标

· 鼓励孩子们通过谈话来组织和澄清他们的想法。

教学资源

1）水果； 2）锋利的水果刀； 3）照相机； 4）折叠的卡片若干和胶水。

教学准备

· 给你收集的水果拍些照片。每一种水果配一张照片。

怎么做

· 鼓励孩子们观察水果并小心地处理它。允许他们在调查研究时看、摸和闻。

· 在他们比较和描述水果时，试着扩大他们的词汇量，例如，

  – 哪个水果最重/最亮/最硬？

  – 有人吃过这些水果吗？

  – 你们能说出它的味道吗？

· 告诉孩子们你要把水果切成两半。询问他们在切开水果后期望发现什么，如颜色、果汁或水果核的大小。确保每个人都有机会解释他们的想法。

· 当孩子们准备好时，把水果切成两半。让孩子们描述他们看到的、闻到的和感受到的。

  – 是你所期望的吗？

· 帮助孩子们拍摄水果的内部。当照片被打印出来时，把它们和水果外部的照片匹配起来。把水果外部的照片贴在折叠卡片的前面，水果里面的照片可以贴在折叠卡片的里面。

· 折叠卡片可以贴在墙上进行互动展示，也可以贴在书上，这样可以创作一本立体翻翻书，孩子们之后会很喜欢阅读。

词汇

坚硬的、柔软的、光滑的、毛茸茸的、重的、轻的、多汁的、果皮、水果核。

小贴士　如果你给水果贴上标签，这将有助于孩子们理解打印工作的过程。

跨领域链接

认识与理解世界：探索与观察。

你感觉怎么样？

· 通过阅读不同的脸部表情来增加孩子们的词汇量和理解力。

教学目标

· 在孩子们的词汇库中引入新的词汇。

教学资源

1）一些不同人物表情的图片； 2）几面镜子。

怎么做

· 解释你们将要思考人们的脸部。当我们看着别人的脸时，我们会看到什么？倾听孩子们的回答。

· 解释当我们的感觉在我们的脸上显现出来时，这就是我们的表情。

· 通过做一张快乐的脸和一张悲伤的脸来说明一下不同的表情。然后鼓励孩子们也使用这些表情。

· 向孩子们展示一张你准备好的照片，鼓励孩子们解释这个人可能会有什么感受，例如：

  － 这个人可能看起来很震惊。

  － 孩子们能否对这个人为什么会感到震惊提出一些想法？

  － 孩子们有没有感到过震惊？

  － 让他们向你展示一下震惊的表情。

  － 说说一些能让你有这种感觉的事情。

  用不同的表情来重复这个过程。

· 把所有的照片放在地板上，然后分发镜子。

· 让每个孩子选择一张照片，然后对着镜子来重现这种表情。

  轮流来相互展示他们的不同表情，并讲述照片中人物的感受，以及为什么会有这种感受。

词汇

不耐烦的、烦心的、震惊的、惊奇的、自豪的、自鸣得意的、开心的、疲惫的、担心的、孤独的、疑惑不解的、生气的、愉快的、兴奋的、害怕的。

小贴士　　　为了扩展这项活动，你可以尝试将两种类似的表情联系起来，并与孩子探索两者的不同之处，例如震惊和惊奇。

跨领域链接

个人、社会和情感的发展：自信与自尊。

玛格丽特·梅奥
《紧急情况!》(2)

 ・ 孩子们描述各种紧急情况和那些会来帮忙的人。

教学目标

・ 使用书籍中的故事来集中孩子们的注意力进行预测和解释。

教学资源

《紧急情况!》

教学准备

・ 和孩子们快乐地阅读这本书。

怎么做

・ 运用书中的插图,让孩子们描述每一个紧急情况。

－ 他们能否解释发生了什么事?

－ 他们能否建议需要哪种紧急救援?

－ 他们能否预测紧急救援将如何提供帮助?

・ 孩子们可能还会谈论谁给紧急服务打过电话,例如,

－ 是沉船中的男子,还是在海滩上打着伞的女士?

・ 用玩具手机让孩子们轮流拨打 110,然后根据书中提到的不同场景选择不同的救援服务。

・ 使用本书第一页和最后一页上的急救车图片。

－ 孩子们能说出每辆车的名字吗?

－ 他们知道谁驾驶每种类型的车辆吗?

－ 他们能记得每辆车该参与哪些紧急救援吗?

词汇

警车、抢修车、救护车、直升机、铲雪车、救生艇、充气艇、警用摩托车、消防飞机、消防车、吊车。

小贴士

我们要意识到，如果孩子们经历过某种紧急情况，这可能对其是一个敏感话题。

跨领域链接

个人、社会和情感的发展：团队意识。

第三章

记忆、反思和复述

在大游行之后

• 和孩子们一起制作一个关于他们所看到的游行的展示。

教学目标

• 通过制作一个关于游行照片的展示来提醒孩子们游行是怎么回事。

教学资源

1）一些有关游行活动的纪念物和照片； 2）在你居住的地区内游行的任何视频剪辑；
3）展示板后附上纸张或布料，加上一个大标签。

教学准备

• 许多节日和仪式都包含游行或队列行进活动。你可以组织一场游行活动作为当地学校或
村庄传统活动的一部分。你甚至可以参与其中。

怎么做

• 通过视频的展示和分享纪念品，鼓励孩子们对游行活动发表评论。
• 提出以下问题，给孩子们时间思考他们的答案，然后参加讨论：
  – 你看到了什么？
  – 你听到了什么了？
  – 游行活动给你带来什么样的感受？
• 让孩子们有时间画或拼贴游行队伍中的表演者。
• 把游行队伍中的人物画像剪下来，并把它们固定在展示板上，指出人们在一个游行
  队伍中是一个接一个的。按从左到右的顺序来做，以加强书写的习惯。
• 将你收集到的任何其他物品添加到你的展示中。

词汇

首先、在前面、在后面、接着。

小贴士　　　　如果孩子们看到不同的游行就对两个游行作一个比较。

跨领域链接

个人、社会和情感的发展：团队意识。

很久以前（1）

· 孩子们制作一些童话故事中的木偶人物来复述他们最喜欢的故事。

教学目标

· 借助木偶来鼓励孩子们复述故事。

教学资源

1）若干木质勺子；　2）若干布条和橡皮筋；　3）记号笔和毛线。

教学准备

· 阅读你想讲述的童话故事，并确定角色。

· 制作这些人物的木偶：

用记号笔在汤勺的勺面上画出一张脸；

加上一些用毛线做的"头发"；

用橡皮筋将一些织物布料当"衣服"固定在汤勺的手柄上。

怎么做

· 给孩子们朗读或告诉他们选好的童话故事。在你朗读的时候，孩子们可以借助木偶把这个故事表演出来。

· 重复这个故事。这一次，当你在讲述中暂停时，孩子们可以为他们的角色添加台词。

　　− 他们能发出合适的声音吗？

　　− 奶奶的声音听起来是怎样的？

　　− 狼假装奶奶时会用什么声音？

　　− 在故事的结尾，当金发姑娘害怕的时候，她会用什么声音？

· 孩子们现在可以借助他们的木偶复述整个故事。

小贴士　　　如果不同小组的孩子关注不同的童话故事，那么你很快就可以收集一系列木偶，将其收在盒子里留作日后使用，在盒子上贴上标签，每一盒代表一组人物。

跨领域链接

沟通、语言和读写能力的发展：角色故事。

很久以前（2）

• 让我们一起讲一个故事。

教学目标

• 鼓励孩子们使用语调和故事语言。

教学资源

准备一本你想复述的带图片的故事书。

教学准备

• 很多机会一起听故事。

怎么做

• 围圈而坐，然后选择一个所有孩子都知道的故事，例如《三只小猪》，问他们是否能记住这个故事。

• 告诉孩子们你们要一起复述这个故事。询问谁愿意开始。提示他们使用"很久以前"开头。

• 第一个孩子说了一句话后，下一个孩子继续，绕着圈子依次讲，直到故事结束。如果一个孩子疏漏了一些情节，要轻轻地提示他们，例如：

"哦，别忘了告诉我们，他用什么建造了他的房子。"

如果一个孩子使用了错误的语法，试着帮助他们重新用词，例如：

"我认为，你可以说：所以他们都跑到了第三个小猪屋里。"

如果一个孩子很难回忆起故事中的下一个事件，就问问是否有人能帮上忙。

• 鼓励孩子们重复故事中的短语，比如：

"他生气了，然后他喘了口气。"

• 提示最后一个孩子使用结束语："……从此以后，他们过上了幸福的生活。"

词汇

"很久以前"、"从此以后幸福地生活下去"，以及你选择的故事中重复使用的短语。

小贴士　　　如果孩子们一开始觉得这个游戏太难，就用这个故事的图画书版本来提示他们。

跨领域链接

沟通、语言和读写能力的发展：故事架构。

转啊转

· 和孩子们谈谈用油、洗涤液和食用色素所能产生的神奇效果。

教学目标

· 通过参与游戏来促进孩子们的思考和讨论。

教学资源

1）一升容量大小的塑料瓶（两个孩子合用一个）；2）冷水；3）植物油；4）洗涤液；5）食物色素；6）吸液管。

教学准备

· 确保孩子们知道如何使用吸液管，在你想做这项活动的前几天，让孩子们玩一下水。

怎么做

· 用冷水装满半个瓶子，滴入一两滴食物色素。观察并谈论你所看到的。

· 或者加一些洗涤液——一到两滴。观察并谈论。

· 或者加一些食用油——一到两滴。观察并讨论。

· 孩子们可以用添加的东西并按不同顺序在水中添加东西，来体验结果是什么。准备好你的问题，这样你可以支持他们的想法。

词汇

一些有用的问题：

你们正在做什么？

接下来你们会怎么做？

你们认为会发生什么？

你们注意到什么了？

和你们先加……的时候一样吗？

你们知道为什么会这样吗？

如果你们加了不止一种颜色会怎么样？

小贴士　　展示一种变化，这样孩子们就可以自由地运用自己的想法用材料来做实验了。

跨领域链接

认识与理解世界：探索和观察。

生日（1）

> • 在为孩子们表演一个故事之前，帮助他们想一想这个故事以及发生了什么。

教学目标

• 鼓励孩子们回应和复述故事。

教学资源

雪莉·休斯的《帮助别人的阿尔菲》（柯林斯图片狮子出版社 1985 年出版）

教学准备

• 将这个故事读给孩子们听。

• 和孩子们讨论：

— 为什么阿尔菲带着他舒适的毛毯去派对。

— 伯纳德在派对上的行为是怎样的？

• 一直问孩子们问题：

— 故事接下来会发生什么？

— 他/她感觉如何？

怎么做

• 让孩子们选择扮演阿尔菲、伯纳德、敏和其他参加聚会的人。成人可以扮演伯纳德的妈妈。

• 表演一下生日聚会。

— 阿尔菲拿着毯子来到伯纳德家，把礼物给了他。

— 所有的孩子都在玩泡泡，然后伯纳德把敏的泡泡弄爆了，她哭了。

— 大家坐下来喝茶，向伯纳德唱歌。

— 伯纳德吓到了敏。

— 阿尔菲拉着伯纳德的手转圈圈，但敏不肯加入。

— 阿尔菲放下他的毯子，这样他就可以抓住敏的手。

— 每个人都玩起了转圈圈的游戏。

• 大家交换角色，再次尝试表演派对场景。

词汇

担心的、沮丧的、震惊的、害怕的、善良的、快乐的。

小贴士

阿尔菲如何是帮忙的？孩子们是否明白这也是一种帮助吗？

跨领域链接

个人、社会和情感的发展：自信与自尊。

生日(2)

· 从一个著名的故事开始，快乐地讨论不同的结果。

教学目标

· 鼓励孩子们预测故事和事件的可能性结局。

教学资源

《帮助别人的阿尔菲》。

教学准备

· 给孩子们朗读故事，讨论阿尔菲、伯纳德、敏的人物感受和行为。

怎么做

· 问孩子们如果有不同的事情发生，故事情节会有什么变化。

 — 如果阿尔菲太担心不能去参加聚会，会发生什么呢？

 — 如果敏没有被伯纳德吓到，该怎么办呢？

 — 如果伯纳德被送到他的房间去冷静，那会发生什么呢？

 那么生日聚会会怎样？

· 选择一个想法去尝试。让孩子们选择在聚会上扮演阿尔菲、伯纳德、敏和其他人的人员。成人可以扮演伯纳德的母亲。

· 表演一个不同的生日派对，然后与原著的结果进行比较。

词汇

担心的、沮丧的、震惊的、害怕的、善良的、快乐的、遗憾的、吝啬的、友好的、生气的。

小贴士　　　这将是第 73 页生日（1）活动的一个很好的延续活动。

跨领域链接

个人、社会和情感的发展：自信与自尊。

玫瑰是红色的

• 示范如何改变传统押韵诗中的单词，并互相传递积极的信息。

教学目标

• 帮助孩子们创作童谣。

教学资源

扩写一首经典的童谣（押韵诗）。

玫瑰是红色的

紫罗兰是蓝色的

糖是甜的

你也是这样的

教学准备

• 教会孩子们这首传统的童谣。

• 如果可能，跟孩子们看一下玫瑰花和紫罗兰花。

怎么做

• 一个班围坐在一起，读这首传统的童谣给孩子们听。让孩子们跟着放大字体的版本阅读。

• 告知孩子们你们将改变童谣的一行，使之成为一首新的童谣。
  解释你要用班上孩子的名字，然后要用押韵的词表达一下美好的事物。

• 通过选择一个孩子的名字，把童谣的第三行改写一下。
  在你说最后一行的时候指着班中的另一个孩子，准备接龙，例如：
  玫瑰是红色的
  紫罗兰是蓝色的
  詹姆斯是快乐的
  你也是这样的

• 鼓励孩子们和你重复说出童谣，这样当他们说最后一句话的时候，每个人都会指向其他孩子。

• 我们会想其他关于彼此的美好的事情。把这些想法用在童谣里，让每个人都重复一遍。

词汇

快乐的、友好的、乐于助人的、善良的、欢快的、机智的、聪明的。

 小贴士　　　对于能力更强些的孩子，你可以写下他们的想法，让他们选择和使用这些词写出自己的童谣。

跨领域链接

个人、社会和情感的发展：建立关系。

取三件物品

· 根据三件任意选择的物品，和孩子们一起编一个故事。

教学目标

· 帮助孩子们用语言来想象角色和经历。

教学资源

1）一些仿真玩具，例如：农场或动物园的动物、车辆、娃娃家的家具和人物；2）箱子或篮子。

教学准备

· 收集大约十件物品，然后把它们放在一个漂亮的盒子或篮子里。

怎么做

· 和一组孩子围坐在一起。

· 选择一个孩子让其闭上眼睛，把手伸到篮子里。让他选择一个物品，然后睁开眼睛，告诉大家它是什么。

  另外两个孩子也这样做一下。

  把选出的三个物品放在圈子中间。

· 然后另一个孩子可以设定故事的场景。可能是，例如：

  海边

  楼梯下的橱柜

  一个陌生的星球

· 鼓励孩子们发挥想象力。

· 向孩子们解释，大家要创作一个包括这三个物件和场景的故事。

· 提醒孩子们使用熟悉的故事开头，例如，

  有一天……

  从前……

  在一个遥远的地方……

· 接着轮流编故事，并且可以互相补充。当快要结尾时，提醒孩子们使用熟悉的结束句型，例如：

  从此以后，他们都幸福地生活着。

  他们激动人心的一天结束了。

小贴士　　　　你可以试着坐在角色扮演区域，帮助设定故事的背景。

跨领域链接

创造力的发展：想象力和想象性的游戏。

大卫·霍伊
《一个更大的水花》

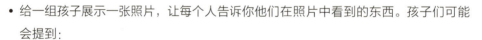

- 谁跳了进去？让孩子们仔细地观察一幅画，描述他们所看到和所想的。

教学目标

- 给孩子们机会去清晰地说话，显示出关注听者的意识。

教学资源

《一个更大的水花》（大卫·霍伊）

教学准备

- 告诉孩子们他们将轮流谈论一张照片。
- 向大家解释，答案没有正确或错误之分。
- 请他们仔细聆听别人的发言。

怎么做

- 给一组孩子展示一张照片，让每个人告诉你他们在照片中看到的东西。孩子们可能会提到：
  - 泳池
  - 蓝色的天空
  - 池子周围的座椅
  - 现代化的房屋
  - 跳板
  - 水花
- 现在让孩子们考虑一下这张照片，给他们提一些问题：

  "在那里感觉如何？"

  "天气怎么样？"

  "水是什么样的？"

  "水花是怎么产生的？"

  "是谁引起的水花？"

  "人们在哪里？"

"谁住在那里？"

"他们认为这个地方是哪里？"

• 通过问问题，鼓励孩子们提出他们的想法：

"为什么？"

"什么触发你这么思考？"

词汇

水花、喷射、跳水、跳板、游泳、水、深的、池子、蓝色、热的、太阳、假日。

小贴士　　孩子们可以继续分享他们在假期或游泳课的经历。

跨领域链接

认识与理解世界：地点。

佐·卡克里斯《全部上车》

 · 使用人员密集的图片组织孩子们玩"我侦察到"的游戏。

教学目标

• 为孩子们的讨论提供一个刺激的焦点。

教学资源

佐·卡克里斯的《全部上车》①。

怎么做

• 要求孩子们仔细观察图片,选择一个特别的人物,并找出他正在做什么。游戏开始时,你可以说:"我发现一个女孩在倒立,你们也能看到她吗?"

• 每个人都会轮流描述他们选择的人正在做什么。其他人应该仔细观察并试图找到这个人。

• 现在鼓励他们去推测:

  − 火车去哪里?

  − 所有的孩子都来自哪里?

  − 你能看到成年人吗?为什么看不到呢?

  − 你看到动物了吗?

  − 火车司机在哪里?

• 也许可以进一步扩大游戏范围,进一步描述在图片中你最喜欢的人物的外表,例如:

  − 男孩还是女孩?

  − 头发是怎样的?

  − 他们穿着什么样的衣服?

  − 他们多大了?

• 你能给这些人起名字吗?

词汇

正在跳、正在吃、正在跳舞、正在唱歌、正坐着、正在走、正在讨论、正在笑、正在爬、

---

① 可将国内绘本《小人儿帮手》(中川千寻文,古寄纯嗣图,蒲蒲兰译,二十一世纪出版社 2013 年版)作为备选。——译者注。

正躺着。

小贴士　　　　　　孩子们可以继续共同合作画一张图画。每个人都在一张大纸上画一个人，你画的人正在做什么呢？

跨领域链接

创造力的发展：创造力。

创作一个角色

- 孩子们穿着制服，站在相框后面，你给他们照相，他们感觉很开心。

教学目标
- 鼓励孩子们利用他们对这个世界的体验。

教学资源

1）几套演出服饰； 2）一个旧相框； 3）照相机； 4）一系列关于人物和他们的职业介绍的非小说类书籍； 5）电脑，或纸和笔。

教学准备
- 阅读有关真人的非小说类书籍。

怎么做

- 和一小群孩子一起看一些关于真人的非小说类书籍。通过互联网了解更多有关人们工作的信息。孩子们认识护士、医生、警察或消防员吗？鼓励他们分享他们的经验。

- 让孩子们打扮成一个新的人物。轮流在旧相框后面摆好姿势。你给孩子们拍照，就好像他们真的在相框里一样。然后鼓励他们谈论其他的角色。
  - 他们是谁？
  - 他们的工作是什么？
  - 他们住在哪里？
  - 他们几岁了？

- 帮助他们写一个关于他们特征的句子，例如：
  我的名字是萨斯卡亚，我是一位消防员。
  你可能希望他们在电脑上写下这句话，或者你可以充当一个记录员。记住要帮助他们写完后重新阅读他们写的话。

- 通过收集几张照片和一些句子，创作一本书。孩子们会喜欢一次次阅读这本书的。

词汇

工作、制服。

小贴士　　　　在选择关于人们和他们所做工作的书籍和信息时，尽量打破原有的认知。

跨领域链接

个人、社会和情感的发展：团队意识。

传统的童话故事

· 以一个传统的童话故事开头，让孩子们在角色扮演中享受乐趣。

教学目标

· 为孩子们提供一个机会，让他们展开想象力，演绎老故事的新版本。

教学资源

1）传统故事书； 2）演出服； 3）匹配你选择故事的角色扮演活动的物品。

教学准备

· 在角色扮演区域做一些简单的调整，比如：

– 拿出三个不同大小的碗和椅子。

– 用一张蓝色的纸条架起一座桥。

怎么做

· 复述一个传统的故事，鼓励他们加入一些重复出现的短语，比如：

"我吹，我吹，我要把你的房子吹倒。"

· 把一小群孩子带到准备好的角色扮演区。询问他们认为什么样的人可能生活在这里。

· 鼓励他们在游戏中套用故事中的事件。试着自己扮演一个角色，例如可以说：

"我要坐在桥边上，看看谁要过桥。"

你戴上狼面具，邀请孩子们扮演三只猪，你要尽力并试着吹倒他们的房子。

· 记住要使用与孩子们相关的故事；另建议使用《排灯节的罗摩和西塔》故事的情景。

词汇

出自不同故事的语言。

小贴士　　　　读和写故事的活动给孩子们阅读和写作的机会，例如妈妈在桌上留下一张纸条给小红帽，让她给奶奶送一篮水果。

跨领域链接

沟通、语言和读写能力的发展：故事事件。

派特 · 哈特金斯
《令人惊喜的聚会》

• 用著名故事中的词汇玩中国的传话游戏。

教学目标

• 鼓励孩子们使用语言做游戏。

教学资源

派特 · 哈特金斯的《令人惊喜的聚会》（红狐狸出版社 1993 年出版）

教学准备

• 向孩子们讲述故事，以帮助他们了解如何表达信息的改变。

• 讨论一些不熟悉的词汇的含义，例如：
"锄欧芹"或"袭击家禽"。

• 观察"我将举办一个聚会"这几个词是怎么写的。

兔子还在轻声传递他的消息吗？

怎么做

• 向孩子们解释，当你低声说话时，别人很难听清楚。
告诉他们，你们要玩一个低声传话游戏，在这个游戏中，信息经常被混淆起来，那就是乐趣之处！

• 大家围圈而坐，大人会从书中选出一个短语，轻声告诉他左边的孩子，例如：
"兔子明天将要锄欧芹。"

• 然后那个孩子会轻声传话给下一个孩子，然后一个接一个传。

• 当信息传回给那个大人时，他会大声重复，以便每个人都能听到。

• 现在告诉孩子原始的信息是什么。
－ 有变化吗？

词汇

书中的短语。

小贴士

如果你使用一个复杂的短语，那样会更有趣，因为它比一个容易识别的信息更有可能被改变，比如"我明天要办一个聚会。"

跨领域链接

个人、社会和情感的发展：建立关系。

将会发生什么?

· 为孩子们提供一个机会，让他们思考并推测下一步会发生什么。

教学目标

· 帮助孩子们得出结论和推测故事的情节。

教学资源

1）伯明翰的《甘伯先生的汽车》（海雀图文出版社 1979 年出版）； 2）伯明翰的《甘伯先生外出》（海雀图文出版社 1979 年出版）

教学准备

· 在和孩子们讨论之前，自己先阅读一下这些故事。

怎么做

· 朗读甘伯先生乘船出游的故事。给孩子们看每个人在船上的照片，了解那时他们快乐地在一起。

  让孩子们猜测他们认为接下来会发生什么事。

· 如果他们猜测船会沉下去，问他们为什么会发生这种情况，然后继续读到故事的结尾。

· 数一数，在翻船前，船上有多少人和动物。

· 轮流看一看每张照片。

  － 他们还记得甘伯先生对孩子和每只动物说的话吗?

  － 为什么他们认为每个人都想上船?

  － 他们愿意去那里吗?

· 现在给孩子们看关于甘伯先生的第二本书。先阅读前两页，然后让他们想一想接下来会发生什么。当他们猜测孩子们和动物们会想加入行动时，继续读故事。

· 当他们愉快地开车时，停止读故事。问孩子们可能会发生什么。他们可能会使用上一本书中的想法，或者他们可能会提出其他建议。

· 继续阅读下一页直到故事中描述的下雨情节，然后询问孩子们的想法:

  － 他们是否注意到汽车没有车顶?

  － 有人想过在雨天车穿过田野时会发生什么事吗?

· 当车轮陷在泥地里，甘伯先生需要有人帮忙推车时:

  － 孩子们认为谁会帮助他，为什么?

- 继续把故事读下去，直到他们把车开起来，太阳出来。
- 告诉孩子们，这个结局将不会和第一个故事相同。
  - 他们认为故事将如何结束？
- 读到故事的最后。
  - 你猜得对吗？这个结局和你想象的一样吗？

小贴士

这项活动适用于其他系列故事书，在两个故事中都有相同的角色。

跨领域链接

交际、语言和读写能力的发展：故事事件。

童谣比赛

 · 借助一项团队游戏来展示孩子们知道多少童谣。

教学目标

• 鼓励孩子们回忆和欣赏熟悉的童谣。

怎么做

• 将孩子们分成三组，每组有一位成人。告诉大家，将有一场比赛来找出谁知道的童谣最多。

• 给每组一个数字。请第一组必须做好准备。

• 鼓励每个人保持稳定的节奏从 1 数到 10。一旦数到 10，第一组必须说出他们的童谣。

• 一旦他们讲完，他们就开始数 1，2，3……当他们数到 10 时，第二组应该立即说出他们的童谣。

• 孩子们又开始数到 10，这是给第三组信号提醒他们说出他们的第一首童谣。

• 继续按这种方法，一轮又一轮地循环，直到：

　　－ 有一组重复一个已经说过的童谣，或者

　　－ 有一组再也想不到其他童谣了，那么这一组就"退出"比赛了。

• 其他两组继续进行比赛，直到胜者产生。每个人都可以参与计数和仲裁！

 小贴士　　　　鼓励孩子们使用他们所知道的任何数字童谣和其他喜欢的童谣。

跨领域链接

个人、社会和情感的发展：气质和态度。

第二部分

读

　　要为儿童营建一个富有标识、符号、告示、数字、词语、押韵诗、读本等学习环境，让他们能够浏览并与成人或者同伴共享这些资源。

——英国皇冠出版社 2008 年版《早期基础阶段实践导引》，第 42 页。

第四章

书的世界

蜡烛（1）

· 当你阅读关于"光"之主题的书籍时探索烛光的魔力。

教学目标

· 鼓励孩子们通过书籍增加他们对世界的最直观的了解。

教学资源

有关"光"主题的书籍，例如：

左克，J.（2002）. 八支蜡烛点燃：一个光明节的故事［M］. 伦敦：弗朗西斯·林肯出版社.

左克，J.（2005）. 点亮一盏灯：一个排灯节的故事［M］. 伦敦：弗朗西斯·林肯出版社.

左克，J.（2005）. 灯笼和鞭炮：一个中国新年故事［M］. 伦敦：弗朗西斯·林肯出版社.

霍勒伯，J.（2000）. 点燃蜡烛：一本光明节的翻翻书［M］. 伦敦：海雀图文出版社.

教学准备

· 在阅读区设置一个展台。

· 用深色布盖住桌子或者用布帘遮住布告板。

· 展示一些蜡烛、烛台、灯笼和代表不同节日使用的灯。

怎么做

· 在天黑的时候安排你的阅读课。

  关掉主灯，在你的阅读区打开一盏灯或点上一支蜡烛。

  每天阅读一本书。

· 问孩子们关于前几天的故事内容。鼓励孩子们比较灯在不同的节日里的使用方式。

  — 他们注意到什么是一样的？

  — 当他们在家时，什么时候点蜡烛？

· 有很多节日都有蜡烛和光，当你开始这项活动的时候，你可以介绍一下光明节、排灯节、圣诞节、生日。

词汇

光、灯、灯笼、蜡烛。

小贴士　　　　如果你想点蜡烛，只有当孩子们都安静地坐在你身边的时候才这样做。

把蜡烛放在一个装有沙子的金属饼干罐里，并把它放在孩子够不到的结实的平面上。把你的灭火毯放在你身边。把火柴递给另一个成年人，等你使用后马上把它们收起来。

跨领域链接

认识与理解世界：交流。

蜡烛（2）

· 和孩子们一起读一首押韵诗，然后把它换成自己的名字进行改编。

教学目标
· 鼓励孩子们开始自己"阅读"。

教学资源
1）包含《杰克要灵敏》这首童谣的书； 2）用大号字体写下这首童谣。

教学准备
· 和孩子们一起念这首童谣，这样他们就熟悉了这首童谣。之后也许孩子们会学着自己说。

怎么做
· 一起念这首童谣，加上一些动作：
  杰克要灵敏——踮着脚尖跳舞
  杰克要快速——在原地尽可能快地小跑
  杰克跳过烛台——跳得很高
· 坐在一起，孩子们看着你用大号字体写下的这首童谣。把孩子们的注意力集中在一首诗的排版上。他们注意到每一行都很短吗？
· 你用手指指着单词，一起说出童谣。
  有的时候，你保持安静，让孩子们说出下一个单词。
  可以请一个孩子站出来，在大家面前大声朗读出来。
· 现在围成一圈。
  孩子们手牵着手，唱着歌，再表演一遍，但每次改换不同的名字，例如：
  大家都要灵敏。
  大家都要快速。
  "弗兰迪"跳过烛台。
  听自己名字的那个小朋友跳到活动圈的中心。

词汇
灵敏的、快速的。

小贴士　　　用硬纸筒和纸板快速制作一个老式的烛台，放在圆圈的中心，让小朋友跳过去。

跨领域链接

身体的发展：运动和空间。

蜡烛（3）

 · 孩子们制作一本关于他们的"光"之主题的书。

教学目标

· 创作一本孩子们能读的"班书"。

教学资源

1）照相机； 2）打印机； 3）影集。

教学准备

· 拍摄一些关于孩子们在节日期间使用的任何蜡烛、灯、灯笼等的照片。

— 可以借用家里用的各种光，在你所处的环境中拍张照。

— 可以从家里带一张照片。

怎么做

· 帮助孩子们在影集的每一页上放一张照片。

· 鼓励孩子们就自己的照片说一个简短的句子，并帮助他们写下来，或者替他们写下来。

把句子剪下来，并把它固定在相册中的这张照片旁边。

· 一起决定一个合适的标题，做一个封面，把书放在蜡烛展示台上。

一起读这本书。

每个孩子可以把自己制作的那一页读给大家听。

· 当你要变换展台的时候，就把这本书放在你的书箱里，这样孩子们就可以随时拿到这本书来看。

词汇

孩子们的名字、节日的名字。

 小贴士 如果你使用每一页都塑封的相册，孩子们就能容易地完成自己的回顾和学习。

跨领域链接

个人、社会和情感的发展：团队意识。

所有的小鸭子

 • 和孩子们一起创立一个以鸭子特点为主题的春天的展台。

教学目标
- 孩子们能阅读大量的关于这一主题的书籍。

教学资源
1）关于鸭子主题的书；2）展板和一个平面；3）黄颜色的布料或纸张；4）鸭子的图片和模型。

教学准备
- 用大小适合的纸覆盖整个展板。很明显，我们要选择黄色。展示一些鸭子的图片和五只小鸭子的文字（见第9章的"五只小鸭子活动"：制作一本书。）
- 找到四到五本关于鸭子的书，甚至可以在阅读区放一些黄颜色的垫子来继续黄颜色的主题。

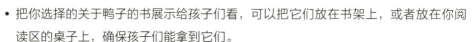

怎么做
- 把你选择的关于鸭子的书展示给孩子们看，可以把它们放在书架上，或者放在你阅读区的桌子上，确保孩子们能拿到它们。
- 在一周内，把这些书都读给孩子们听，鼓励孩子们自己去读或看这些书。
- 孩子们可以把其他的关于鸭子主题的书加入到收集库——有些书来自你的阅读区，有的书来自孩子们家里。
- 孩子们可以把自己画的关于鸭子的铅笔画和水彩画放在墙上展示，把玩具鸭子带来，或者把鸭子模型和书一起放在书架上。

 小贴士　　　　包括一些非小说类的书籍以及故事和童谣。

跨领域链接
认识与理解世界：探索与观察。

如何去做……

- **在父母或老师烹饪的时候让孩子拍一些照片，帮助孩子们用这些照片制作一些食谱类书籍。**

教学目标

- 帮助孩子们学习从书中获取一些信息。

教学资源

1）数码相机； 2）有粘性的便条。

教学准备

- 决定你要做什么菜，然后准备好食材和用具。
- 和孩子们分享一些有关食谱的书籍，让他们认识到这些书籍的用处。

怎么做

- 在你烹饪过程的每一个阶段，选一个孩子拍照。

  拍摄的内容是：

  - 食材；

  - 穿上围裙的孩子们；

  - 烹饪的每一个阶段；

  - 清洗/整理；

  - 完成的食物。

- 帮助孩子们打印出照片。

  把照片摆出来，这样每个人都能看到它们。

  照片的顺序是正确的吗？

- 要求孩子们把照片按正确的顺序分类。解释一下这样做很重要的理由。

  "如果你按错误的顺序烹饪，会发生什么呢？"

- 现在，在照片上打几个洞，然后把它们绑在一起。

  帮助孩子们为每幅图片配一个简单的句子。

  把这个句子写在一个贴纸上，然后每个孩子都可以在相关的照片上贴上一张贴纸。

  缺少什么？一个书名或是封面。

  孩子们可以制作缺少的部分，并把它添加到他们的说明书中。

小贴士　　　　每次你烹饪的时候都要做这个活动，这样在孩子的童书角建立一个食谱区。也许他们可以借一个食谱，然后带回家试着再做一次。

跨领域链接

认识与理解世界：信息通信技术（ICT）。

假日（1）

•根据度假目的地，制作一本明信片集，和孩子们把明信片分类，创建一个展板。

教学目标

• 通过使用标签和书籍，为孩子们创造有大量打印文字的环境。

教学资源

明信片集。

教学准备

• 和孩子们聊聊假日和外出旅行的日子。

问问他们去过哪儿了。

• 鼓励他们带上他们去过的地方的明信片。

给孩子们的父母发个通知，允许孩子近几天收集所有的明信片。

怎么做

• 当你收集好明信片后，把它们铺在地板上。

让一组孩子探索卡片上的图片。

将其作为交流和分享经验的另一个机会。

• 然后使用分类环或大张纸将明信片分为三到四组。分组的创意可以包括：海边、酒店、主题公园或村庄。

鼓励孩子们决定如何分类，然后接受他们的创意。

• 让孩子们为每一组提出建议并且将其写在标签上。它应该是什么？

当你为他们每一组写上一些合适的标签时，要求孩子们认真看着。

• 展示每一组的明信片。

现在让孩子们去找到与自己小组主题相关的书籍，也将其加入到展示中。尽力把小说类和非小说类书籍都包括进去。

• 鼓励其他孩子来看看这个展示。

解释一下明信片已经被分类了。

－ 他们能读懂标签吗？或者他们能猜出标签的意思吗？

词汇

海边、山、湖、镇、村、酒店、游泳池、主题公园。

小贴士　　　　　　在故事时间里阅读这些书。

跨领域链接

问题解决、推理和计算的能力：计算。

我的曲调

• 孩子们创作和阅读自己的音乐。

教学目标
• 给孩子们提供一个机会练习从左到右跟踪符号。

教学资源
1）纸条若干； 2）带粘性的圆圈； 3）乐器。

教学准备
• 将纸带折叠成四部分，以形成一条线条。

怎么做
• 给每个孩子一张纸条和三个有粘性的圆圈。向孩子们解释一下：
  "你可以把你的一个圆圈贴在纸上的某一方块中。选择你喜欢的任何方块。"
  "在另两个方块中粘贴另两个圆圈。"
  "这时应该有三个方块有圆，一个方块是空的。"

• 向孩子们解释：
  "当你看到一个圆圈时，你就演奏你的乐器。"
  "当你看到这个方块是空的时，你就休息。"
  用一种乐器演示，让每个人都能理解。
• 孩子们将使用打击乐器演奏他们自己的音乐作品。
  从左侧开始，然后一直到纸条的右边，孩子们会为每个圆圈打一个节拍，并在空格处休息。
• 你数出一个强有力的 1—2—3—4 节奏来帮助他们掌握时间。
  当你数数的时候，几个小朋友可以同时演奏自己的曲调。
• 一旦他们熟悉了这个过程：
  − 就让孩子们交换纸条，或者
  − 把他们的纸条反过来，演奏新的曲调
  为更有能力的孩子创造一些变化：

- 把纸条一个接在另一个下面，演奏更长的曲调。一个成年人可以依次指向每一个纸条，让孩子们可以一起演奏。
- 你可以做一些有八个方块和六个圆圈的纸条。

小贴士　　如果你想使用钟音条，可以让孩子从 C、G、D、A、E 中选择。它们构成的五声音阶永远是和谐的。

跨领域链接

创造力的发展：音乐和舞蹈。

故事场所

• 使用适合教学主题的图画书来帮助孩子思考故事场景的设置。

教学目标

• 帮助孩子们意识到故事是有场景的。

教学资源

几本关于该主题的故事书，例如：

场景：在花园里。使用书籍：

巴特沃斯·N.，印克潘·M.（2006）.雅斯贝斯的豆茎 ［M］.伦敦：霍德儿童读物出版社.

卡尔·E.（2002）.饥饿的毛毛虫.伦敦：海雀图文出版社.

卡尔·E.（2009）.小小的种子.伦敦：西蒙和舒斯特儿童出版社.

法兰西·V.，巴特利特·A.（1995）.奥利弗的蔬菜.伦敦：霍德儿童出版社.

怎么做

• 把选好的故事书展示给孩子们看，提示孩子们所有故事内容。

• 取其中一本书，问孩子们故事发生在哪里。对其他书籍重复此操作，并说道：

"谁注意到了什么？"

"所有这些故事都发生在……"

• 解释一下，这就是所谓的"背景环境"。这就是故事发生的地方。想想你在这个环境中可能会发现什么，例如在公园里，你可能会发现花、甲虫、秋千或沙坑。

• 其他环境呢？如果故事发生在如下的背景环境里，你会发现……

－ 森林：狼、树、鸟；

－ 大海：美人鱼、贝壳、鱼；

－ 家：妈妈、床、电视。

• 孩子们能想到任何有这些背景环境的书吗？孩子们可以翻遍班里的书柜来找到他们记得的故事发生在某个这样的场景中。让孩子们每天阅读一些这样的书。把这些书放在一起，这样孩子们就可以随时阅读。

词汇

背景环境。

小贴士　　　　你的出发点可以是任何适合你当前工作的主题或环境。

跨领域链接

沟通、语言和读写能力的发展：故事场所。

我的祖母

• 为孩子们制作一本故事集，让他们想一想自己的祖母。

教学目标

• 鼓励孩子们增加自己对这个世界的体验。

教学资源

1）故事书《小红帽》； 2）其他有祖母人物的故事书：

海德威克·M.（2010）. 凯蒂·莫拉和两位祖母. 伦敦：红狐狸出版社.

巴特威克·N.（2008）. 我的祖母真棒. 伦敦：沃克书籍出版社.

艾斯利·H.（2006）. 我和我祖母. 沃特福德：艾斯利出版社.

教育准备

• 要求孩子们去收集有祖母主题的故事。

怎么做

• 要求孩子们复述《小红帽》故事。
  向他们展示故事书中祖母的图片。

• 让孩子们查看其他的书，找到关于祖母的图片。
  问问是否他们有一位祖母（要了解其他替代词）
  收集所有孩子们称呼祖母的单词，例如：奶奶……

• 关于他们的祖母，有什么特别之处吗？
  − 她长什么样子？
  − 她平时为他们做什么？
  − 她会来看望他们吗？
  − 她看上去像故事书中的祖母吗？
  − 他们喜欢和祖母一起干什么事？
  − 他们会像小红帽一样从自己家走到祖母家吗？

• 孩子们理解他们和他们祖母之间的关系吗？例如：
  − 她是爸爸的妈妈或是妈妈的妈妈？
  − 他们能否告诉你他们是祖母的孙子（外孙）或孙女（外孙女）？
  也许你可以展示一张你小时候和祖母在一起的照片。

- 打印并展示出所有祖母的其他用词（见提示）。

  用你已经收集到的故事书来展示这些词汇。
- 如果孩子们热衷于更深入地讨论这个话题，你不妨也制作一本关于祖母的故事集。

词汇

奶奶、姥姥、外婆。

小贴士　　展示用来表示"祖母"的各种词汇，这些词汇是你所处的家庭环境中的口语表达，这样可以提升对不同语言和剧本的意识。例如：

Mamie（法语）、 Abuela（西班牙语）、 Oma（德语）、 Babcia（波兰语）

跨领域链接

认识与理解世界：时间。

家中的书

 • 每个人都会阅读他们带回家的书籍并且选出他们最喜欢的书。

教学目标

• 强调家长与孩子们一起阅读的重要性。

教学资源

1）一系列的书籍，例如关于狗熊的书； 2）用 A3 大小的纸，展示每本书的标题。每本书用一张纸； 3）三种颜色的贴纸若干。

教学准备

• 选择一套由一个主题贯穿的七八本书。

• 准备一张通知，告知家长本周孩子们在学校有借书的活动。

• 用书本制作出吸引人的展示，让孩子们从中选择一本。

• 将 A3 纸放在孩子可以拿到的地方，便于孩子们可以记录下他们借了哪本书。

怎么做

• 让一组孩子聚集在一起看这些书。让他们拿着这些书，谈论一下哪些书是他们熟悉的，哪些书是他们喜欢读的。

• 告诉孩子们可以把这些书中的一本带回家，和他们的父母一起阅读。解释一下，你将会发现大部分人最喜欢哪本书。

• 帮助孩子们选择一本书带回家，并在 A3 纸上的书名下写上自己的名字。

• 第二天，鼓励家长和孩子们选择一个标签来表明他们对他们读过的书的看法，例如：

   绿色：很棒——非常喜欢阅读；

   黄色：不错——值得一读；

   红色：还好——不是我最喜欢的书。

• 然后将这些书介绍给另一组孩子阅读。重复这个活动直到每个孩子至少带过一本书回家。

• 鼓励孩子们去数每本书上的彩色贴纸。看看哪一本是全班最喜欢的。

词汇

非常好、非常喜欢、值得一读、推荐、最喜欢的、有趣的。

小贴士　　尝试提供双语书籍来匹配孩子们家中的语言，并对并非所有家庭的家长都有读写能力这一事实敏感——你可以在某个环境中与助手们一起做这项活动，可能这样更合适些。

跨领域链接

个人、社会和情感的发展：自信与自尊。

谁说的?

 · 用传统故事向孩子们介绍"讲话泡泡"。

教学目标
- 去创作一项展示，鼓励孩子们去了解印刷的书籍，然后讲述故事。

教学资源
1）选择一些熟悉的故事书，例如：传统的故事书； 2）从 A3 纸上剪下一些大泡泡。

教学准备
- 在"讲话泡泡"里，写下一些某些角色重复使用的短语，例如，

奶奶，你有大大的眼睛。

谁在吃我的粥？

小猪，小猪，让我进来，

有人一直在吃我的粥，所以粥不见了！

- 把这些"讲话泡泡"展示在阅读区展板上，把选好的书放在附近。用"谁说的"这几个词作为展示的标题。

怎么做
- 把一组孩子聚集在一起。问他们是否知道"讲话泡泡"是什么。有些孩子会从卡通故事或漫画中识别出什么是"讲话泡泡"。
- 向孩子们解释，"讲话泡泡"向你展示人们说的话。告诉他们这些"讲话泡泡"来自他们所知道的故事。当你问到"我想知道，是否有人知道谁说的那句话"时指向标题词。
- 现在一起朗读"讲话泡泡"中的一句话。
  "有人知道这句话是谁说的吗？"
  和孩子们一起阅读其他的"讲话泡泡"，然后确定是哪个人物和故事。
- 鼓励孩子们在提供的故事书中找到角色，帮助他们用"讲话泡泡"来展示。
- 有人能用故事书中的不同例子来展示讲话吗？如果可能的话，用孩子们的建议来扩充你的展示板内容。

词汇
讲话泡泡、谈论、词汇、说（原形）、说（过去式）、人物。

小贴士　　在你阅读所展示的单词时，指着这些单词，这将帮助孩子们回忆这些单词，并鼓励他们加入讨论。

跨领域链接

交际、语言和读写能力的发展：故事人物。

我们要去动物园

· **帮助孩子们选择和复印他们自己版本的故事。**

教学目标
- 帮助促进孩子们对故事结构的理解。

教学资源

1）为制作故事书，准备好纸张（见教学准备）； 2）一台可用的复印机。

教学准备
- 在每一张 A4 纸上写下：

一句开场白，例如：有一天我们都去了动物园。

一句结束语，例如：我们都回家喝茶了。

还有几页纸写着动物的名字，可能是一张图片，还有一个数字，例如：两只大象。

对于稍大一些的孩子，可以自己选择开场白和结束语。

- 把每一页纸放在一个塑料文件包里，然后保存在一个活页夹里。

怎么做
- 向孩子们解释，他们要自己编故事。

  "什么是开始故事的好方法？"

  听听孩子们的建议。
- 和孩子们一起，复印出今天故事的开场白，给每个孩子自己的复印件，帮助他们读出句子。
- 现在看看收集的动物页面。

  "谁能读一下他们说的话？"

  鼓励所有的孩子参与进来。
- 他们需要从动物的页面中选择三页，并将其复印出来，加入到开场白页面，然后开始制作一本书。
- 现在要讨论，故事必须结束了。

  "谁能想到一些结局？"

  复印并分发今天的结尾句，一起阅读。
- 把你所有的书页放在一起，制作出一本你自己的书。

- 过几天，再重复这个过程，创作一个不同的故事，例如：

  我们要去野餐，我们要带……

  从而逐步建立起你的故事创意源文件。

 小贴士　　当孩子们复印好这些页面后可塑封，这样可以保护原页面。

跨领域链接

认识与理解世界：信息通信技术（ICT）。

我是谁？

- 拍摄装扮成故事书中人物的孩子们，再制作恰当的"讲话泡泡"一起展示。

教学目标
- 鼓励孩子们复述故事和讨论人物。

教学资源
1）选择一些熟悉的故事书，例如：传统的故事书；2）装扮用的服饰；3）照相机；4）制作"讲话泡泡"的纸张或电脑上的书写程序。

教学准备
- 运用第115页"谁说的？"活动向孩子们介绍"讲话泡泡"。
- 确定孩子们都熟悉你所选择的故事。

怎么做
- 和一组孩子一起进行这个活动。

  让他们从准备好的故事中选择一个最喜欢的故事。

  鼓励孩子们复述他们最喜欢的一个故事。

  他们能按先后顺序告诉你故事的主要内容吗？
- 让他们装扮成一个角色，谈一谈他们所选择的角色。

  拍摄一张已装扮好的孩子们的照片。
- 现在告诉每个孩子，他们要想起他们的角色在故事中所说的话。

  帮助他们选择一个著名的或重复的短语。

  要么让孩子们帮你在电脑上输入单词，然后打印出人物说的话，然后把它们剪下，粘贴在一个"讲话泡泡"里。

  要么让孩子们看着你把他们的话写在纸上的"讲话泡泡"里。
- 把"讲话泡泡"展示在孩子的照片旁边。

  其他孩子能猜出他们是哪个故事书中的人物吗？
- 使用"我是谁？"作为展板的标题。

词汇
你选择的故事书中的对话。

小贴士　　　　　选择适合你班级的故事，能反映学生们的文化多样性。

跨领域链接

沟通、语言和读写能力的发展：故事人物。

户外阅读

• 在一个晴朗的日子里，把你的读书角移到室外。

教学目标

• 创建一个吸引人的读书区，供孩子们和成年人一起享受阅读书本的乐趣。

教学资源

1）一些垫子；2）一些毯子；3）一些书；4）放书籍的可移动推车、装置、架子或箱子。

怎么做

• 告诉孩子们，这是一个大晴天，你认为把读书角移到室外将很有乐趣。

• 带一组孩子到室外讨论哪里是最好的地方。鼓励孩子们为自己的想法辩护，并倾听彼此的建议。

"我们能不能把读书角放在太阳底下吗？为什么不呢？"

"坐在小路上怎么样？会舒服吗？"

"我们能靠近自行车或门口吗？是否安全？"

"在树底下或雨篷下怎么样？那里会是安静的地方吗？"

• 当你们选择了最好的地方后，帮助孩子们规划他们需要什么，如果可能的话，让孩子们把东西搬到室外。让孩子们把物品放在适当的地方，让他们在舒适、安全的地方阅读。他们是否想要有什么特别的规则来规定如何在外面使用这些书？

• 然后让他们坐下来，享受阅读的乐趣。

词汇

垫子、毯子、手推车、盒子、装置、架子、书。

小贴士　　　　给确定读书角区域的小组提供时间，让他们告诉其他孩子关于他们的选择。

跨领域链接

个人、社会和情感的发展：行为和自我控制。

书签（1）

 • 做一个书签，帮助孩子们记住他们在书本中阅读的位置。

教学目标

• 创建一个资源来帮助孩子阅读。

教学资源

1）闪光粉；　2）层压纸和塑封机。

怎么做

• 帮助孩子们在一张层压纸膜上洒上闪光粉。把上方的层压纸盖起来，根据你的设备进行层压塑封。

• 把它剪成可以用来做书签的长条，放在你书旁边漂亮的罐子里，让任何人都可以使用。

• 和一群孩子坐在一起。确保每个孩子都有一本书和一张书签。

• 练习使用书签来指出你正在阅读的单词。利用这个时间强化从左到右，从页面的顶部到底部的阅读方式。

小贴士　　　因为这些书签几乎是透明的，所以它们不会妨碍能够"往前阅读"的孩子。他们仍然可以阅读下一个单词或者查看延续到下一行的句子。

跨领域链接

认识与理解世界：设计与制作。

书签(2)

· 孩子们制作属于自己的特别的棒棒糖粘纸书签。

教学目标

· 制作个性化的书签来鼓励孩子们阅读。

教学资源

1) 一些棒棒糖的棒子；2) 选择1：毡尖笔（粗头笔）；3) 选择2：若干条毛毡、毛线和旧手套。

怎么做

· 选择今天和孩子们一起使用哪一个想法。

选择1——适合可以写自己名字的孩子们

帮助孩子们用毡尖笔沿着棒棒糖的棒子长度写下自己的名字。如有必要的话，在一张草稿纸上练习一下。

· 在他们名字的末尾留出一点空间，在那里他们可以添加一些小图片，例如一朵花、一面旗帜或一辆小轿车。

选择2——制作一个手偶

· 从手套上剪下手指套，给每个孩子一个。这些手指套应该是2—3厘米长。

· 帮助孩子们把特征粘在他们的手偶上，例如：

  - 在红手指上涂上黑点，制作出一只瓢虫。

  - 在绿手指上画上两只大眼睛，制作出一只青蛙。

  - 用一些毛发做出鼻子、眼睛和嘴巴，成为一张脸。

· 将棒棒糖的棒子塞到手偶里并粘上胶水固定。

小贴士　　　　孩子们可以用他们的棒棒糖书签来识别他们今天选择带回家的书。

跨领域链接

认识与理解世界：设计与制作。

第五章

发现

花园中心(2)

· 使用标签来标识向日葵的各个部分，并且帮助孩子们阅读。

教学目标
• 帮助孩子们理解一个单词的概念。

教学资源

　　1）埃里克·卡尔的《小小的种子》西蒙和舒斯特儿童书籍出版社 2009 年出版； 2）一盆向日葵花； 3）放书籍的可移动推车、装置、架子或箱子； 4）黄色和绿色餐巾纸， PVA 胶水可食用的种子（例如南瓜种子）； 5）一些大大小小从卡片上剪下的标签。

教学准备

• 阅读和享受埃里克·卡尔的《小小的种子》故事。仔细观察和思考作者是如何创作书中的图画的。

• 给孩子们时间仔细观察向日葵。他们能识别出这些植物的不同部分吗？

怎么做

• 和一组孩子在墙面上创造一幅巨大的向日葵拼贴画。让孩子们依次识别花的各个部位。把单词清楚地写在标签上，然后用可剥离粘合剂把它贴在花各部分的旁边。

• 一起朗读这些标签。朗读的时候观察每一个单词的初始字母。

• 把标签拿开，打乱，然后把它们交给孩子们。让每个人依次阅读他们的标签，并告诉你把它放在哪里。把标签贴回去。重复这个活动，直到每个孩子人都轮到一次。从能力较强的孩子开始，给其他人一个机会去学习或记住标签的内容。

• 拿出几组使用相同单词的小标签，以便孩子们可以选择去制作小的拼贴画，然后贴上标签。这些拼贴画可以用在你的花园中心角色扮演活动中，或者作为不同花卉的目录，顾客可以来购买。

词汇

　　花茎、叶子、芽、花、种子。

小贴士　　　　在向日葵花上安放种子是相当复杂的。向孩子们展示如何做，但不要期望他们能在轮到自己时也能重复做好。

跨领域链接

认识与理解世界：探索与观察。

你的名字里有什么?

• 孩子们通过向领队走去，对有他们名字中的字母作出回应, 这个字母识别游戏孩子们会玩得很开心。

教学目标

• 帮助孩子们记住他们名字中的字母。

教学资源

1) 一组塑料字母放在一个袋子里，只要你有这组孩子名字中的所有字母，你可能不必使用字母表中的所有 26 个字母； 2) 用来书写他们名字的纸张。

教学准备

• 确保每个人都知道他们自己名字中的每一个字母。

• 孩子们可以把名字写出来放在身边, 以备玩游戏的时候需要查看。

怎么做

• 选出一个人担任领队。这个领队，或者是一个成人，或者是孩子，站在装有字母袋子的前面。其他的孩子们横着排好队面对领队站立，距离 6—7 步远。

• 这个领队手伸入袋子中，随意拿起一个字母。他们知道这个字母是什么吗？如果不知道，准备好去帮助他们。

• 然后领队大声说出这个字母，并且展示给大家看。任何一个孩子，如果名字中有这个字母，就向前跨出一步。

"如果你的名字中有两个这个字母，你可以跨出两步。"

• 领队继续挑选并说出字母的名字。第一个到达领队的孩子接任领队。余下的每个人都回到出发地。

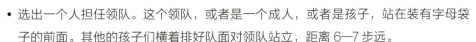

小贴士

成人需要监控游戏的准确性，并帮助那些仍然在学习如何拼写他们自己名字的幼儿。

跨领域链接

个人、社会和情感的发展：建立关系。

早餐时间

• 使用谷物盒帮助孩子们辨认单词或符号。

教学目标

• 鼓励孩子们回忆他们经常看到的单词或符号。

教学资源

1）谷物包装袋；2）谷类植物的照片或放种子的容器，谷物包括：燕麦、大米、小麦和玉米；3）一些大圈和标签。

教学准备

• 在每一个大圈内放置一种谷物的图片或容器以及合适的标签。

怎么做

• 让孩子们花些时间观察一下谷物的包装袋。通过谷物的包装和标签，孩子们能辨认出不同的谷物吗？可以讨论一下：
  – 你最喜欢哪一种？
  – 你今天吃了哪一种？
  – 哪一种你从来没尝过？

• 给孩子们看谷类植物的照片，或者植物种子的容器。向他们解释包装里的谷类食品是由这些植物的种子或谷物制成的。

• 观察和识别植物中的一种，例如：大米。
  孩子们能否说出哪些谷类食品可以用大米做？线索通常在名字里。帮助孩子们发现这一点。找到由大米制成的谷物盒子，把它们放在"大米"的圈子里。

• 重复这个顺序，放好其他谷物盒子。

词汇

燕麦、大米、小麦、玉米。

小贴士 你可以用你的盒子做一个展示，或者在你的商店中使用它们。

跨领域链接

问题解决、推理和计算的能力：计算。

130

狂欢节头饰

 · 孩子们自己制作在狂欢节游行时戴的帽子。

教学目标

• 帮助孩子们通过阅读指令开展一个活动。

教学资源

1）卡片或坚固的纸张，长度要够围住孩子的头；2）拼贴材料，包括长条绸带、花、亮片和发光小饰物；3）胶带和胶水。

教学准备

• 写出三条符合孩子能力的指令。

• 使用一个表格，或者贴有标签的表格，或是几句简单扼要的句子。

— 选择纸带。

— 装饰纸带。

— 把两端固定在一起。

怎么做

• 把指令读给孩子们听，要求他们告诉你指令的意思。

他们是否能排列出指令的正确顺序？

把指令页按照顺序装订在一起，这样可以在制作时看到指令。

• 核实孩子们都理解了指令。

现在他们可以使用这些简单的指令来制作自己的帽子了。

不断地问孩子他们正在做的是哪一条指令。

• 帽子做完后，要求孩子们检查是否完成了所有的指令。

词汇

指令。

 小贴士　确认孩子们装饰纸带所使用的物品可以在游行舞蹈中随风飘舞摆动。

跨领域链接

认识与理解世界：设计与制作。

我们在哪里？

 · 和孩子们一起散步，在街上拍摄所有你所看到的熟悉的标志。

教学目标

• 给孩子们机会辨认标语或符号中的词汇。

教学资源

数码照相机和打印机。

教学准备

• 你将带孩子们外出，所以让孩子们提前做好充分的准备，并提醒他们需要遵守外出教学活动的规则。

• 环顾一下所在地，以便计划一条最佳路线，可以识别标记和符号。

怎么做

• 和孩子们一起在你所在的地区周围的街道上散散步。

• 拍摄一些标志的照片，这些标志能让你知道你在哪里。尝试拍摄：

– 街道的名称；

– 到镇上、电影院等地方的指向箭头；

– 写着你所在地区名字的指示板；

– 写有学校等的类似的指示板；

– 商店、工厂、停车场和公司的名字。

• 留心注意一些相似的标志，例如：

– 汽车站。

– 显示孩子通行的路标。

– 外卖餐厅。

• 一回来，孩子们可以和一位成人一起指着照片说话。

• 孩子们可以朗读和辨认任何符号吗？你可以提供一些线索。

– 如果有帮助，可以提供开头字母。（提供"主大街"中的"M"是有帮助的，但提供"肖迪奇"中的"S"没什么帮助）

– 孩子们可以辨认出快餐店、汽车经销店和加油站等的标志。

词汇

　　方向、符号、标志。

小贴士

　　　　你可以制作一个展板，通过剪旧的街道地图来为你的照片制作背景，或者作为一个展板四周的装饰。

跨领域链接

　　认识与理解世界：地点。

生日(3)

 · 泰迪将举办一个生日派对。他向每个人发出邀请。请帮助孩子阅读他们收到的邀请信。

教学目标

- 提供一些孩子们可以看懂的简单文本。

教学资源

聚会邀请函和信封。

教学准备

- 选择一种聚会邀请函，或是通过电脑程序打印的，或是一些简单的、买来的纸质邀请函。
- 填写泰迪写给每个孩子的邀请函。
- 把邀请函放在写有每个孩子名字的信封里。

怎么做

- 向孩子们展示留在教室里的信封。如果他们能辨认出自己的名字，就让他们把寄给他们的信封收集起来。能力较弱的孩子也许能从三至四个为一组的信封里挑出自己的名字。
- 以小组的形式活动，鼓励孩子们打开信封，去发现里面的内容。谁能辨认出这是一个生日会的邀请函吗？
- 鼓励孩子们尽力读懂邀请函是谁发出的。
  "这是泰迪发出的，他将要举办一个聚会。"
- 然后尽力搞清楚聚会的日期和时间。
  "泰迪将过几岁生日呢？"
- 在之后的一天，举办一个聚会，这样孩子们也可以提前在家里和家长阅读他们的邀请函。

词汇

信封、姓名、聚会、泰迪、星期一/星期二/星期三/星期四/星期五、 1 点钟、 2 点钟、 3 点钟。

小贴士　　　　对于大一些的孩子，你可以帮助他们在日历上找到泰迪的生日。他们知道他们自己的生日吗？

跨领域链接

问题解决、推理和计算的能力：用数字来标签和数数。

波利·阿拉基亚
《抓住那只山羊!》(1)

• 观察这本超级棒的绘本插图。然后帮助孩子们建立他们自己的市场摊位。

教学目标

• 鼓励孩子们用书中的插图来寻找信息。

教学资源

1)《抓住那头山羊!：在尼日利亚逛市场的一天》（波利·阿拉基亚（2007）．巴斯：贝尔福特出版社.）； 2）纸张和颜料； 3）一些桌子和角色扮演的资源。

教学准备

• 快乐地阅读这个故事。

怎么做

• 花些时间观察插图以了解不同的市场交易者在卖什么。使用商店的标志，注意文字和图片。利用另外的线索来观察陈列的商品。

• 现在可以建造你们自己的市场。

　－ 把桌子排成一排。

　－ 使用班级或托儿所的资源，比如模型水果和蔬菜、商店里的包装袋、家里的盘子等、装扮的衣服和乐器，来布置你的摊位。

• 孩子们可以两两合作，为他们的摊位画一个记号。他们可以尝试构词或使用符号。帮助孩子们在他们的桌子或摊位前贴上他们的牌子。

• 你的市场现在已经准备好开始角色扮演活动了。

词汇

市场、摊位、市场交易者。

小贴士　　　如果你附近有一个街市市场，在开始活动前，可以去看一看。

跨领域链接

认识与理解世界：交流。

除旧换新

> • 更换房间里的旧标签，并当孩子们制作新的标签时，提醒他们涉及的日常行为。

教学目标

• 为孩子们创造了一个拥有大量打印文字的环境。

教学资源

1）数码相机； 2）打印机； 3）塑封机。

怎么做

• 要求孩子们看一下房间里各种各样的标签。他们是否注意到这些标签被撕破，损坏或变脏了？向他们解释，现在是时候用新的标签了。

• 告诉孩子们，你们要使用照片和文字来获得信息，或者提醒他们如何用动作表示或如何使用资源。讨论一些可能性。

准备好一些可以帮助孩子们的想法，例如：

照片：某人的手放在盆里，水龙头开着，同时手上沾满了肥皂

文字：请洗手。

这个标签放在哪里呢？

照片：有人在沙土附近扫地。

文字：当你完成了，请离开。

这个标签放在哪里呢？

照片：穿着围裙的孩子。

文字：你需要穿一件围裙。

这个标签放在哪里呢？

• 现在，和孩子们一起拍照。让他们尽可能多做一些。

• 写下这些单词，让孩子们复制在电脑上。打印并塑封，然后贴上你的新标签。

词汇

标签、信息。

小贴士

在任何一个学期开始的时候，这都是一个很好的活动。这是一个明确你所处环境中的日常事务的机会。

跨领域链接

个人、社会和情感的发展：行为和自我控制。

词汇袋

 · 一个帮助孩子们创造句子的生动游戏。

教学目标

• 为孩子们提供了一个机会去广泛阅读词汇和简单句。

教学资源

1）不同颜色的六个可提的袋子，贴上数字"1"至"6"的标签； 2）一个大的骰子；
3）标有数字"1"至"6"的卡纸纸条； 4）选择与你的主题相关联的简单句子，每次使用五个单词，例如：

− 我会演奏鼓/三角铃/吉他。

− 我喜欢吃比萨/薯条/蛋糕。

− 我可以看到蝙蝠/球/猫/房子。

− 我正在汽车里/屋子里/房间里/床上。

注意，每个句子中的最后一个词每次应该是不同的。

教学准备

• 把每个句子分割成五个单独的单词和一个句号。把每句话的第一个词放在1号袋子里，第二个词放在2号袋子里，以此类推，把所有的句号放在6号袋子里。

• 把这些袋子挂在你所在的场地四周上方。

怎么做

• 每个人都坐在一个圆圈外围，给每个孩子一张编号为"1"至"6"的纸条。他们拿着这些纸条要去摆出他们的句子。

1　2　3　4　5　6

• 第一个孩子在圆圈中心掷骰子，然后读出数字。
他们必须跑去找上面有那个数字的袋子，收集一个单词，或者一个句号。

• 如果一个孩子已经有了这个数字，他们就不用找了。
可以这么玩，例如：
这个孩子必须站起来在地板上贴上这些数字，然后把骰子递给旁边的孩子。

• 一直继续这个游戏，直到每个人都组成了一句话。现在朗读给大家听。

词汇

任何你在阅读或写作中关注的单词。

小贴士　　使用那些你希望孩子们在他们阅读中能识别出来的单词。如果你想重复使用这个活动，就把这些单词卡片塑封一下。

跨领域链接

问题解决、推理和计算的能力：用数字来标签和数数。

小型动物（3）

- 在书签上写出孩子们的问题，以此来鼓励孩子们在简易、非虚构类书本中搜寻信息。

教学目标

- 通过从非虚构类书本中搜索信息来加强和运用孩子们的阅读能力。

教学资源

1）关于小型动物主题的非虚构类书籍； 2）卡片条。

教学准备

- 在新的话题开始前，问问孩子们，关于小型动物，他们想发现什么。把他们的想法提炼简单的问题。

- 沿着卡片的长度方向，写下每一个问题：

— 所有的七星瓢虫都是红色和黑色的吗？

— 一只蜘蛛有几条腿？

- 现在把一张像书签的卡纸放在非虚构类书的某一页，你知道这页有答案。

怎么做

- 放置一箱子的书，每个人都坐一个圆圈外围，给每个孩子一张编号为1—6的纸条。他们拿着这些纸条要去摆出他们的句子。他们必须跑去找上面有那个数字的袋子，收集一个单词，或者一个句号。
- 孩子们两人一组选择一本书。帮助他们去读懂问题，然后在指定页寻找答案。
- 鼓励孩子们快速浏览关键词，例如：蜘蛛、腿。
- 帮助他们去读相关的句子，辨认熟悉的单词。接着，讨论意思。
- 放一些可以用的纸、铅笔盒、蜡笔。当你在帮助另外两个孩子读问题的时候，他们可以记录他们的信息。

词汇

如何？什么？在哪里？什么时候？为什么？

小贴士　　　在书签反面写下标题和页码以便在有人帮你整理书籍后，你可以迅速把书本归位。

跨领域链接

认识与理解世界：探索与观察。

寻宝线索

• 孩子们根据线索找到宝物，这个游戏让阅读变得令人激动。

教学目标

• 帮助孩子们迅速理解词汇。

教学资源

1）用孩子正在学习的词汇在卡片上写一些简单的线索（不超过六个），例如：

— 看看门后。

— 看看车垫子下面。

— 看看玩沙子工具附近。

— 看看书盒子内。

2）财宝为这一天准备的水果小吃/一个丢失的玩具/一个新的玩具/一本为故事时间准备的新书。

教学准备

• 把卡片放在标有名字的物品后面，然后把最终的宝物藏起来。

• 记得保留游戏开始时的第一条线索。

• 如果天气好的话，可有室外的线索。

怎么做

• 和一组孩子一起玩这个游戏，告诉孩子们他们将要寻找的宝物，例如：

去找找今天的小零食

• 向孩子们解释这个游戏，让孩子们理解如何按照线索来做。一起朗读第一条线索，例如：

看看门后面

让孩子们开始寻找。

当他们发现了那扇正确的门时，他们将找到第二张线索卡。

• 让孩子们从隐藏处找到下一个线索。

— 谁可以读一下这条线索？

• 这将带领他们到达下一个隐藏着线索卡的物体。

• 一直继续这个游戏直到所有的线索都被找到而且孩子们都朗读了。

• 当宝物被找到后，和班里其余的小朋友一起分享。

词汇

看、在……后面、在……顶部、在……下面。

小贴士　　　　当孩子们熟悉了寻宝游戏后，你可以加入一些包括猜测等更有挑战性的线索，例如：看看又高又红的东西后面。

跨领域链接

问题解决、推理和计算的能力：形状、空间和测量。

关键词游戏

> • 在操场上用粉笔在格子里写下一些词，创造一种有趣的方式在室外练习关键词汇。

教学目标

• 加强孩子们的字母对应能力，以便他们识别词汇。

教学资源

1）粉笔； 2）一组关键词（看反面的词汇表）； 3）一个晴天。

教学准备

• 在一个坚硬的平面画两个网状格子，每一网状格子有 6 个格子。

• 在两个网状格子的每一格中写上一个关键词。

• 确保这 12 个关键词都在你准备的那套关键词卡片上。

怎么做

• 把孩子们分成 6 人一队的两个小组，让他们站在网状格子的旁边。如果他们以前没有玩过这个游戏，就向孩子们解释一下。

• 向孩子们展示一张关键词卡片。

  − 谁可以朗读一下？

  − 这个单词在你的格子里吗？

  如果这个单词在一个格子里，则该小组中的一个孩子站在格子里。

• 然后展示下一个单词卡片。

  − 谁可以朗读一下？

  − 它在你的格子里吗？

• 一直继续这个游戏，如果哪一个小组站满了他们格子的 6 个单词上，那就获胜了。

• 小组交换位置，用不同的格子再玩一遍。每个人都能读出他们新的格子中的单词吗？

词汇

从附录 1 的词汇表中选出 12 个高频词汇，例如：这个、和、一个、给、说过、在……里面、他、我、的、它、是、你。

小贴士 再多准备一些关键词（这些词不是格子中的词汇），以进一步提高兴趣。

跨领域链接

沟通、语言和读写能力的发展：阅读大量的简单词汇。

猜猜这是谁?(1)

 • 当孩子们玩这个游戏的时候，他们会很喜欢阅读自己的名字。

教学目标
- 帮助孩子们理解用在名字里的单词。

教学资源
　　铭牌（名字卡片）。

教学准备
- 确保每一个人知道全班孩子的名字。

怎么做
- 大家围圈而坐，所有的名牌放在中间。
- 提问孩子们这些单词。
  - 他们能辨认出这些作为名字的词汇吗？
  - 他们能辨认出自己的名字吗？
- 孩子们依次找到他们自己的名字，然后拿着名牌回到自己的位置。当每个孩子都有名牌的时候，让他们将名牌举高以便大家可以看见。
- 选择一个孩子把名牌放回到中间，然后让这个孩子挑选下一个孩子把名牌放回来，一直继续，直到每一个孩子都把名牌放回来。
- 现在让第一个孩子选择别人的名字。
  - 他们可以读出这个单词吗？
  - 这个单词是以什么音开头的？
  - 这个音和第一个书写的字母符合吗？
- 当这个孩子读出这个名字时，他可以把名牌交给它的主人。
  现在轮流玩这个游戏，直到每一个孩子都取回了名牌并且读出了别人的名牌。
  保留这些名牌之后可以再玩一次。

词汇
　　孩子们的名字。

小贴士　　利用这个游戏可以促进孩子们的语音知识。

跨领域链接

个人、社会和情感的发展：团队意识。

猜猜这是谁？(2)

 • 给几组面部不朝着照相机的孩子们拍照。孩子们能从人的背面认出彼此吗？

教学目标
• 帮助孩子们理解用在名字里的单词。

教学资源
1）名牌； 2）照相机。

教学准备
• 确保每一个人知道全班孩子的名字。

怎么做
• 和一组孩子玩这个游戏。小组有一个名牌。
• 从讨论拍照开始。

你们通常做些什么游戏？

今天我们玩拍照游戏，你们不看着相机微笑，你们将转过身去！

• 让两个孩子站在一起，把背展示给班里余下的小朋友看。

你们觉得还能知道这是谁吗？

你们怎么区别谁是谁？

鼓励孩子们讨论身高和他们的着装。也可以想一想头发的颜色和长度。为这些小朋友找到名牌，然后其他孩子也成组玩一下这个游戏。

• 要求孩子们去选择一个与自己长相很不同的伙伴。然后拍摄一张两人的背部照片。如果可能的话，让孩子们观察照片打印的过程。

• 向孩子们展示照片，这样孩子们可以观察到这些照片。把可重复利用的粘纸贴在名牌反面，把这些名牌放在旁边。

词汇

孩子们的名字。

小贴士　　第二天，把名牌放在错误的照片旁边，要求孩子们把错误挑出来。

个人、社会和情感的发展：团队意识。

关键词隧道

• 带一组孩子外出举行球类比赛，也包括阅读练习。

教学目标

• 给孩子们提供机会阅读一些熟悉的词汇。

教学资源

1）一组关键词的放大词卡，这些关键词是孩子们正在学习的；2）容器；3）球。

教学准备

• 把关键词卡片放在容器里，确保孩子们看不见。

• 一起带出去。

怎么做

• 选择三个孩子组成隧道。他们应该站成一排，面对其他小朋友，腿部大大地分开，相邻小朋友的脚与脚靠拢接触。他们用打开的腿组成三个隧道。

• 当你把容器递给他们的时候，他们三个每人从容器里选一张卡片。他们必须捂住卡片，这样其他孩子看不到。

• 余下的孩子站成一排。第一个孩子上前将一只球从一个"隧道"中滚过。
  – 它将穿过哪个隧道？

• 如果这个球穿过一个"隧道"，那个孩子举起手中的关键词卡片。
  – 那个滚球的孩子能读出这个词吗？

• 如果能读出，他们俩交换位置，那个滚球的孩子做"隧道"。

• 在扮演"隧道"角色前，他应该从容器里再选择另一张关键词卡片。

• 一个孩子可以当小助手，把球放回原处，把刚用过的卡片放回在容器里，和其他卡片放在一起。原来做隧道的孩子排到滚球的孩子队伍最后。

词汇

任何关键词、例如：我、在……上面、这个、这儿、是。

小贴士　　把卡片放回去再玩，意味着多一次机会去强化知识，同时也可以帮助任何觉得这个任务有困难的孩子。

跨领域链接

身体的发展：运动和空间。

这一周的关键词

• 孩子们从你已经选择好的报纸标题上裁剪和粘贴关键词。

教学目标

• 帮助孩子们识别一些关键词。

教学资源

1）A4 纸；2）剪刀、胶水；3）报纸、杂志和宣传册上标题和题目；4）一组关键词。

教学准备

• 剪下报刊上的大标题或是粗体且清晰的印刷字。检查一下这些标题中包含你想要练习的关键词，并且内容是适合幼童阅读的。

• 摆好剪刀、胶水、纸张和关键词。

怎么做

• 向孩子们展示一个关键词，并且一起朗读。

• 一起看一些从杂志上剪下的页面。

• 询问孩子们是否可以在那里找到相同的关键词。

• 孩子们现在可以剪下这个单词，然后贴在一张纸上。他们最终有一组纸张，每一张上是同一个单词，以不同的字体、字号和颜色，排满整张纸面。

• 每个孩子都粘贴完他们的单词后，一起朗读这个词。

• 当大人指出一个孩子自己贴上的词时，这个孩子要读出这个词。当然，这些词都是一样的。

• 用另一个关键词，再做一遍这个活动。

  你可以让一组孩子关注一个单词，也可以在每一张纸上写上一个单词，留下这些纸，让孩子们找到这些单词，剪下然后粘贴在正确的纸张上。

词汇

任何你想要关注的关键词，例如：这个、和、是、在……上面、这里。

小贴士   对于大一些的孩子，给每个孩子一张纸，让他们去收集一组关键词。

154

跨领域链接

身体的发展：探索媒介与材料。

关键词竞赛

• 一种充满活力的跑步和阅读游戏。为了赢得比赛，每一队需要读出 8 个关键词。

教学目标

• 发展孩子们的字母对应能力，以便于他们可以理解单词。

教学资源

一组关键词（教师事先准备词汇表）。

教学准备

• 放大和复印一些关键词放在 A4 卡纸上。

• 如果你想重复使用，可以将卡纸塑封使其更耐用。

• 你需要为每一组准备 8 个关键词（每一组可以是相同的 8 个单词）。

怎么做

• 摆好 8 个单词，使它们形成一个 1 米宽的正方形边框。

• 把孩子们分成几个小组，然后要求他们面对正方形排好队伍，与边线保持一定距离。

• 第一个孩子跑向关键词方形，挑选一个他们会朗读的单词。这个孩子大声说出这个单词，随后和他的队伍（或一个大人）确认正确性。

   然后在这个孩子跑回队伍之前，把这个单词放在正方形中间。

• 第二个孩子跑去关键词方形，挑出一张卡片朗读。如果读错了，大人可以告诉这个孩子这个单词的读音，但是这个孩子在跑回队伍之前，必须把这个单词卡片放回到方形原来的位置。

• 一直继续比赛，直到所有的单词被正确朗读且放在中间位置。

• 第一个读完全部单词的小组获胜。

词汇

教师事先准备词汇表。

小贴士　　　　选择对孩子们来说越来越熟悉的关键词。

跨领域链接

身体的发展：运动和空间。

假日（2）

> • 孩子们把照片贴在盘子上，然后使用一些句子开头的单词来写一个假期日记。

教学目标

• 给孩子们机会写一些简单句。

教学资源

1）7 个纸盘子；　2）假期目的地和房屋的图片；　3）句子卡片。

教学准备

• 准备一些句子开头：例如：

星期一她去了……

除了周日，一周的每一天都准备一下。

可以这样写：*星期天她又回家了!*

• 剪好一些旅游目的地的图片。这些地方可能是公园、海边、森林或山脉。

• 剪好一些房子室外的图片。

怎么做

• 和一组小朋友一起玩这个游戏，告知他们将为弗洛姨妈写一篇度假日记，或者可以自己设计一个有趣的名字。

• 让孩子们选择一个房子的照片，然后把它贴在一个纸盘子上。这就是弗洛姨妈的房子。

• 一起观察目的地的照片，识别出是哪些地方。每一个孩子为弗洛姨妈选择一个假期旅游的地方。他们把选择的照片贴在另外一些盘子上。现在，把这些贴有旅游目的地和房子照片的盘子都排成一排，就完工了。

• 接着，给孩子们展示句子的开头，朗读并且辨认一周的每一天。

• 每个小朋友都能按照正确的顺序说出一周的每一天吗？

• 把开头的句式放在纸盘子下面。第一个盘子下是这个句式：*星期一她去了……*
第二个盘子下是这个句式：*星期二她去了……*一直到最后一个盘子下面是*星期天她又回家了。*

- 帮助孩子写下弗洛姨妈要去的地方的名称，把这些单词接在合适的句子开头后。
    - 你们可以朗读弗洛姨妈的日记吗？
- 打乱这些盘子，然后组合句子，去制作一篇不同的假日日记。

词汇

一周的每一天、日记。

小贴士 　　　　在你的读书角备有一套以一周的每一天为特征的书籍。

跨领域链接

认识与理解世界：时间。

词汇墙

> • 在讲授新的主题或话题前使用这个活动。孩子们作画，老师做好标签，一起创立一个词汇库。

教学目标

• 鼓励孩子们去使用语音知识朗读简单词汇。

教学资源

1）孩子们可以使用的展示板和背景纸； 2）美术材料； 3）制作标签用的纸张和笔。

教学准备

• 用非彩色的背景纸盖住你的展示板。

怎么做

• 和孩子们解释一下今天活动的新主题，例如：沿着我们的街道。

他们觉得会发现什么？

记录他们的想法，例如：汽车、公交车、超市、商店、（行人自控）人行道、交通信号灯、人们。

• 孩子们可以用颜料、拼贴画或从杂志上剪下来的画来创作自己的图画，展现自己的想法。让孩子们帮忙去找到这些素材，粘贴在展示板上。

• 和孩子们聚在展示板旁边。你可以指着图片中的一个物体，让孩子们告诉你这个什么。

• 在一张大纸上写下这个单词。当你写的时候，鼓励孩子们给出建议：

－ 这个单词的开头是怎么发音的？

－ 你将如何把这个单词写下来？

－ 这个单词的中间是怎么发音的？

－ 最后怎么发音？

• 当你写好这个单词后，一起朗读这个单词，然后依次对每一幅图片做相同的活动。

• 当所有的单词都写好时，挑一个孩子上前，选择一个标签展示给大家看。

－ 谁可以朗读一下？

－ 谁可以指出这个单词对应的图片？

把单词贴在那里，然后继续游戏，直到这个词汇墙完成。

• 现在，当孩子们要写相关主题的句子时，可以使用这个词汇墙了。

词汇

任何与你的主题相关的词汇。

小贴士

如果可能的话，把这个活动中的一个展板作为平时课程的开头活动。采用粘贴和方便移去的方式来粘贴图片和文字，这样你可以经常更换。

跨领域链接

创造力的发展：创造力。

高登的修理厂（1）

· 和孩子们搭建一个可以进行角色扮演活动的车库围栏。

教学目标

· 在角色扮演区域，要布置可供孩子们阅读的打印文字。

教学资源

1）车辆的图片； 2）纸筒； 3）马克笔、胶水和剪刀。

教学准备

· 和孩子们讨论各种陆地上的车辆：小轿车、货车、自行车、卡车等。

他们能说出一些小轿车的品牌吗？

· 鼓励孩子们用 A4 纸自己去创作一些个性车辆的图片。

· 从纸筒上剪下一张纸条，长度要可以沿着角色扮演区域的墙壁围一圈，或将堆放在一起的桌子一起围起来。

怎么做

· 提醒孩子们，他们正在帮忙布置一个新的角色扮演场地：高登的修理厂。跟他们说："高登在他的车库里修车。他可能会修哪一辆？"

· 让孩子们向你展示他们的图片，告诉每一个小朋友，这个什么车，甚至可以说说小轿车的品牌和型号。

· 用大的粗体字，从纸张的左手边开始写：

高登可以修理……

鼓励孩子们去识别你正在写的字母。

－ 他们能猜出这些词汇的意思吗？

－ 写完后一起朗读一下。

· 现在选择一张图片。选好的孩子把图片贴在围栏上，跟在对应的单词后面。如果孩子愿意，还可以在图片下方写上车辆的名字/型号/品牌。现在，朗读这些单词。例如：

高登可以修理一辆迷你宝马车。

· 加上第二张图片和名称，然后再一起朗读。

高登可以修理一辆迷你宝马车、一辆公交车。

以这样的方式继续下去，直到用完所有的图片。

· 在高登的车库四周，把围栏布置好。

词汇

小轿车、自行车、摩托车、长途大巴、公交车、两厢货车、重型卡车等。

小贴士　　　　如果你不想花费时间制作车辆图片，则汽车杂志是一个很好的图片资源可供裁剪。

跨领域链接

沟通、语言和读写能力的发展：角色扮演。

第六章

欣赏故事和诗歌

小餐馆（2）

· 让孩子们分享一下像沃波尔太太那样摇晃的经历。

教学目标
· 鼓励孩子们把自己的经历和角色的感受作比较。

教学资源

1）艾伦·亚伯格的《女招待沃波尔太太》（海雀图文出版社 1980 年出版）； 2）托盘；3）不易碎的盘子、杯子或平底锅。

教学准备

· 和孩子们一起分享这个故事，一直到沃波尔太太丢了她的工作，全家人都很沮丧。

－ 孩子们理解沃波尔太太为什么哭吗？

－ 如果他们看到别人哭，他们有什么感受？

－ 他们曾经摔过东西吗？

－ 摔的是什么？

－ 发生了什么事？

－ 他们的感受是什么？

怎么做

· 告诉孩子们他们将成为男服务员或女服务员。谁认为他可以拿稳一个带托盘的茶壶？

· 一起整理一些不易碎的盘子、杯子或平底锅。数一数，然后把它们堆放在一个小托盘上。

· 让孩子们依次在房间里穿行，保持堆满东西的托盘平衡。如果他们可以设法做到，给予他们掌声。

· 如果他们的托盘掉了，大家一起大喊："沃波尔太太抖动了！"

词汇

人物角色的名字、平衡、小心、抖动、掉落、翻倒、倒地、多少。

小贴士　　　　拓展这个游戏：让孩子们预估自己能平衡地托住多少物品，然后鼓励他们计数，记录他们能不摇晃地拿多少物品。

跨领域链接

问题解决、推理和计算的能力：用数字来标签和数数。

今天谁在小木屋里？

 · 孩子们将热爱以这种方式来介绍一个故事。

教学目标

· 提供一些道具来鼓励孩子们识别故事中的角色。

教学资源

1）一些小木屋图片上的卡片（详见教学准备）； 2）故事书中人物角色的小图片。

教学准备

· 将一张很大的卡纸折叠，使它站立起来——像一张生日卡片。在卡片的前面，画上一间传统的童话故事中的小木屋，并涂上颜色。

· 把门的三条边剪开，让它可以开关——像一扇基督降临期的日历门。

· 选择一张角色图片固定在卡片内部，当你打开门时，可以看到它，关上门就看不见了。固定的方式是，它可以方便地换成另一张图片。

· 孩子们可以使用剪贴画材料参与制作小木屋，但人物需要你自己制作，这样就不会泄露答案！

怎么做

· 当孩子们坐好准备听故事的时候，给孩子们看这间小木屋。问问他们谁可能住在这样的小木屋里。尽可能鼓励孩子们说出更多的答案，例如：

－ 金发姑娘；

－《三只小熊》中的一只；

－《三只小猪》中的一只；

－ 装扮成奶奶的大灰狼；

－ 奶奶自己；

－ 小红帽；

－《糖果屋》中的女巫.

为什么你认为这个人会住在这里呢？有没有什么线索？

· 现在邀请一个小朋友出来，打开门揭晓今天故事中的人物。

－ 有没有谁猜对了？

－ 你可以提醒大家：这个人物发生了什么故事？

－ 在这个故事里，谁常常住在小木屋里？

• 现在向孩子们讲述或朗读这个故事。

小贴士　　　　你可能想通过一扇开着的窗表达想法，那就把一张线索图片放在窗户后面，在你开门之前先讨论一下。

跨领域链接

创造力的发展：想象力与想象性游戏。

艾玛·加克莱
《突突嘀嘀》(2)

 · 孩子们识别各种表示声音的词汇，然后在故事合适的地方复述这些词汇。

教学目标

· 帮助孩子们去配对、识别和阅读一些简单的词汇。

教学资源

1）艾玛·加克莱的《突突嘀嘀》（博克思出版社 2009 年出版）； 2）若干卡纸。

教学准备

· 在每一张卡纸上写上表达一种声音效果的词组，例如:（车辆高速驶过时发出的）呜，呜。制作尽可能多的卡片，使得孩子们每人有一张。

怎么做

· 把这本书介绍给孩子们，然后花些时间观察第一张双线页面。鼓励孩子们通过颜色和类型来辨别每一种车辆。

· 观察第二张图片，在繁忙的天桥上，这次他们可以看到哪种车?

· 继续阅读，当朗读到印刷体的文字时，你可以鼓励孩子们配合你。你指着这些放大的印刷体词汇，让孩子们做出相应的音效。

· 当你们读完这整个故事后，翻到任一页，指着表示音效的大印刷字，这样说:

"谁记得这个词怎么念?"

"第一个字母怎么发音?"

在其他页面重复这个练习。

· 发给每个小朋友一张写有一种声音的卡片。要求孩子们朗读并记忆并一一检查。

· 现在再一次朗读这个故事——不让孩子们看书。在恰当的地方，孩子们应该配出写在他们卡片上的音效的词汇。

· 使用所有的车停在车库的那一页完成这个活动。

词汇

书中所有的音效词汇。

小贴士

创作彩色词汇的展板：

• 在纸上印出图案，方法是：用手指把颜料涂在可洗的表面上。

• 干了后，剪出形状，这样可以制作出故事中的车辆或者你自己设计的其他图案或卡片。

• 添加你的彩色姓名标签。

跨领域链接

认识与理解世界：地点。

艾玛·加克莱
《突突嘀嘀》(3)

 · 用书中的想法写一些简单的句子，帮助孩子们根据这些想法创作自己的句子。

教学目标

· 鼓励孩子们去写一些简单句子。

教学资源

1) 艾玛·加克莱的《突突嘀嘀》(博克思出版社 2009 年出版)；2) 七张卡纸条。

教学准备

· 你将使用如下从书中改写的七个句子：

这辆红色吉普车快速开走了。

这辆黑色小轿车加速开走了。

这辆蓝色面包车缓缓地开走了。

这辆黄色出租车急速开走了。

这辆粉色豪华轿车慢慢滑动着开走了。

这辆绿色露营车发动后开走了。

这辆紫色小轿车猛冲地开走了。

把其中 5 个句子写在卡纸条上，2 条卡纸空着备用。

· 在重读这本书之前，一起回顾一下这个故事，鼓励孩子们在你停下来的时候，说出一些词汇。尝试在一些表示颜色和动作的词汇处停顿。例如：

"嘀嘀，嘀嘀，……开过来了……城市出租车,接着后面是……"

如果有需要，可以说出每一个单词的第一个发音，帮助孩子们记忆。

怎么做

· 孩子们一边看着，你一边在一条空白卡纸上写下一句话，例如：

这辆黄色出租车急速开走了。

请会读的小朋友朗读一下这个句子。让每一个孩子轮流读一下。

- 现在把卡片剪成三部分：

  这辆/黄色出租车/飞驰而过。

  把这些卡纸打乱后，递给三个小朋友，问问他们是否可以把这些卡纸以正确的顺序排列好。要求其他小朋友朗读并检查他们做得是否正确。
- 使用另一个句子重复这个过程。
- 现在，和其他孩子阅读其他的句子。
- 把所有的卡纸条剪成三个部分，然后把纸条堆放成三堆：

  一堆是："这个"；

  一堆是： 车辆的颜色和名字；

  一堆是： 动作。
- 向孩子们解释，他们应该从每一堆卡纸条中选出一张，然后使用三张组成一个句子。
- 挑战一下孩子们，看看他们可以从这些破碎的句子中组成多少个不同的句子。
- 之后，确保那些孩子们能够复述和解释他们组成的句子。

词汇

句子、表示颜色的词汇、表示动作的词汇。

小贴士

- 制定一个更简易的版本，去掉表示颜色的词汇。
- 制定一个难度更大的版本，为每一辆车子加上第二个描述性的词汇，这个单词在书中可以找到。

跨领域链接

认识与理解世界：地点。

猜猜这个故事

· 提供给孩子们物品，看看他们是否能识别出这些物品来自哪些故事。

教学目标

· 鼓励孩子们从熟悉的故事中回忆细节。

教学资源

1）一个篮子或吸引人的容器； 2）一组故事书； 3）解释故事人物和一些小物件，例如：

- 《灰姑娘》：一只参加聚会的正装鞋子，一只老鼠，一根魔杖。

- 《小红帽》：一些花，一个篮子，一条披巾或是一副老式眼镜。

- 《金发女孩和三只熊》：三只不同大小的碗，一把破旧的椅子（放在洋娃娃屋里的），一盒燕麦片。

教学准备

· 选择三本书——一本是你将要读的，任意其他的两本。

· 把你将要朗读的故事书的代表物品放在篮子里，拿一张人物照片做准备。

怎么做

· 当每个人做好准备听故事时，给孩子们看篮子，然后辨认篮子里的东西。

- 这能让孩子们想起任何他们知道的故事吗？

- 这些物品扮演了什么角色？

- 它们属于谁？

如果他们需要进一步的线索，向他们展示人物角色的图片。

· 一旦孩子们已经识别出这故事，则向他们展示这三本书。

- 他们能从封面辨认出正确的一本书吗？

- 向孩子们提问，是什么线索让他们从封面就可以辨认出来。

· 现在，阅读这个故事吧。

词汇

封面、标题、图例。

变化

• 把你的线索物品制作得主题更模糊一些，例如：为《金发女孩和三只熊》的故事准备盐和糖。

跨领域链接

沟通、语言和读写能力的发展：故事人物。

高登·亚当斯《商店，商店，去商店买东西》

 • 帮助孩子们写他们自己的诗歌。

教学目标

• 给孩子们一个机会实践运用词汇和文本内容。

教学资源

高登·亚当斯的绘本故事《商店，商店，去商店买东西》，选自沃特斯，F.《是读诗的时候了》，猎户座儿童书籍出版社 1999 年出版。

教学准备

• 和孩子们快乐地阅读这首童谣。

• 他们能找到押韵的词汇吗？

• 再次朗读，观察是否有孩子预料到这是一首童谣。

怎么做

• 重复这首童谣的开头，然后要求孩子们帮助你制作一张购物清单。
  "当你去购物时，你会买什么？"

• 当你有一些建议时，把它们写下来，然后尽力想出一些押韵的词汇。

• 然后，选择一组押韵的词汇，在每个物品前加上一个形容词，例如：
  − 一条红色的短裙；
  − 一件校服衬衫。
  使用两个或三个押韵的组合继续这样的练习。

• 使用原来的童谣结尾来结束你的诗歌。

词汇

几组押韵的词汇，例如：

调羹—气球；

饼—领结；

短裙—衬衫；

鱼—盘子；

晾衣夹子—鸡蛋；

水壶—马克杯；

地图—鸭舌帽；

巧克力—盒子；

厢式车—平底锅；

猪—假发。

小贴士　　　下次，试着将把这个游戏当作锻炼记忆的游戏：你说出第一个单词，看看孩子们是否能说出押韵的词。

跨领域链接

认识与理解世界：交流。

故事示意图

• 帮助一小组孩子一起合作制作一幅故事的图片。

教学目标

• 鼓励孩子们讨论一个故事中的按顺序发生的一系列事情。

教学资源

1）一大张纸； 2）水笔和蜡笔。

教学准备

• 选择一个故事读给孩子们听。

怎么做

• 安排一小组小朋友围绕在一张大纸的周围，告诉他们，你们将要制作一幅很大的画，来表现这个故事。

• 问问哪个小朋友记得这个故事的开头。鼓励两个孩子们画故事的开头部分。

• 然后，问问大家，接下来发生了。鼓励另两个孩子画这个故事的第二部分。一直继续下去，直到这个故事的主要事件都被记录下来了。

• 现在要求孩子们指着他们画的图来复述这个故事。当他们复述的时候，使用一支粗头笔在一张图片和下一张图片中画上箭头，表明事件发展的顺序。

• 问问孩子们是否这个故事已经完成了。

  − 有什么地方还要改进吗？

  − 我们可以怎样展示这个故事的大意呢？

  − 加个标题怎么样？

  − 这个故事示意图能清晰展示事情发展的顺序吗？

  − 在图片边上加上数字有没有用处呢？

• 孩子们可以决定他们对他们的图片是否还要加入更多的细节或颜色。

词汇

开始、下一个、结尾、顺序、标题、示意图。

 小贴士　　当幼幼童们按事情发展顺序复述故事时，一位成人可以帮忙画画。

跨领域链接

沟通、语言和读写能力的发展：故事架构。

约翰·福斯特 《十头跳舞的恐龙》

 · 改变恐龙发生的状况，帮助孩子们用经典的格式创作一首新的童谣。

教学目标

给孩子们一个机会实践运用词汇和文本。

教学资源

约翰·福斯特的《十头跳舞的恐龙》选自《是读诗的时候了》，猎户座儿童书籍出版社1999 年出版。

教学准备

• 阅读和欣赏这首童谣或者另选一首相同格式的童谣，例如：《五只小猫咪》（选自 E·麦特森改编的《这只小猫咪》，企鹅出版社 1991 年出版。

怎么做

• 鼓励孩子们在读童谣的时候找出押韵的词汇。
• 注意第一行最后的单词和数字的发音押韵，例如：
  "线"—"九"。
• 写出童谣的第一行。
• 现在向孩子们建议，改变一下一头恐龙发生的状况。
• 提出另一个想法，例如：
  一头恐龙脚下滑了一下，撞到了头。
• 写下这些新的词汇，但是用原来的词汇结尾。
• 在整个童谣中继续用新的想法写出每一头恐龙发生的状况。

词汇

在这首童谣中用到的许多有趣的词汇，例如：旋转的、被强行控制的。

小贴士　　　打印出这些跳舞的恐龙会很有趣哦!

跨领域链接

问题解决、推理和计算的能力：计算。

波利·阿拉基亚
《抓住那只山羊！》(2)

· 接下去会发生什么？当你们一起阅读一个故事的时候，在插图里找到线索。

教学目标

鼓励孩子们提出一个关于故事将如何发展的想法，并思考如何结尾。

教学资源

波利·阿拉基亚的《抓住那只山羊！：在尼日利亚逛市场的一天》（贝尔福特出版社 2007 年出版）。

教学准备

• 在你准备和孩子分享一个故事之前，朗读书本最后几页上的信息。这将帮助你为不是来自尼日利亚的孩子们设定一个语境。

怎么做

• 故事书中的每一张图片上都有线索，如山羊去哪里了、什么物品不见了。缓慢地朗读，给孩子们一个机会去仔细观察插图。

   – 谁发现线索了？

   – 他们可以看见山羊或山羊身体的一部分吗？

   – 他们可以看见丢失的物品吗？

• 花些时间去数一下市场里的商人留在摊位上的物品数量。

• 当你读到妈妈大声叫唤阿尤卡的这一页时，停下来向孩子们提问：

   – 谁能猜出山羊在哪里？

   – 你能猜出山羊去哪里了吗？

• 在你回到这一页故事前，鼓励孩子们猜猜结果是什么。

小贴士

这可能是用到"言语泡泡"的一个机会。大多数口语词汇在长方形的"言语泡泡"格子里。孩子们能用这些凌乱的"泡泡"语言说出故事的结尾中妈妈的话吗？

跨领域链接

认识与理解世界：交流。

使用手偶

· 根据你的手偶人物和孩子们一起创作一个故事。

教学目标

· 鼓励孩子们运用故事中的句型，并按照故事正确的发展顺序复述。

教学资源

动物手偶。

怎么做

· 和一小组孩子一起开展这个活动，让每一个孩子选择一个动物玩偶。

· 大人带头开始创作一个简单的故事，鼓励孩子们移动手偶，并且重复说出词汇，
例如：

一天，一头小象感到很孤单无聊，所以他走出去散散步，想找找新朋友。

他遇到了一只猴子。

"你想和我一起玩吗？"小象问。

"我没空，"猴子说，"我正在找坚果。"

小象继续走，直到遇到了一头河马。

"你愿意和我一起玩吗？"小象问。

"我没空，"河马说，"我正在泥里打滚儿呢。"

所以小象继续走，直到遇到了一只企鹅……

· 用其他动物玩偶，继续陈述。

直到，最终有一个动物同意了！

确保每个成员都参与了这个活动。

词汇

动物名字、问题、借口。

小贴士　　　　这可以提供一个机会和孩子们聊聊交朋友的话题。

跨领域链接

个人、社会和情感的发展：自信与自尊。

贾尔斯·安德烈和
尼克·沙拉特《裤子》

· 当孩子们创作关于袜子的故事时，和大家一起阅读一下这个吸引人的故事。

教学目标

· 用声音、词汇和语篇来帮助孩子们探索和实践。

教学资源

贾尔斯·安德烈，尼克·沙拉特的《裤子》（柯基犬图画出版社 2002 年出版）。

教学准备

· 和孩子们愉快地阅读这个绘本。

· 依次在插图的帮助下复述每一页故事的内容。

怎么做

· 用"袜子"代替"裤子"，阅读绘本的前几页。

· 然后要求孩子们一起参与（等他们笑停）。

· 当你重新朗读这个绘本的时候，使用相同的形容词和短语，但是把"裤子"一词改成"袜子"。

· 现在问问孩子们，是否可以想到用其他的方式来描绘袜子，例如：

－ 厚袜子；

－ 洞洞袜；

－ 臭袜子；

－ 圣诞袜；

－ 公主袜。

如果他们需要进一步线索，则向他们展示人物角色的图片。

· 尽力让替换的词汇押韵。

· 告诉孩子们需要为你们已经编写好的新书配一些不同的图片。

· 让孩子们用粗线笔装饰一下袜子的外形。在晾衣绳上展示这些袜子图片，用配有放大的词汇描述袜子。

· 可以让更有能力的孩子在电脑上打印出这些图片和文字。

词汇

书中的形容词。

小贴士　　　　当你取下晾衣绳时，把袜子图片和描述袜子的形容词图片粘在一起，制作好一本书供孩子们自己阅读。

跨领域链接

创造力的发展：创造力。

和我一起唱歌

• 孩子们录音并制作自己的录音带。

教学目标

• 强化孩子们关于韵律和诗歌的知识。

教学资源

1）磁带播放器； 2）空白磁带——小型的磁带更利于孩子使用。

教学准备

• 唱出并说出童谣，数数的童谣和短诗。

怎么做

• 设定一个地方，孩子们可以一起过来并且录制他们喜欢的童谣。

• 决定一下你们想如何完成录制。例如：

  − 一盘磁带录制数数的童谣，一盘录制动物的童谣。

  − 每个小组录制一盘磁带——可能按年龄分组，或是在活动中分组。

• 确定这些磁带都清晰地贴上标签了，以便于孩子们知道如何使用。大人可以提供帮助，这样孩子们可以理解他们必须录制好一盘再做第二盘。

  "如果想跳过别人的童谣录制自己的，什么事情将会发生？"

• 一旦完成了，则所有磁带都可以被留在音乐区域或读书区域，以供其他人欣赏或参与录制。

• 在你的磁带上画上密码，并留下一把"钥匙"，这样孩子们可以自由选择。

• 告诉孩子们需要为你们已经编写好的新书配一些不同的图片。

• 你有设备可以录制光碟或者使用电脑来代替磁带播放器。

小贴士　　如果你剪下卡纸来用，孩子们会乐于自己制作磁带的封面。

跨领域链接

认识与理解世界：信息通信技术（ICT）。

贝斯·秀珊
《那是我开心的时候》(1)

· 演绎故事的各个事件，使用一些简单的道具来帮助孩子们记忆。

教学目标

· 给孩子们提供道具来谈谈故事中的人和事。

教学资源

1）两个大的和一个小的泰迪熊；2）贝斯·秀珊的《那是我开心的时候》（小蜜蜂出版社 2005 年出版）；3）一片叶子、一颗星星、一本小的书、一张小床和一个小垫子。

教学准备

· 阅读故事。

· 问问孩子们为什么小熊会感到有点儿悲伤。

怎么做

· 给孩子们展示泰迪熊，并且问他们这是谁。

· 他们能否记得熊爸爸为鼓励小熊做的两件事情？
  向孩子们展示叶子和星星。

· 他们能否记得熊妈妈为鼓励小熊做的两件事情？
  向孩子们展示小书和垫子。

· 他们能否记得小熊为他自己做了什么？
  向孩子们展示小床。

· 现在让孩子们利用道具依次复述故事。

词汇

快乐的、兴奋的、沮丧的、遗憾的、欢呼起来、微笑、记得。

小贴士　　　问问孩子们关于让他们快乐的事情。

跨领域链接

个人、社会和情感的发展：自理能力。

贝斯·秀珊
《那是我开心的时候》(2)

 • 孩子们分享故事中描绘的经历，来发现他们快乐的方式。

教学目标
- 鼓励孩子们运用文本探索和实践。

教学资源

1）贝斯·秀珊的《那是我开心的时候》； 2）叶子、可粘贴的星星、大张的深色彩纸、垫子和书本。

教学准备
- 阅读故事。
- 谈论一个中心主题，当你感觉有一点悲伤的时候回归到快乐。

怎么做
- 告诉孩子们你们将要试试故事中的这些想法，然后谈谈自己的感受。
- 走到室外，踢开树叶，选出一片特别的树叶展示给大家看。选择一些树叶放在袋子里拿回来制作一张拼贴画。
- 和朋友们坐在垫子上。从图书角选择一本最喜欢的书和一位朋友一起阅读。你能找到和你的名字相同字母开头的单词吗？
- 让孩子们把上百颗星星粘贴在一大张黑色纸上。
  一起从一数到一百。
- 每个人躺在地板上准备睡觉！
- 你觉得这些想法可以成功地让你变得快乐吗？
- 让孩子们投票选出最让他们兴奋的方式，记录下他们的发现，例如：
  - 每个人有一个笑脸，可以粘在标有各种活动的表格里。
  - 运用一个电脑程序帮助你用图表来记录信息。

词汇

大笑、微笑、咯咯笑、快乐的。

小贴士　　　　让一大群孩子参与这个活动，然后在一个成人帮助下完成所有的活动，最后报告感受。

跨领域链接

个人、社会和情感的发展：建立关系。

《早上好，母鸡太太》

 · 在这首童谣中改变颜色词汇，和孩子们创作出你们自己的小鸡彩虹。

教学目标

• 帮助孩子们理解一个词的意义。

教学资源

绘本《早上好，母鸡太太》。

教学准备

• 制作这首童谣的放大版本。

• 把两张可粘贴的卡纸粘贴在童谣中的词汇处。

怎么做

• 和孩子们朗读和学习这首童谣。当你们一起朗读的时候，手指着这些词汇，鼓励他们去辨认词汇。

• 重点突出表示颜色的词汇——黄色、棕色和红色。

• 解释这些词汇是母鸡和小鸡的颜色，但是你们将玩玩变成其他颜色的游戏。

• 告诉孩子们，他们可以改变两个颜色词汇。

• 谁可以指出"黄色"和"红色"两个词？
用小卡纸盖住这些词汇。

• 再次朗读这首童谣，在空着的单词处停下，问问孩子们有没有建议用其他词汇，然后写在你的卡纸上。接着再朗读一下你的童谣。例如：
他们中四个是粉色的。

• 用不同的颜色词汇来重复这个活动，这样可以创作出许多新的童谣。

词汇

黄色、棕色、红色、粉色、绿色、橙色、蓝色、青绿色、紫色、黑色、白色。

 小贴士　　　画出十只小鸡并剪下，交给不同的小组，使它们凑起来是十，例如：一个小组有 7 只，另一个小组有 3 只；或者一个小组有 2 只，一个小组 3 只，另一个小组 5 只。

跨领域链接

问题解决、推理和计算的能力：计算。

罗伯特·罗菲尔德 《帝达里克》（1）

• 孩子们从这个澳大利亚的传统故事中演绎出各个事件。

教学目标

• 帮助孩子们开始识别故事是怎样构建的。

教学资源

罗伯特·罗菲尔德的《帝达里克，这只造成水灾的青蛙》（伦敦海雀图文出版社 1980 年出版）。

教学准备

• 选择一则土著梦幻传说，这个传统的故事结构是：
- 有一个问题。
- 尝试用不同的策略去解决问题。
- 最终一个策略有效并且有一个好的结果。
• 在标题页上，我们可以看见所有出现在这个故事里的动物。帮助孩子们去记住这些名字。
• 和孩子们分享这个故事。

怎么做

• 依次思考故事中每一个角色，以及它们说的话和做的事：
- 每一个人可以尝试变成一只小青蛙，然后变得越来越大，之后又迅速缩回到他们正常的大小。
- 每一个人可以假装讲一个有趣的故事。选择一个孩子会讲的简单的笑话，然后当他们讲的时候，他们就会大笑。
- 做"青蛙跳"可能不太合适——所以或者用两个毛绒玩具去做这个动作，或者每个人可以做"兔子跳"。
- 像蜥蜴一样挺着肚子，趾高气扬地走。
- 每个人可以像鳗鱼一样跳舞。
• 现在再次朗读这个故事，当故事每一部分发生的时候，让孩子们演绎出来。
• 孩子们现在可以分小组自己复述这个故事了——不需要你的朗读了。只要鳗鱼排在最后，其他动物的出场顺序不重要。

词汇

角色的名字、"从前"或者"很久以前"——常用的故事开头。

小贴士

"梦幻时间"是土著创造世界的一个概念，它包括许多故事，一些故事解释了人们应该如何行为处事。如果你在网上搜索"土著梦幻时间"，则你可以找到更多关于此的信息。《帝达里克》是一本有用的书籍，表达了分享的想法以及贪婪的后果。

跨领域链接

个人、社会和情感的发展：建立关系。

罗伯特·罗菲尔德
《帝达里克》(2)

 • **帮助孩子们给怪兽们创立新的名字。**

教学目标

• 鼓励孩子们运用文本探索和实践。

教学资源

1）罗伯特·罗菲尔德的《帝达里克，这只造成水灾的青蛙》（伦敦海雀图文出版社 1980 年出版）；2）如果有条件的，可以准备一个柔软的玩具或是故事中角色的玩偶。

教学准备

• 朗读这个故事。

• 讨论故事中角色：他长得怎么样，做了些什么。

怎么做

• 围坐成圆形。问问孩子们，谁记得怪兽的名字。孩子们依次用怪兽的声音说出他的名字。

• 为什么我们叫他帝达里克呢？
  如果孩子们有一些想法，比如用"里克"做一些活动，那么用这个词去写出不同的名字，如里克莱克或者比戈里克。

• 当孩子们笑停了，问问他们是否可以想到他的另一个名字。表扬每一个大胆尝试的小朋友。

• 如果你有一个玩偶或者是柔软的玩具，当每个人提出想法时，让这个玩具点点头。

词汇

不要尽力把新的词语写下来！

跨领域链接

创造力的发展：创造力。

杰克和杰尔

· 有顺序地表演出故事的发展过程来解释说明一首熟悉的童谣的开头、中间和结尾。

教学目标
· 帮助孩子们理解故事的各个要素。

教学准备
· 确保孩子们都很熟悉这个童谣，而且可以回忆起来反复诵读。

怎么做
· 一起说出这首童谣。
· 问问孩子们，在童谣的开头发生了什么。

    杰克和杰尔正在往山上爬。

· 选两个孩子表演一下。
· 问问孩子们，接下去发生什么？

    杰克掉了下来。然后杰尔也掉了下来。

· 选更多一些孩子表演故事。
· 结尾是什么呢？

    杰克爬了起来，回家了。

· 另一个孩子表演一下这段故事。
· 他们认为杰尔会怎样呢？
· 现在分配好三组"演员"，每一组负责一个部分：开头、中间和结尾。这些孩子可以在恰当的时候做无声表演，同时其他孩子重复这个童谣。

词汇

开头、中间、结尾。

小贴士　　你可以用其他童谣来尝试一下，在这个童谣的三个部分可以清晰地识别出来，例如：

《轻拍蛋糕》，《轻拍蛋糕》，《面包工人》（童谣名）

《两只小鸟》

《小小蜘蛛》

跨领域链接

沟通、语言和读写能力的发展：故事架构。

越来越大（1）

· **帮助孩子们在一本熟悉的绘本里朗读和理解重复出现的短语。**

教学目标

· 促进孩子们对故事语言和印刷作用的理解。

教学准备

· 柔丝·M. 的《我们去捉狗熊》（沃克出版社 1993 年出版）。

· 其他的书，其中重复出现的短语字体在印刷时逐渐扩大。

怎么做

· 在孩子们已经听过这个故事很多次之后，仔细看一看描写人物动作的每一页，
例如：

  跌跌撞撞，跌跌撞撞，跌跌撞撞

· 孩子们能看见重复三遍的词汇吗？帮他们一起数一数。

· 问问孩子们是否注意到被重复的词汇有什么不同。向孩子们展示词汇是如何变得越
来越大的。

  - 你们知道为什么词汇这样印刷吗？

· 听取孩子们的建议，然后让他们说出他们的想法，例如：他们可能建议在故事中人
物累的时候，词汇被念得越来越慢，或者在加快速度的时候，词汇会被念得越来
越快。

· 第一遍朗读的时候，试着轻声一些，然后越来越响，这样来阐述一个想法。

· 再次朗读这本书，鼓励孩子们加入一起重复词汇，开始声音轻一些，最后大叫
出来！

· 让孩子们去找找其他的书中像这样扩大印刷文字的地方。

· 留下一些例子给孩子们去探索。

词汇

  小、大、更大、安静、响亮、更响亮。

小贴士　你可以在课堂宝典系列丛书的《幼儿自然拼读的游戏，想法和活动》一

书中得到更多的灵感。

跨领域链接

跨领域链接

问题解决、推理和计算的能力：形状、空间和测量。

越来越大(2)

 • 帮助孩子们创立自己的重复短语，并且在电脑中放大粗体字。

教学目标
• 促进孩子们对故事语言和印刷作用的理解。

教学资源
1）一些书，这些书中将重复出现的短语字体逐渐放大；2）有书写（文字处理）程序的电脑。

教学准备
• 帮助孩子们理解放大字体的惯例，阅读几本展示这些文字的书或者使用"越来越大（1）"这个活动。

怎么做
• 当孩子们已经阅读过这个选择好的故事多次之后，看着书中每一页，解释印刷字体逐渐变大。
• 讨论如何将这个故事制作得更加吸引人，例如：
  "这将帮助我们知道豆茎正长得越来越高。"
• 让孩子们选择一个起始的单词，将它打在电脑上（参见下方的词汇表）。向他们展示如何在词尾加上"er"。
• 帮助他们在电脑上打出或复制这个新词汇三次。
• 然后告诉他们如何改变字体的大小，使字变得更大。
• 让孩子们一直实践下去，直到他们选择了最适合的字体大小。
• 打印出他们重复的短语，然后展示给其他人朗读。

词汇
小—更小
大—更大
轻声—更轻声
响亮—更响亮
高—更高
近—更近

小贴士

如果有的小朋友想无限放大字体，你需要解释一下，这个字体在你需要打印出来的时候，必须大小适中才可以打印在纸上。

跨领域链接

认识与理解世界：信息通信技术（ICT）。

越来越大(3)

• 用孩子们自己的想法为重复的短语创作音乐，让音乐越来越响或越来越轻。

教学目标

• 促进孩子们对故事语言和印刷作用的理解。

教学资源

1）打击乐器； 2）有书写（文字处理）程序的电脑。

教学准备

• 运用"越来越大（2）"的活动介绍印刷字体被放大的想法。

怎么做

• 演奏一种乐器。要求孩子们想出一个词汇来描述这种声音，例如：砰（击打声），砰（冲撞声）。

• 把这个单词写三遍，一次用小号字体，一次用大一些的字体，然后再大一号。用演奏乐器的声音变大或变小，来指出重复这些印刷字体的大小。

• 让孩子们两两合作练习并选择一种乐器。

• 现在让他们想出一个词来描述他们乐器发出的声音。

• 帮助孩子们在电脑的书写程序中写单词。

• 让他们打出这个单词三遍，然后改变字体的大小，这样单词会变得越来越大。

• 打印出孩子们想出的词汇。

• 然后一个孩子指着三种大小的重复单词，同时他的搭档演奏出与字体大小匹配的乐器音量。

• 让孩子们轮流玩这个演奏和指点的游戏。

• 然后孩子们尝试演奏另一种乐器来表达另一组词汇。

• 当他们确信小的字体等于轻声，那么一个大人可以指挥一群孩子演奏各种乐器来表达一组词：

玩，玩，玩

真好玩呀!

词汇

砰砰、轰隆、隆隆声、叮叮、丁零零、咔嚓、呼呼、咯咯、吱吱、嘟嘟。

 小贴士　　　也许你可以给孩子们介绍渐强的音乐符号。

跨领域链接

创造力的发展：音乐和舞蹈。

第三部分
写

要让儿童观察成人阅读和写作，鼓励他们通过做标记、使用自己的写作符号和惯用的写作方式去尝试自己写作。

——英国皇冠出版社 2008 年版《早期基础阶段实践导引》，第 42 页。

第七章

手指游戏

蜡烛（4）

· 孩子们喜欢用手指作画来创作他们自己的蜡烛设计。

教学目标

· 鼓励孩子们在玩的时候制作字母形状。

教学资源

1）颜色鲜亮的手指颜料； 2）大开本的纸张。

教学准备

· 给桌上蜡烛形状的模具填上颜料。

· 剪出一张更大的纸。

怎么做

· 鼓励孩子们用他们的指尖在颜料上做设计。尝试：

　— 画圈；

　— 画长短直线；

　— 画曲线；

oooo

lili

ww

这些是我们用来写字母的基本形状。

· 现在把纸小心地放在颜料上。

· 轻按，然后取出蜡烛。

· 孩子们现在可以用颜料和刷子，或者从黄色纸上剪下的形状给他们的蜡烛加上黄色
的边框。

词汇

圆的、笔直的、联合的。

小贴士　　　　一些孩子可能喜欢在桌上准备他们自己的蜡烛形状。

跨领域链接

　　创造力的发展：媒介与材料。

让手指移动

· 在孩子们开始写字之前，试着用一些简单的娱乐练习活动手指肌肉。

教学目标

• 鼓励孩子们练习手部控制技能为写字做准备。

教学资源

大量的带动作的韵律诗。

怎么做

• 就像比赛前运动员热身一样，在孩子们期望锻炼写字技能之前，值得做一些手指练习。任何带有手指运动的动作韵律诗都可以被使用，例如：

两只小鸟；

大拇指汤姆；

飞碟里的五个小矮人。

• 或者创作自己的一套练习。下面有两个想法开始这个活动：

－ 张开你的手放在桌子上，手掌朝下。

谁可以在不移动其他手指的情况下，依次抬起每一个手指？

你可以做到多快？

你可以做到多慢？

你比你的朋友更快吗？

－ 你的拇指可以一个接一个碰到其他手指吗？

其他手指必须是拇指所在的同一个手上的！

你可以用另一只手做到吗？

你可以做到多快？

词汇

拇指、手指、摆动、伸直、蜷曲。

小贴士　　当你要求孩子们做写字前的热身活动时，孩子们渐渐可以独立完成了。

跨领域链接

身体的发展：媒介与材料。

丝带舞蹈

 • 孩子们一边跳舞一边挥动他们的丝带。

教学目标
- 创造机会让孩子们使用肩膀的大动作。

教学资源
1）大长条丝带； 2）录制好的音乐。

教学准备
- 录制一些活泼但是节奏均衡的音乐。华尔兹是一个很好的选择范围。
- 和孩子们谈谈假日游行中的舞蹈者们，他们是如何挥动丝带，并且在空中舞出各种形状。

怎么做
- 孩子们可以用一些时间自由随着音乐跳舞，把丝带高高地在空中挥舞，练习这个动作。
- 等他们熟悉了如何舞动丝带后，要求他们跟着你到处走走，挥动丝带。让他们感觉自己是游行队伍中的舞者。
- 要求孩子们尽力把丝带舞动在空中形成一个圆形。鼓励所有的孩子们都以相同的方向舞动。
- 当你给他们一个信号时，他们就改变丝带的舞动方向。你可以举起一只手或换另一只手，或者吹口哨。
- 当大家坐下休息时，问一下孩子们：
  "用一只手完成容易吗？"
  "哪只手？"
  "和你写字画画时是同一只手吗？"
- 下一次，试着用丝带舞出"Z"的形状再来一遍。

词汇
左边、右边、高的、低的。

带头者可以拿棒子、旗子或是花作为游行进行中的指挥棒，指挥丝带挥舞的方向。

跨领域链接

认识与理解世界：交流。

条形旗子

· 当孩子们使用电脑鼠标制作旗子的时候，让孩子们锻炼手部控制。

教学目标

· 给孩子们机会用越来越强的控制力来操控物体。

教学资源

1）带鼠标的电脑； 2）简易的绘画程序，例如：第一幅画。

教学准备

· 向孩子们展示如何用鼠标点击他们想要使用的颜色。

· 创造机会让孩子们用不同的颜色玩乐或是做记号。

怎么做

· 告诉孩子们他们将制作一些旗子。

· 展示如何使用电脑程序：

－ 在电脑程序中选择最宽的刷子符号。

－ 提醒孩子们如何选择他们想要的颜色。

－ 使用鼠标在屏幕的上方画一条水平线。

－ 然后选择第二个颜色在第一条线下面画一条相似的线条。

－ 选择第三、第四种颜色划线，一直继续这个过程。

· 打印出你的设计，向孩子们展示你制作的旗子。

· 现在轮到孩子们制作他们自己的旗子了。

· 当孩子们制作旗子的时候，你可以把旗子固定在一根绳上，挂在教室门上或是展板上。

词汇

点击、压、握着、穿过、下面。

小贴士　　　　为了控制他们画的线条平稳，鼓励孩子们慢慢地画线。

跨领域链接

认识与理解世界：信息通信技术（ICT）。

生日（4）

 • 用一个有糖衣的蛋糕来庆祝，并且利用这个机会锻炼孩子们写字母。

教学目标
• 锻炼孩子们正确地写字母。

教学资源
1）买来的或是提前制作好的蛋糕，一个或多个； 2）糖粉和水的混合物； 3）食用色素和串签（去掉尖锐的头部）或是糖霜笔。

教学准备
• 选择一款你想要孩子们装饰的蛋糕：
— 一个大一点的蛋糕，大小可以写下一个名字。
— 一些小蛋糕。
• 选择使用糖霜管或是让孩子们使用干净的串签蘸一下食用色素，在糖衣还未干的时候在上面写字。
• 让孩子们用一层糖衣给蛋糕上糖霜。

怎么做
• 给孩子们看一下蛋糕，解释一下你们将要用字母装饰蛋糕。
• 展示如何用糖衣写字，提醒孩子们字母的正确写法。
• 帮助孩子们用写好的糖衣装饰蛋糕。
• 如果你选用多个小蛋糕，试试这些想法：
— 每个孩子有一个蛋糕，然后把自己名字的第一个字母写在上面。
— 每个孩子可以在他们的蛋糕上写一个字母，这样合在一起拼写出"生日快乐"或是一个玩具的名字。他们能自己排好字母拼写出单词吗？
• 如果你决定使用一个大蛋糕，可让孩子们依次在蛋糕上写出字母，拼出一个玩具的名字或"生日快乐"字样。

词汇
开始、顶部、向下、上方、圆形、向上、挤压。

小贴士　　　先利用防油纸模仿练习在糖衣上写字。

跨领域链接

认识与理解世界：交流。

音乐记号（1）

· 孩子们喜欢随着一些舒缓的音乐做动作，然后当听第二遍的时候，画出来。

教学目标

· 鼓励孩子们用他们的双手做左右移动。

教学资源

1）舒缓的音乐，例如：德沃夏克的《新世界交响曲》； 2）大开本的纸、颜料和笔刷。

教学准备

· 在被覆盖的表面上准备好纸和颜料。

怎么做

· 给孩子们播放音乐。

· 鼓励孩子们用合适的方式随着音乐做动作，例如：挥动手臂或慢慢转圈。

· 告诉孩子们你将再播放一遍音乐，但这次是边听边画。

· 播放音乐，鼓励孩子们在整张纸上画出长长的、光滑的有颜色的波浪线。鼓励孩子们从左边开始画，在右边结束。

· 颜料干了之后，讨论一下像什么，例如：

　蓝色的颜料： 水/大海/天空；

　绿色的颜料： 草地/小山；

　橙色/红色： 日落。

词汇

光滑、长的、柔和的、缓慢的、流动的、升和降。

小贴士　　　　用这些颜料的颜色作为背景，让孩子们加入一些小细节，例如：小船、花朵和绵羊等，来匹配背景颜色的主题。

跨领域链接

创造力的发展：创造力。

音乐记号(2)

· 孩子们在听欢快激动的音乐时，喜欢做一些快速移动的动作。

教学目标

· 鼓励孩子们用他们的手指在空中做出形状，同时做一些记号。

教学资源

1）激动欢快的音乐，例如：里姆斯基·科拉科夫《大黄蜂的飞翔》； 2）大开本的纸、粗头记号笔。

教学准备

· 在被覆盖的表面上准备好纸。

怎么做

· 给孩子们播放音乐。鼓励孩子们用合适的方式随着音乐做动作，例如：用手指、手臂和腿做快速移动的动作。

· 告诉孩子们你将再播放一遍音乐，但这次是边听边画。鼓励他们在纸上画出快速移动的记号。允许他们使用大量明亮的颜色随意地在纸上画出记号。

· 或者提供一张纸，中心有一个模板，之后可以被移走，显示出太阳光的图案。

· 向孩子们展示如何从纸上的圆形开始，然后从圆形的边缘向外拨出去。

词汇

快速、移动、尖的、短的、锋利的、快速的、急促的。

小贴士　　　　　用粉笔在深色的纸上再试一下，创作一张烟花的图片。

跨领域链接

创造力的发展：创造力。

纸张游戏

• 孩子们通过撕纸来办一个展示。这可以促进孩子们手部和手指精细肌肉的发展。

教学目标

• 鼓励孩子们锻炼手部控制技能。

教学资源

1）做底板的纸盒、胶水； 2）图片 1：有绿色和棕色阴影的糖纸； 3）图片 2：报纸。

教学准备

• 剪出一张足够大的纸可以覆盖你的展示板。

怎么做

图片 1：

• 告诉孩子们你们将在展板上展示一个森林的图案。

• 向他们展示如何通过撕纸用糖纸做出一些树。解释一下如何撕可使纸的边缘呈锯齿形，这样看上去更像生活中真实的物体形状。孩子们可以把绿色的纸撕成大大的云的形状，放在树的顶部。他们还需要用棕色的纸撕出长条形做树干。

• 帮助孩子们把这些纸片粘在底板纸上，让其看上去像一片森林。

• 孩子们还可以加入上好色的小孩子的形象在走路，或者加入住在树林里的动物形象，或是汉塞尔、格雷特尔和女巫的小木屋——任何适合当前图片主题的东西都可以。

图片 2：

• 告诉孩子们你们将只使用旧报纸，展示一个繁忙的城镇。讨论一下镇上可能有什么，例如：楼房、交通设施、道路。在展板的下面部分用黑色马克笔画出一条马路横跨展板。

• 孩子们用报纸撕出不同大小的长方形图案。

• 帮助他们在底板纸上贴上大一些的长方形，看上去像镇上的楼房。使用小一些的长方形代表小轿车、公共汽车等。

• 等胶水干了，帮助孩子们在报纸图片上用黑色记号笔画上轮子和窗户。

词汇

撕开、撕裂的/破旧的、裂口/裂缝。

 小贴士　　撕东西锻炼的手部肌肉和握笔相同。

跨领域链接

身体的发展：媒介与材料。

字母形状

· 把写字练习转变成孩子们的艺术活动。

教学目标

· 鼓励孩子们练习形成字母的形状。

教学资源

1）若干马克笔；2）图片1：亮棕色、绿色和粉色的纸；3）图片2：粉色和亮棕色纸。

教学准备

· 图片1：用纸剪出屋顶的形状。尽力剪出各种不同的形状。

· 图片2：用纸剪出长方形。

· 在每一张纸左手边的角落放上一个小的记号，这样孩子们知道从哪里开始。

怎么做

图片1：

· 告诉孩子们，他们将在屋顶样子的纸上加上瓦片。一开始，你先画一片瓦片，让孩子们仔细观察，这样接下去他们可以自己完成了。

· 向他们展示如何画出一排"U"，连接在一起，从屋顶开始，从左到右画。提醒他们应该从你标过点的地方开始。

· 现在，一排接一排往下画。当整个图形画满了"U"字母之后，整个设计应该看上去像屋顶的瓦片。

· 现在让孩子们选择一个屋顶形状的图形和一只彩色的记号笔。鼓励他们要小心画，但是要让笔在整个图形里移动。

· 孩子们可以完成任意数量。空白图形的数量要足够多，以满足任何人要重新画。

· 所有的图形都完成后，孩子们可以帮忙一起把屋顶贴在深色底板纸的下半部分的地方，加上烟囱、星星、一些雪花和圣诞老人的形象来完成你的冬季夜景图。

图片2：

· 告诉孩子们他们可以完成一幅拥挤人群的图片。

· 展示图片1的制作过程，这样孩子们可以想象完成的作品的样子。

· 给每个孩子一张粉色和亮棕色的纸。

- 鼓励他们用他们的水笔在整张纸上，从左往右画圆。他们可以在整张纸上画尽可能多的行数。
- 纸张画满圆形之后，孩子们可以加上眼睛嘴巴和一些头发来画出一张张有趣的脸，这样可以创作自己的一幅拥挤人群的画。

词汇

左边、右边、上面、下面、上方、圆形。

小贴士　　　　鼓励孩子们在纸张上从左到右移动画笔和从上到下移动画笔。

跨领域链接

身体的发展：媒介与材料。

小型动物（4）

• 当孩子们练习从左到右在纸上写字画画时，他们可用银色的笔制作自己的蜗牛小道。

教学目标

• 鼓励孩子们用越来越强的控制力来用手控制物体。

教学资源

1）蜗牛——如果可能的话；2）银色的马克笔；3）深色的糖纸；4）有对比色的糖纸。

教学准备

• 准备一些花园蜗牛供孩子们观察。

• 让孩子们观察蜗牛从深色的纸向诱人的黄瓜片移动。指出它们的路线。

怎么做

• 告诉孩子们，他们将制作自己的蜗牛小道。他们将使用银色的马克笔来制作路线。

　－ 他们能否思考为什么笔是这个颜色的？

　－ 他们是否记得真正的蜗牛路线看上去的样子？

• 提醒孩子们从纸的左边开始画路线，一直画到右边。他们可以尽力画一些圈形或弧形的线，画这些图形都是为写字做准备的。

• 小朋友们完成银色路线后，他们可以在路线的右手边结尾处粘上一个纸圆。

• 作品干了以后，孩子们可以用亮色笔在纸圆上画一个螺旋型。

• 加上一些物件来完成这幅蜗牛作品，可以给它加上一片黄瓜。

词汇

圆形、穿过、左边、右边、圈形、螺旋型。

小贴士　　　使用你的蜗牛小道来练习一系列押韵的词汇，完成发音练习，例如：一条苍白的鲸和蜗牛的轨迹。

跨领域链接

认识与理解世界：探索与观察。

室外写字

• 孩子们可以在室外练习写字的一系列的方法。

教学目标
• 给孩子们提供各种写字工具。

教学资源
1）粉笔；2）干净的空瓶子；3）粘纸、鹅卵石、树叶和圆锥形球果。

教学准备
• 一起收集今天你要使用的写字工具。
• 去室外之前：
− 确保每个人穿着恰当——一些孩子可能需要带围脖。
− 解释一下为什么自然材料适合室外写字。
− 帮助他们理解，他们只能在你展示的地方，用你给他们的工具写字。

怎么做
• 告诉孩子们他们今天要在室外写字。
• 提醒孩子们你希望他们练习的一个单词（例如他们的名字）或是字母的形状。
• 在外出前提醒他们从左边开始写。
 − 他们能记住左边是哪一边吗？
 书空一下写字的方法。
• 在室外，你需要展示每一种写字工具怎样和在哪里被使用：
 − 粉笔和带喷嘴的水瓶适合在坚硬的表面写字。
 − 用钝的木棒在沙坑里写字。
 − 鹅卵石、球果和树叶可以摆在草地上拼出字母的图案。

词汇
左边、右边、上面、下面、圈形、上方。

小贴士　　　如果要培养孩子们良好的写字习惯，这个活动（和其他大部分写字活动一样）应该严格把关。

跨领域链接

　　身体的发展：运用工具与材料。

快乐的拼图

· 孩子们完成一幅画，然后把画剪开，制作自己的拼图。

教学目标

· 鼓励孩子们运用精细运动控制技能。

教学资源

1）浅色大卡纸； 2）孩子们用的粗头记号笔和剪刀； 3）成人用的铅笔和尺子。

教学准备

· 玩拼图的经验。

怎么做

· 在你们的教学环境里，和孩子们聊聊拼图。

– 他们最喜欢哪一种拼图？

– 哪一个最难拼？

· 告知他们将自己制作拼图。

· 要求每个小朋友在一张卡纸上画出一个彩色的图案或图片。鼓励他们填满卡纸上而且用上盒子里所有的颜色！图片完成后，提醒他们写上自己的名字。

· 然后把卡纸翻过来，当你用铅笔和尺子在卡纸反面画上 4—5 条连接线时，让孩子们仔细观察。

接着，孩子们用记号笔沿着这些线再加深一下，然后你帮助他们用剪刀沿着线仔细剪下来。

· 现在他们可以再次制作拼图，然后和其他小朋友一起玩。

词汇

直的、线、剪刀、剪。

小贴士　　　这个活动可以根据不同能力的孩子变换形式，例如：对于幼童们，3—4 块拼图比较合适。

跨领域链接

创造力的发展：探索媒介与材料。

《小蜘蛛》

 · 孩子们在一起分享这首童谣前，一起用羊毛和通管器自己制作蜘蛛。

教学目标
- 鼓励孩子们运用精细动作控制技能。

教学资源
1）若干通管器； 2）羊毛； 3）亮片； 4）剪刀和胶水。

教学准备
- 确保每个人都知道这首童谣《小蜘蛛》。
- 讨论一下真正的蜘蛛：
- 谁看见过蜘蛛？
- 它们是什么样的？
- 它们怎样移动？
- 它们有多大？
- 它们有几条腿？

怎么做
- 告诉孩子们，他们将自己制作蜘蛛。
- 帮助每个孩子数出 4 根通管器备用。
- 向他们展示如何在绑在一起的 4 根通管器周围包上羊毛。他们应当一直缠绕直到羊毛形成了蜘蛛身体的形状。然后帮助孩子们用剪刀剪断羊毛，但记住要留出一长段羊毛，这样可以提着蜘蛛晃动。大人可以帮忙打个结，这样羊毛不会散开。
- 现在让孩子们选择一对亮片做蜘蛛的眼睛。
- 帮助他们把眼睛贴在蜘蛛的头部。
- 当孩子们背诵童谣的时候，移动他们的蜘蛛。
- 用大字写下童谣，并且在周围晃动蜘蛛，这样做一个展示。

词汇
数字 1—4、缠绕、羊毛、剪刀、剪、亮片、晃。

小贴士

把这个活动延伸为写字活动——在一张张纸条上写下制作蜘蛛的说明，然后要求孩子们以正确的顺序排列。

跨领域链接

身体的发展：运用工具与材料。

小餐馆(3)

• 孩子们制作一些菜单的时候，是一个有趣的写字机会。

教学目标

• 鼓励孩子们运用尽力听单词开头的音节。

教学资源

1）打印好或画好的关于食物的图片； 2）若干对折好的 A4 卡纸； 3）胶水、记号笔； 4）艾伦·亚伯格的《女招待沃波尔太太》（伦敦海雀图文出版社 1980 年出版）。

教学准备

• 读完这个故事后，关注沃波尔太太和孩子们列菜单的那一页。

怎么做

• 向孩子们展示折叠的卡纸将成为菜单纸。

• 讨论故事中菜单是由图片和旁边的文字构成的。

• 摆出食物的图片，鼓励孩子们辨认这些物品。

• 让每个孩子选择一些图片制作自己的菜单。

• 帮助孩子们把图片粘在菜单上，留出空间写字。

• 鼓励他们试着在恰当的图片旁边写上文字。

词汇

各种各样的食物名称，例如：茶、奶昔、可乐、果汁、汤、汉堡、三明治、水果、冰激凌。

小贴士　　　　选择开头字母不一样的单词有助于才刚开始使用拼读知识写字的小朋友。

跨领域链接

身体的发展：健康和身体意识。

第八章

写下来

灰姑娘忙碌的一天

• 和孩子们玩一个记忆游戏，然后他们写下一连串灰姑娘要做的事。

教学目标

• 鼓励孩子们尝试用罗列清单的方式写作。

教学资源

1）卡纸条和马克笔； 2）磁力板和磁铁； 3）预先准备好的写清单的纸。

教学准备

• 为角色扮演活动作准备：打印一些长条的纸备用。

— 在纸的顶部写："灰姑娘，今天你必须做……"

— 在纸的底部写：姓名。

— 在中间，按序写好"1"，"2"和"3"，然后留出空间。

怎么做

• 和一组孩子围坐成圆形，玩游戏。告诉他们，他们准备扮演丑陋的姐姐们。提醒他们，姐姐们是怎样欺负灰姑娘的，希望她为她们做任何事情。

• 你用这句话开始这个游戏："今天上午，我想让灰姑娘做……"然后加上一件让她做的杂事。

• 每个孩子重复灰姑娘之前做过的事，然后在清单上再加上一件事。你可以给出 4—5 个建议来做个限定。

• 孩子提出每一件杂事后，一个大人就迅速把它写在每个人的卡纸条上。然后把这些卡纸条粘贴成一个清单。你可以使用如下的表达：

— 拖地板；

— 擦桌子；

— 洗碗碟；

— 点壁炉；

— 喂猫咪；

— 洗裙子；

— 削土豆；

— 给面包涂黄油；

－ 买东西;

　　　－ 洗鞋子。

　　孩子们可以使用清单来提醒他们已经说的内容。

- 现在，拿走清单再玩一次。孩子们可以用相同的想法但是以不同的顺序表达，或者你可以写下他们想到的新的想法。同样的方式可以创作一个新的清单。
- 给孩子们看写着他们想法的准备好的纸条，读给他们听。
- 给他们解释一下，在角色扮演区玩游戏的时候，他们可以制作一张要求灰姑娘做的事情清单，然后张贴在磁板上。之前游戏中你制作好的清单可以贴在旁边，万一孩子们想要使用这些想法，可以看到。

小贴士

　　如果这个群体中只有你一个大人，那么在游戏前先写下一些普通的杂事，这样可以加快游戏的进程。一些孩子可能喜欢在桌上准备他们自己喜欢的形状的蜡烛。

跨领域链接

沟通、语言和读写能力的发展：角色扮演。

盒子里有什么？

• 如果在收获的季节，你们将要准备给社区居民准备一盒盒水果作为礼物，帮助孩子们用简单的句型结构记录下内容。

教学目标

• 鼓励孩子们组织简单的句型。

教学资源

1）纸条；2）贴好标签的水果图片；3）若干小盒子。

教学准备

• 每个孩子需要两张纸条，一张上写"我有"，另一张上写"在我的盒子里"。不要忘记加上句号。

• 收集水果的图片。把图片粘贴在每个人的卡纸上，水果的名字写在背面。用"一个"或"一些"表达恰当的数量，例如："一只梨""一只苹果""一些葡萄"。

怎么做

• 在期望孩子们自己完成这个活动之前，和一组小朋友先开展一次。

• 把一张"我有"的卡纸放在前面。现在选择一张图片卡放在旁边，然后在它上面放一张"在我盒子里"的纸条。

• 读出这句话，包括这个水果的名称。让孩子们注意关于句子的开头单词要大写，然后结尾用句号。

• 现在孩子们可以开始写下这句话。给每个孩子他们自己的句子开头和结尾的单词。他们可以选择画出水果或写出水果的名称作为句子的一部分。

• 孩子们可以任意造句，然后用盒子里的水果来解释，但是……必须确保文字和图片是匹配的！

词汇

句子、句号、大写字母。

小贴士

能力强一些的孩子可以在水果名称前加上颜色词，例如"我有一个黄色的香蕉""我有一些绿色的葡萄"。

跨领域链接

个人、社会和情感的发展：团队意识。

亲爱的熊

• 以泰迪熊的名义写一封信给你的孩子们去阅读。利用这个机会加强他们对另一个国家的理解。

教学目标
• 给孩子们一个理由让其在游戏中锻炼写作。

教学资源
1）一个新的泰迪熊或相似的毛绒玩具； 2）纸张、水笔和铅笔。

教学准备
• 大人假扮泰迪熊写一封信，并把它留在教室里让孩子们找到。
• 泰迪熊告诉孩子们，他来自另一个国家，要来拜访他们。
• 在信中尽力问一些简单的问题，例如：你们能猜出我住在哪里吗？

怎么做
• 一旦孩子们找到了这封信，请帮助孩子们阅读内容。向孩子们展示纸和笔，鼓励他们写回信。允许孩子们以自己的方式自由写作。
• 第二天，泰迪熊回信告诉他们关于这个国家事情，然后让孩子们猜一猜，从他的窗户往外看可以看到什么？
• 一直持续交换信件，直到孩子们热衷这件事，问一些如下的问题：我的工作是什么？你猜猜我穿了什么衣服？然后问一个最终的问题，例如：我怎样找到你的学校？
• 安排一天接待来访的新朋友泰迪熊。讨论如何欢迎这位新朋友——也许新朋友来访时可以举办一个茶话会。

词汇
根据你选择的国家，词汇可以各不相同，例如：
澳大利亚：海滩、冲浪、阳光、防晒霜、野餐和救生员。
挪威：山、高的、爬、湾峡、小船、渔夫和山中救援。

小贴士
不要忘记，孩子们在交流时可以画画。

跨领域链接

认识与理解世界：交流。

婚礼 (2)

> • 假定有客人来参加婚礼，和孩子们写下客人的名字卡片来安排座位表。

教学目标
- 帮助孩子们识别和写下自己的名字。

教学资源

1）卡片和水笔； 2）2—3 个小桌子和椅子。

教学准备
- 帮助孩子们在卡纸上写下自己的名字。
- 向他们展示名字卡片，帮助他们识别自己的名字。

怎么做
- 告诉孩子们，在婚礼仪式后，大家通常会聚餐。
  解释一下，新郎和新娘将安排客人的座位——称为座位表——在桌上的名字卡片就表示每个人就坐的位置。
- 选择名字卡片中两个为新郎和新娘。让一个孩子把这些卡片放在该放的地方。
- 现在说明一下，新郎希望每一个女孩旁边坐一个男孩。帮助其他孩子按这个方式把名字卡片放在桌上。
- 和孩子们一起读一下名字，检查位置摆放是否正确。现在每一个孩子找到自己的名字然后就坐。说说谁坐在谁的旁边。
- 拿走名字卡片，以其他的座位安排方式再玩一遍，例如：所有的男孩一桌，所有的女孩在另一桌。

词汇

名字、旁边、谁、在哪里。

小贴士　　　　能力强一些的孩子可以用简明的图片来制定座位表，并确定桌子上的名字卡片位置。

跨领域链接

个人、社会和情感的发展：团队意识。

假期(3)

• 帮助孩子们制作明信片，一面贴上度假照片，另一面写上信息。

教学目标
• 给孩子们一个机会让其独立完成写字。

教学资源
1）若干空白明信片或卡片； 2）度假宣传册。

教学准备
• 从你假期去过的地方，寄一张明信片给学校。
• 把明信片内容读给孩子们听。
• 解释一下照片中显示的是你所去过的地方。

怎么做
• 如果孩子们度过假，问问他们：
　　－ 你们去过哪里？
• 给孩子们看一看度假宣传册，讨论不同类型的地方，如：海边、主题公园。
• 让孩子们剪下最喜欢的地方的图片。
• 示范如何把图片贴在卡片的一边，制作一张明信片。讨论将寄给谁。
• 现在让孩子们在明信片的背面写上一条信息。讨论一下写什么，例如：我们去游泳了。
  提醒孩子们如何用自己的名字结束他们的信息。
• 向孩子们展示哪里写他们父母和朋友的名字。
• 展示明信片的时候，把它们挂在长绳子上，这样卡片两面都可以被看到了。

词汇
海边、宾馆、泳池、别墅、主题公园、游乐场、度假村、山脉、湖泊。

小贴士　　　　　虽然大一些的孩子可以在明信片上写地址，但我们不建议这么做，这样可以使活动简化一些。

跨领域链接
认识与理解世界：地点。

关于攀爬墙

• 享受室外写字的乐趣。帮助孩子们使用分割句来描述他们在攀爬墙上的位置。

教学目标

• 鼓励孩子们将写的字再读一遍。

教学资源

1）记号笔和纸；2）写在卡纸条上的句子。

教学准备

• 在卡纸条上写一些简单的句子，描述你在攀爬架上和周围的位置，例如：

− 我在……上（这根绳子）。

− 我在……下面（这个滑滑梯）。

− 我在……旁边（这根木头）。

• 按如上指示，把卡纸条分成两部分，这样孩子们可以重新编排，创作出各种不同的句子。

怎么做

• 向孩子们解释他们将要玩攀爬架的游戏，但你会随时叫停，然后问他们的位置。边做，边让孩子们说出许多写在卡纸上的词汇。

• 现在把孩子们聚集起来，朗读你准备好的句子。向孩子们展示他们可以如何交换句子的某些部分来创作新的句子。

• 让孩子们选择他们愿意写哪一句话，使用句子的开头部分和结尾部分。

• 鼓励孩子们朗读他们已经写出的每一句话。现在他们可以罗列出攀爬架上的位置。

• 让孩子们在攀爬设备上自由游玩一会儿，然后再把他们叫到一起，用另一个分割句子的开头和结尾来创作一个不同的句子。

• 朗读这个句子，再一次找到攀爬架上的位置。

词汇

在……上面、在……下面、附近、在……后面、在……前面、高的、低的、旁边。

小贴士　　　　　创作一幅攀爬架的小图片，然后复印出来，这样孩子们在写位置的时候，可以画出这个位置。

跨领域链接

问题解决、推理和计算能力：形状、空间和测量。

十根肥香肠

 · 使用这个熟悉的童谣来激发孩子们写"巨响"或"爆裂",然后在一起背诵这个童谣时使用他们的作品。

教学目标

· 鼓励孩子们写一些简单的单词。

教学资源

10 张 A4 纸。

教学准备

· 把 5 张纸剪成圆形,5 张纸剪成"爆炸"形(锯齿形)。

怎么做

· 和 10 个孩子一起玩这个游戏,确保他们都知道这首数数的童谣《十根肥香肠》。
"当香肠在盘子里的时候,它们做什么?"
"有时它们会发出巨响,有时它们会发生爆裂。"

· 下发纸张,告诉孩子们,如果他们拿到了一个圆形,就用黑色粗体字写"巨响",但如果他们拿到了像爆炸的锯齿样纸张,他们就写"爆裂"。

· 向孩子们解释他们将成为依次要爆炸的香肠!当轮到他们时,他们要举起他们的单词,大声说出这个单词,然后坐下。

· 现在你要手握着这些纸,站在一个圈里,交替出示"巨响"和"爆裂"两个单词,一起说出这个童谣。

· 即使在你的节奏被打乱了,也不要忘了帮助大家说出童谣。

 小贴士 这是一个很好的让孩子们练习如何自己拼写单词的机会。

跨领域链接

问题解决、推理和计算能力:计算。

你做了什么?

• 让孩子们给自己做的面团作品做标签。

教学目标
• 给孩子们一个理由让其写简单的说明文字。

教学资源
1）面团，模具； 2）若干硬纸或卡纸条，将其折叠起来，使它们能竖起来。

教学准备
• 给孩子们大量的时间自由玩面团。
• 在做面团的桌子旁放一张写字桌。
• 有一个准备好的空间展示面团作品和他们的标签。

怎么做
• 鼓励孩子们用面团创作作品。他们可以选择创作人物、动物、怪兽等。作品完成后，他们可以把作品放在展示台上。
• 现在，他们去写字台做标签了。向他们展示如何确保纸条顶部折叠起来，这样标签可以站立起来。
• 他们决定想采取哪一种方法去写字。这将取决于孩子们的能力和经历：
  - 鼓励孩子们自己拼写单词完成标签，例如：
  （汤姆做了一个可怕的恐龙）
  - 让孩子们看着，你为他们写出单词。
  - 准备一些句子，孩子们可以复制和运用，例如：
  ……做了一个……
  ……的作品是一个……
  这里有一个……
  - 和孩子们讨论这些句子，一起朗读一下，然后写下来。
• 然后孩子们把标签放在自己的作品旁边。

词汇
推、拉、挤、做。

小贴士　试着给面团上色，在面团和水混合之前加入食用色素。

跨领域链接

身体的发展：运用工具与材料。

清理你的牙齿

• 和将开始独立写作的孩子们创建一个特殊的词汇库。

教学目标

• 建立一个资源库来帮助孩子们写作。

教学资源

1）若干小卡纸； 2）一套用英语字母作为标签的空袋子。

教学准备

• 把空的字母口袋放在写字桌旁边，和孩子们一起坐在桌子旁。

怎么做

• 和孩子们聊聊如何爱护自己的牙齿，然后让他们写一写。

• 问问孩子们是否能想到一些他们今天写作要用到的单词，例如：
  牙刷、牙医。

• 用粗体字把这些单词写在一张卡纸上。
  – 它以什么音节开始呢？
  在你写的时候大声读出来，让这些孩子理解即可。

• 现在，给孩子们展示这个单词。一起朗读，识别开头字母。说出这个单词的孩子可以走出来，把这个单词放入标有这个字母的袋子里。如果有需要，其他小朋友可以帮忙。

• 继续这样下去，直到你已经对于这个主题有充足的词汇储备。

• 要求任意一个小朋友出来，从口袋中挑选一个单词，大声朗读出来。
  – 大家都同意这么读吗？

• 这个孩子把这个单词再放回正确的袋子。
  – 这个孩子还能记得哪个袋子吗？

• 现在这个孩子可以利用这个资源帮助自己完成今天的写作。提醒他们哪里可以找到其他的关键词。
  "这些只是适合今天的词汇。"

词汇

牙刷、牙膏、牙医、冲洗、不吃糖、水。

小贴士　　　　　活动最后取走所有的卡片，这样袋子空了可以为下一次或下一组有自己想法的小朋友做好准备。

跨领域链接

身体的发展：健康和身体意识。

欢迎!

• 帮助孩子们给新加入这个场所的孩子做卡片。

教学目标

- 向孩子们介绍有目的的写作，同时让其学会使用清单。

教学资源

1）将要加入你们的新的小朋友名字的清单；2）可用的电脑和写字程序。

怎么做

- 告诉孩子们有新的小朋友将要加入你们，他们要来参观一下。

- 向他们展示名单并且读给他们听。要求他们仔细看一下，并且注意名字的排序。

- 告知他们你们想要设计一个欢迎卡片送给每一个清单上的人。
  孩子们可以在电脑前一起完成，从图片库里选择和下载图片。

- 然后他们可以帮助你创建一则信息，例如：
  亲爱的……我们在星期三上午十点期待你过来和我们一起玩。爱你的……

- 留出空白处写上收信人和寄信人的名字，之后，你将信息填在空白处。（如果你不想用现在孩子们的名字在信息最后署名，那么用团队、班级或场所的名字代替。）

- 鼓励孩子们在你给出的界定范围内自己选择字体、颜色和布局等。最后打印出卡片。

- 团队中的每一个孩子现在都可以选择清单中的一个名字，填入卡片中，然后在结尾处写上自己的名字。

- 提醒孩子们勾出你在清单中已经选好的名字，这样没有一个人会被遗漏。如果使用清单的话，这是一个比较有用的方法。

- 和孩子们一一朗读卡片，再一次检查一下清单，确保每个人都能拿到卡片。

小贴士　　你可以用家庭用语写一些卡片，不一定是英语。

跨领域链接

个人、社会和情感的发展：建立关系。

回答问题

· 请孩子们写下答案来回答你的问题。

教学目标
· 提供一个机会让孩子们独立写作。

教学资源
1）一个收集答案的外表吸引人的盒子； 2）纸和铅笔。

教学准备
· 选择一个开放性问题向孩子们提问，例如：

你最喜欢在学校做什么？
· 用大的字体打印或写出答案。

怎么做
· 给孩子们看问题，问问他们是否有人会朗读。鼓励他们试一试，然后你把问题读给他们听，一边读一边指着每一个单词。
· 向孩子们解释你对他们的答案很感兴趣，但是现在你没有时间听每一个人说出来。提问：
   "能否请你们写下答案，然后放在盒子里，我以后再阅读？"
· 给孩子们看一下放答案的盒子。
· 把问题钉在盒子旁边的墙上。
· 提醒孩子们写上他们的名字，否则你将不知道谁喜欢什么。
· 稍后，你和孩子们一起打开盒子，阅读答案。表扬孩子们的尝试。
· 下一次，问一个不同的问题，例如：
   "今天你和谁一起玩了？"

词汇
问题、回答、什么、谁、什么时候、在哪里、怎样。

小贴士　　　　这是一个让孩子们运用发音规则进行写作的好机会。

跨领域链接
个人、社会和情感的发展：团队意识。

跳圈圈游戏

 · 一种边来回跳边组织句子的游戏。孩子们从一个圈跳到另一个圈来，同时选择他们的词汇。

教学目标
- 帮助孩子们形成简单句。

教学资源
1) 五个圈；2) 若干大开面的纸。

教学准备
- 在每一张纸上写一个关键词，例如：
汤姆、可以、看见、一只、狗。
- 把圈圈摆成一个圆。
- 把每一张卡片放在每一个圈里。

怎么做
- 告诉孩子们他们将用圈圈里的单词来造句。花些时间朗读一下每一个单词。
- 你通过再一次大声朗读所有的单词来展示一下这个活动，然后介绍一下你选择句子的全过程。你可以用这五个单词造出如下句：
汤姆可以看见一只狗。
一只狗可以看见汤姆。
汤姆可以看见一只狗吗？
一只狗可以看见汤姆吗？
- 现在踏进你选的第一个单词的圈里，然后大声读出来。寻找一下你的第二个单词，跳到那个圈圈里，并且大声说出来。一直持续到讲完你的句子。
- 选一个孩子来完成。帮助这个孩子用现有的单词造一个句子，然后让孩子跳到相应圈圈里，同时大声说出单词。
让每一个孩子依次来完成。
"你要造什么句子？"
- 鼓励其他的孩子认真看，仔细听。

词汇

句子。

小贴士   给能力强一些的孩子增加选择的词汇，或是增加标点符号卡片和一些单词的大写字母卡片。

跨领域链接

身体的发展：运动和空间。

沙子里的字母

· 把字母藏在沙子里，观察孩子们能否欢快地拼出由辅音、元音、辅音组成的单词。

教学目标

· 鼓励孩子们运用他们的音标知识拼写简单的单词。

教学资源

1）三个洗净的不同颜色的碗，盛满沙子；2）带磁条的字母；3）单人使用的磁性板。

教学准备

· 把字母放在三个碗的沙子里。

· 两个碗藏有相同的辅音字母组，例如：

s, t, p, n, c, d, g, h, m, r。

· 一个碗里有五个元音字母。

· 从这些字母里，你至少可以组成：

能、猫、切、狗、挖、人、垫子、坐、坐（过去式）、遇见（过去式）、网、平底锅、别针、钢笔、水壶、太阳、跑、帽子、热的、母鸡。

怎么做

· 和孩子们围坐成一个圈，碗放在中央。

· 选择一个孩子出来，从每一个碗里依次选出一个字母。识别一下选出来的字母，然后把字母放在磁板上。向孩子们展示，你将如何把这些字母组成一个简单的单词。通过分割和连接字母的声音来朗读。

· 现在孩子们可以两人一组，从每一个碗中选出一个字母（看不见字母），然后再组成一个单词放在他们的板上。

　－ 你们可以朗读一下吗？

　－ 这是一个现存的单词吗？

· 每个人都组了一个单词后，让孩子们举起他们的板，这样大家可以看到他们的单词。大家一起朗读一下这些单词。

　－ 有人可以用相同的字母组一个不同的单词吗？

词汇

辅音、元音、声音、字母、单词。

小贴士

把碗放在大磁板的旁边，收集尽可能多的单词。在活动最后，一起朗读这些单词。

跨领域链接

沟通、语言和读写能力的发展：阅读大量的简单单词。

高登的修理厂（2）

 · 使用破旧且损坏的玩具车和孩子们一起制定一个修理价目表。

教学目标

- 鼓励孩子们在角色扮演中运用读和写的能力。

教学资源

1）破损的玩具车若干辆； 2）大开面的卡纸和水笔。

教学准备

- 在卡纸的上面部分写上"高登修理厂价目表"。
- 在卡纸上画上辅助写字的淡淡的线。

怎么做

- 孩子们围坐在一个桌子边。这个桌子上放有完好或破损车子的盒子。
- 让孩子们检查车子的损坏情况。讨论一下车子出了什么问题。
- 告诉孩子们，他们将决定高登汽车修理的收费情况。让一个孩子描述一下，他挑选的车子的问题，例如：

  它需要一个新的轮胎。
- 问问大家，换一个新轮胎，高登应该收多少钱。以英镑为单位，使用孩子们可以理解的数量，确定一个金额，例如：

  10英镑。
- 向孩子们展示大卡纸，朗读上方的文字：高登修理厂价目表。
- 用一张纸去练习如何写价目表，例如：

  一个新轮胎……10英镑。

  一个孩子现在可以用粗头彩色笔把这些字抄写到价目表上。
- 大家轮流这样做，描述车辆损坏情况，写出价格，最后将其写在价目表上。

词汇

损坏、修理、价格、车辆的部件、轮胎、雨刷、车灯等。

 小贴士　　　这个活动比较吸引男孩子。

跨领域链接

问题解决、推理和计算的能力：用数字来标签和数数。

今天谁成了好心人？

• 写下一个问题，请孩子们留心并记录身边善意的行为。

教学目标

• 给孩子们一个机会让其读和写熟悉的单词。

教学资源

一块白板和一些水笔。

教学准备

• 在白板的上面部分写一个问题，例如：

今天谁是好心人？

怎么做

• 让孩子们看白板并一起朗读问题。向他们解释，今天他们将观察所有对别人做好事的人。

• 如果看到有人在做好事，他们应该把这个人的名字写在白板上，例如：

如果你看见杰米帮山姆捡起他掉在地上的铅笔——没人要求杰米这么做——那么杰米就是在做好事。你可以把杰米的名字写在白板上。

• 鼓励孩子们说出他们看见的善举。

• 在这一天快结束的时候，和孩子们围坐在一起。看着白板，数一数所有的名字。

• 问问谁在白板上写过名字。孩子们依次走出来告诉大家是他们写的，以及他们认为的善举。大家为他们的关注善举而鼓掌。

• 然后每一个在名单中的孩子都起立，大家为他们鼓掌。

词汇

善良的、友好的、帮助他人的、有礼貌的。

小贴士　　　下次再搞这个活动的时候，改变白板上面的问题，用"勤奋"和"忙碌"来代替。

跨领域链接

个人、社会和情感的发展：建立关系。

幸运抽签

・玩一个简单的幸运抽签游戏，给孩子们一个好玩的理由让其写下他们的名字。

教学目标

・帮助孩子们识别并写下自己的名字。

教学资源

1）若干小纸片和铅笔； 2）一个可回收的塑料冰激凌筒或带拉绳的袋子可以放下所有的名字。

怎么做

・告诉孩子们你们将玩幸运抽签的游戏。
　"有人知道这个游戏吗？"

・解释一下规则。将每个人的名字——写在一张纸上——将放入一个筒或袋子里，然后每个人闭上眼睛从纸堆中挑出一张纸。
　他们将打开这张纸然后读出名字。
　"如果这是你的名字，那你就赢啦！"

・帮助孩子们在小纸片上写下他们的名字。提醒他们书写清晰，可以让别人读懂。然后向他们展示如何折叠，最后放入筒或袋子里。

・当每个人都把名字放入后，你把筒或袋子充分摇一下。
　"大家都知道我为什么摇袋子吗？"
　大家都知道这是抽签的一个公平的方式吗？

・现在就是激动人心的时刻了……要求一个大人闭上眼睛，把手伸到袋子里，选一张纸片。小心地打开纸片，读出名字。为他们鼓掌！

・那个叫到名字的孩子可以第一个去拿外套、得到点心或是吃中饭。在他们离开之前，他们必须闭上眼睛，手伸到袋子里选择一张纸。然后打开这张纸。
　"你能读出这个名字吗？"
　继续玩下去，猜 3—4 个名字。

・把这个袋子留在边上，这样如果孩子们想玩就可以玩。

词汇

幸运抽签、名字、折叠、打开、第一、第二、第三、第四。

 小贴士　　　　请记住选到过的名字要拿走，这样它们就不会再被挑到。

跨领域链接

个人、社会和情感的发展：建立关系。

制作一个棋盘的游戏（1）

· 帮助孩子们用包装纸制作一个简单的棋盘游戏。

教学目标

· 给孩子们一个机会让其写说明。

教学资源

1) 一张彩色的包装纸（剪成和适合你的塑封机的尺寸）； 2) 20张小正方形纸，用来做棋盘路线（15张小正方形纸一个颜色，5张为另一种不同的颜色）； 3) 水笔，纸和胶水。

教学准备

· 经常和孩子们玩棋盘游戏。

怎么做

· 和一小群孩子围坐在桌边。告诉他们，你们将自己制作棋盘游戏。

· 摆开包装纸，向他们展示如何用小正方形来制作棋盘路线。
    - 他们是否理解为什么需要不同颜色的正方形？

· 帮助孩子们在每一个正方形中写上一个数字。然后把这些格子贴在包装纸上。

· 帮助孩子们在合适的地方写上"起点"和"终点"。

· 现在和孩子们计划一下，在5个不同颜色方块旁边，写一些说明，例如：
  轮空一轮、退回一格、再走一步、再走一个方块。

· 帮助孩子们仔细写说明，这样其他人可以读懂，然后把这些说明贴在彩色方块旁边。如果可能，把游戏用的纸张都塑封一下，这样可以更耐用。

· 用计数器和骰子一起玩。

词汇

说明用语有：轮空一轮、退回一格、再走一步、再走一个方块。

小贴士　　　　根据孩子们的能力可以改动这个游戏，例如：对于低龄幼儿，你可以把数字事先写好，方便他们直接排序，你可以帮他们记下说明的文字。

跨领域链接

问题解决、推理和计算的能力：用数字来标签和数数。

制作一个棋盘的游戏（2）

· 使用孩子们自己为棋盘画的画来制作一个棋盘游戏。

教学目标
· 制作和玩一个游戏，孩子们可以识别字母的发音。

教学资源
1）A3卡纸； 2）20张小正方形纸，其中10张一个颜色，10张另一种颜色； 3）一套字母卡片； 4）记号笔和胶水。

教学准备
· 选择你需要孩子们练习发音的字母。

怎么做
· 和一小群孩子围坐在桌边。告诉他们，你们将自己制作棋盘游戏，还要识别字母的发音。
· 选择一个游戏的名字，例如："什么声音"，然后用粗体字写在卡片上。
· 要求孩子们在A3卡纸上画一些图片，灵感来自一个故事或是你们正在讨论的主题，例如：小型动物。
· 向他们展示如何用小方块做棋盘路线。
· 帮助孩子们沿着棋盘路线安排方格的图案，例如：两种不同颜色的方格间隔排列，或者两个相同颜色的接着两个另一种颜色的。
· 帮助孩子们在每一个方格上写一个数字，然后贴在装饰好的卡纸上，形成一条路线。帮助孩子们在合适的地方写上"起点"和"终点"。
· 要求孩子们选择一种颜色。向孩子们解释，只要停在这个颜色上，就要挑选一张卡片，向孩子们展示字母卡，并且告诉他们，他们必须说出字母的发音。然后把卡片放回这堆卡片的底部。
· 告诉孩子们如果他们读错这个字母，那么留在原来的方格里，但如读对了，那么就可以移到第二格。孩子们依次拿到字母卡片后，检查他们是否理解规则。
· 然后用计数器和骰子来玩这个游戏。
· 第一个到达终点的即为获胜者。

词汇

数字 1—20、字母发音。

 小贴士　你也可以使用关键词汇卡片。

跨领域链接

个人、社会和情感的发展：建立关系。

第九章

制作一本书

花园中心（3）

· 向孩子们介绍这首数数的诗歌，在图片中加入数字词汇，创作属于你们自己的诗歌。

教学目标
- 和孩子们一起写一首诗。

教学资源

1）《花园童谣》（选自 N. 托慈， P. 库森的《把我大声读出来：为每一天说唱、低吟或高歌的诗歌》第 125 页，麦克米伦儿童出版社 2007 年出版）； 2）十张装裱纸； 3）涂色材料。

教学准备

- 孩子们可以创作一些和花园相关物品的图画。
- 把物品剪下来，成组地装裱一下以便备用，例如：一个植物房、两个独轮手推车、三把铁锹等，十样东西为一组。
- 使用任意余下的图片来做封面，配上题目《一首数数的诗歌》。

怎么做

- 将《花园童谣》读给孩子们听。
- 要求他们识别出诗歌的写作类型：每一行由一个数字开头，这些数字都是按序排列的。练习一下数数。
- 有几行诗是押韵的。在你读出押韵的词之前停下来，孩子们能猜出这个押韵的单词吗？
- 多朗读几次这首诗歌，让孩子们熟悉它。
- 现在拿出你们画的画。
    - 孩子们能找到只画了一个物品的纸吗？
    - 你为这个图片写上标签，例如：一个植物房。
    - 他们能找到有两个物品的纸吗？
    - 你再次记下物品，例如："两个独轮手推车。"
  以这种方式继续下去，直到在一页上写下十个物品。
- 现在你们可以一起朗读你们集体创作的这首诗。
- 这是一个有用的模式，可以用在你们关注的任何主题上。

词汇

数字单词、韵律。

把每一页订在一起，封面在最上面，将其制作成一本数数的书。

跨领域链接

问题解决、推理和计算的能力：用数字来标签和数数。

花园中心(4)

• 和孩子们一起制作一本手风琴样式的书，来展示植物的生长周期。

教学目标

• 孩子们参与的写作。

教学资源

1）6 张厚 A4 纸； 2）在"花园中心（1）"的活动中做好的 5 个植物生长阶段的模型。

教学准备

• 把 6 张较厚的 A4 纸边与边黏合在一起，形成手风琴的样子。

• 给孩子们展示他们已经做好的植物生长的各阶段模型。一边展示，一边组织孩子们讨论植物生长过程中的变化。

怎么做

• 鼓励孩子们把植物生长不同阶段的 5 个罐子排个序，强调从左到右排序的重要性：让它们与文字匹配。

• 问孩子们：

"第一个罐子里的种子在哪里？"

"在泥土里。"

把文字"种子在泥土里"记在手风琴书的第一页。

• 问问孩子们，他们是如何知道种子什么时候开始生长的。

"它发了一个芽了。"

把"它发了一个芽"写在第二页。

• 一直这样写下去：

它在泥土里。

它发了一个芽。

它长了一片叶子。

它有一个花苞。

这棵植物有种子了。

• 给孩子们看你如何把最后一页和第一页粘在一起，这样形成一件事情的循环——一个生命周期。

词汇

种子、芽、叶子、花苞、泥土、花。

小贴士　　　在写字桌上留下一些小的手风琴书给那些想自己做书的孩子们作为参考。

跨领域链接

认识与理解世界：探索与观察。

大的书，小的书

• 为"三只熊"做一些书，鼓励孩子们写的字和书的大小匹配。

教学目标

• 鼓励孩子们在游戏中练习写字。

教学资源

1）纸和卡片； 2）水笔、铅笔和蜡笔。

教学准备

• 把折叠的纸和亮色的封面装订在一起，做出一些书，让其有三种不同的大小。

• 在每一种大小的书里写和画相同的信息，例如："这是我的床""这是我的碗""这是我的椅子"。图画和文字大小要和书的大小匹配。

怎么做

• 给孩子们展示你做的三本书，和孩子们讨论：

 — 他们注意到这三本书有什么特点？

 — 他们能识别出大号书、中号书还是小号书吗？

 — 哪个家庭可能拥有这些书？

• 现在观察一下书的里面。鼓励孩子们观察相同的文字和图片。

• 描述一下写的字——是小字、大字还是介于中间呢？鼓励孩子们用尽可能多的表达来描述字的大小，或是对比大小。

• 告诉孩子们他们会在写字桌上发现这样的一套套书，如果他们愿意，可以为小熊家做更多的书。

• 提醒孩子们画的画和写的字的大小要和他们选的书的大小匹配。

词汇

大的、很大的、中等的、介于中间的、小的、更小的。

小贴士　　　　在你们角色扮演时用的小木屋里，给小熊们准备一个"书架"，然后鼓励孩子们在那里玩的时候读一读这些书。

273

跨领域链接

问题解决、推理和计算能力：形状、空间与测量。

我的家

· 孩子们唱一首歌和写一本书，记录住在他们家里的人的数量。

教学目标
· 帮助孩子们用写作的方式来记录。

教学资源
1）《多少人住在你家里》（选自《火绒盒：66 首写给孩子的歌》， A&C 布莱克出版社，1983 年出版）； 2） 每本书需要的 3 张普通的 A4 纸和 1 张 A4 卡纸，足够每个孩子做一本书。

教学准备
· 为了做好每一本书：
— 在每一张卡纸上铺上 3 张普通的纸。
— 把卡纸和普通的纸对折，中心对齐后用订书机订起来。
— 然后剪去上面的两个角，制造出屋顶的样子。
— 在最后一页写上： ×××住在我的家里。
· 给你自己再做一本书用来展示。

怎么做
· 唱这首歌——多少人住在我的家里？
和孩子们聊聊关于住在他们家里的人。
告诉他们你们将制作一本关于多少人和动物住在他们家里的书。
· 让孩子们观察你做的书。展示一下：
如何用门和窗装饰书的封面和封底。
怎样在新的一页上画上人或动物。
你完成了关于你的家这本书中的图画之后，数一数，然后完成最后的句子。
· 鼓励孩子们在他们的书中画和写。通过数数，帮助孩子们完成最后一句话，然后在他们的房子里写下数字。

词汇
妈妈、爸爸、姐妹、兄弟、婴儿、狗、猫、兔子、豚鼠。

小贴士　　　记得对于缺失父母等家人家庭的孩子要特别留心。在计算家庭成员数量的时候，加上动物的数量会很有帮助。

跨领域链接

问题解决、推理和计算能力：用数字来标签和数数。

五只小鸭子

· 帮助孩子们做一本属于自己的童谣书。

教学目标

· 强化孩子们对于书本制作的熟悉度。

教学资源

A4 纸和卡纸。

教学准备

· 为孩子们做的书：

— 一张卡纸对折，两张相同大小的纸放在里面，订在一起。

— 把"五只小鸭子"作为题目写在每一本书的封面上。

· 确保每个人知道这首童谣。

怎么做

· 给每人一本书，告诉他们你们将制作一本童谣书。

他们都能找到封面吗？

· 鼓励孩子们打开书，在第一页上画一个小池塘。问问孩子们诗歌的开始有几只鸭子在池塘里。帮助他们在池塘里画 5 只鸭子。

· 鼓励孩子们翻到第二页，再画一个池塘。问问孩子们这次多少鸭子回来了，帮助孩子们在池塘里画 4 只鸭子。

· 继续把整本书画下去，书页上依次出现 5 只、4 只、3 只、2 只、1 只、0 只、5 只鸭子等。确保最后一页和第一页一样，5 只鸭子游回来了。

· 能力强一些的孩子可能喜欢在每一页上写上数字。

· 在封底写上孩子们的名字，把书放在孩子们方便阅读的地方。

词汇

5、4、3、2、1、0、封面、标题、作者、页、翻页、下一个、封底。

小贴士　　　　提醒孩子们仔细一些，不要一次翻两页。

跨领域链接

问题解决、推理和计算能力：计算。

出去散步

- 和孩子们散步回来后，根据派特·霍金斯的《柔斯的散步》制作一本班级的书。同时孩子们可以制作一个在整本书里一直散步的卡纸人物。

教学目标

- 做一本书记录孩子们已经参加过的活动。

教学资源

1）普通 A3 纸若干； 2）两张 A3 卡纸做封面和封底； 3）一些小的卡纸； 4）派特·霍金斯的《柔斯的散步》（红狐狸出版社， 2001 年出版）。

教学准备

- 带孩子们在附近散散步。
- 谈谈你们走过的地方。

怎么做

- 回来后，和孩子们聊聊你们的散步，然后把《柔斯的散步》读给每个小朋友们听。
- 使用介词有序地列出你们走过的地方，例如：
    - 大门外；
    - 小山下；
    - 穿马路；
    - 经过商店；
    - 公园周围；
- 让孩子们选择一个走过的地方画下来。然后大人可以在它们的图片下方写上恰当的描述性短语。
- 将这些页面和封面、封底订在一起形成一本书。标题写上"我们走的路"，鼓励每个人都阅读一下。
- 现在每一个孩子在一张小卡纸上画一张自画像。然后他们可以依次来朗读这本书，并带着卡纸人物走过书本的每一页。

词汇

通过、周围、经过、穿过、往下、在……下面。

小贴士　　　　　卡纸人物可以放在封底内侧制作的小口袋里。

跨领域链接

认识与理解世界：地点。

玛丽·奥尼尔
《什么是白色的?》

 · 用这首诗作为一个启发，和孩子们写下自己创作的表达颜色的诗歌。

教学目标

• 和孩子们写一首诗，你替他们记录下来。

教学资源

玛丽·奥尼尔的诗《什么是白色的? 》（选自 A. 让波《毛毛虫怕痒吗? 》，海雀图文出版社 1989 年出版）。

教学准备

• 这首诗中列举的东西都是白色的。在你们一起朗读这首诗的时候有很多有趣的词可以讨论。

• 如果你教的孩子年龄很小，最好只使用诗歌的一部分。

怎么做

• 告诉孩子们，你们将写一首关于颜色的诗。
  一起为你们的诗选一个标题，例如:
  什么是红色的?

• 收集有颜色的物体，用介词有序地列出你们走过的地方，例如: 交通信号灯（见下一页词汇表）。记下孩子们的想法。

• 然后帮助孩子们把这些想法扩展成描述性短语，例如:
  红色意味着停止。

• 再扩展孩子们的短语，例如:
  一种警告我们有危险的持续闪烁的红灯

• 提示孩子们在描述和拓展他们想法的时候，使用描述五官感觉的短语。

• 然后，写下一列短语来创作一首简单的诗，例如:
  什么是红色?
  一种警告我们有危险的持续闪烁的红灯，
  在田野中生长的红色的罂粟花，

用别针可佩戴的纸罂粟花，
鸣笛而过的红色巨型消防车。

词汇

消防车、罂粟花、邮箱、泛红的脸颊、火、交通信号灯、危险、落日、血、心脏、玫瑰花、苹果、唇膏、小丑的鼻子。

 小贴士　　　　　孩子们可以给他们诗歌的每一行配插图，来创作一本诗集。

跨领域链接

认识与理解世界：地点。

我们的一天

· 和孩子们一起拍照记录你们每天的日常生活，并把这些照片装订成一本书，来讲述"我们的一天"。

教学目标

· 制作一本书，来记录孩子们正在参加的各种活动。

教学资源

1）照相机； 2）一大本剪贴本。

教学准备

· 帮助孩子们在一天中重要的时刻拍一些照片，例如：到校挂起衣服时、讲故事时、游戏时、午餐时。

怎么做

· 一起看着照片。鼓励孩子们说出每一张照片发生的事情。确定哪张照片是一天的开始。

· 然后把照片按序排好，展示一天的日常活动。问问大家：

"下一张照片是什么？"

"在这个之前或之后，我们做了什么？"

"那之后发生了什么？"

"我们的一天是怎样结束的？"

· 让孩子们按正确的顺序将照片贴在书里。

阅读这本给孩子们听，注意使用故事语言和表示时间的连接词，例如：

首先、接着、最后。

· 鼓励他们依次讲述一天的故事。

词汇

首先、然后、接下去、之后、以后、最后。

小贴士　　　对于大一些的孩子，大人可以在每一张照片边上写下这个故事。

跨领域链接

问题解决、推理和计算能力：形状、空间与测量。

在我的午餐盒里

 · 帮助孩子们根据自己的午餐盒中的食物来制作简易的活页书。

教学目标
- 培养孩子们如何建构故事的意识。

教学资源

1）关于食物的书；2）一本活页书；3）用来做书的 A4 纸和卡纸；4）若干小纸片和胶带。

教学准备
- 制作一本午餐盒样子的书：
  - 将三张 A4 纸放在两张卡纸之间，然后装订纸的下边缘，这样打开书本时，顶部像一个午餐盒。
  - 第一页写上"在我的饭盒里，有⋯⋯"。

怎么做
- 给孩子们看一本活页书，观察它是怎样展示内容的。
- 向他们展示你准备好的午餐盒书和一些小的纸片。示范如何将小纸片粘贴在书里，使它们可以竖立起来，看上去就像书摆动的翅膀。
- 读一读你在饭盒书上的第一页写的文字。鼓励孩子们说出一些饭盒书里可能有的东西。

  一起看看你的食物书和图片字典并说说其他的东西。
- 孩子们现在可以在每一页的午饭盒里的东西上画一张图片。然后，帮助他们把食物的名字写在小纸片上。

  记得一张纸片上只写一个单词！
- 帮助他们将纸片藏在图片后面作为一个活页。

  "你们可以阅读自己做的书吗？"

  "你们可以阅读你的朋友的书吗？"

词汇

任何被孩子们选择的食物名称。

小贴士　使用事先剪好的胶带，这样孩子们在粘贴书页的时候可以更独立一些。

跨领域链接

身体的发展：健康和身体意识。

你知道你的 ABC 字母吗?

 · 孩子们将在他们小小的字母书里选择配图。

教学目标
- 给孩子们一个机会让其使用词汇库和其他资源。

教学资源
1）图片字典； 2）教室词汇库； 3）A4 纸。

教学准备
- 把 A4 纸裁成两半，将 7 张这样的纸对折，订在一起，做成一本小书。
- 打印好标题"字母书"，每一本小书准备一份。
- 确保孩子们知道字母歌，或者在进行这个活动前让他们对字母有一些了解。

怎么做
- 和一组孩子一起玩这个游戏。

  让孩子们用图片字典两两结对活动。

  要求他们寻找以"a"开头的物品。

  提醒孩子们这是这个字母的名字。

  "你们可以找到以"a"开头的物品吗?
- 鼓励孩子们两两之间可以说出不同物品，这样完成的书可以各不相同。

  "尽量选择和你搭档不一样的物品。"

  例如：苹果和鳄鱼。
- 向他们展示你已经做好的小书。要求他们把标题"字母书"贴在封面上，然后在标题下写上他们的名字。
- 帮助孩子们在他们书的第一页上方写上字母"a"。然后他们可以画出他们选的物品。
- 你们可以一次选 6 个字母，在其他时间再完成其他页。
- 或者你可以先帮孩子们把 26 个字母写在每一页上，他们可以在写字桌上选择性完成。

词汇
字母表中单词的名称。

小贴士　　　　在孩子们写字母的时候，要观察他们，对于任何字母拼写中的出现问题都要做好记录。

跨领域链接

个人、社会和情感的发展：建立关系。

乔的太空旅行

> • 鼓励孩子们想象奇怪和有趣的事情，那是乔在他参观的星球上所发现的。

教学目标

- 能用词汇库来写出一个故事。

教学资源

1）一张大开本黑色的纸； 2）星星贴纸——金色和银色； 3）颜料； 4）标签贴纸； 5）火箭形状的书。

教学准备

- 用普通纸和卡纸做一些火箭形状的书。
- 让孩子们在黑色的纸上画出 5—6 个亮色的星球。
- 在这些星球周围贴上星星，然后等着晾干。

怎么做

- 和一组孩子一起玩这个游戏，帮助他们给这些星球起名字，名字可以是自创的词汇。
- 尽力去创造一些小朋友利用语音知识可以拼出的词汇，例如： Zar、 Bod、 Lub、 Niz。
- 鼓励小朋友们在标签贴纸上写下这些名字，然后贴在被选出的星球旁边。
- 使用一个模型太空人物乔，确定他住在一个星球上。

  告诉孩子们:

  "乔将开启一项空间探索，我们将讲述他的故事。"
- 从乔的家出发，他将穿越太空到另一个星球上。

  问问孩子们，

  "他将在那里看到什么？"
- 把他们的建议写在标签贴纸上，贴在这个星球旁边。

  例如:

  － 蓝色的树。

  － 一条有着绿黄条纹的狗。

一起阅读这些文字，提醒每一个人他们所说的话。

• 给每个孩子一本火箭样子的书，写下他们自己的关于乔旅行的故事，使用图片上的单词作为词汇库。

词汇

任何孩子们想使用的单词。

小贴士　　　这个活动适合那些已经可以写一些关键词的孩子们。

跨领域链接

沟通、语言和读写能力的发展：故事场景。

特殊的外出日

• 鼓励孩子们在家里举办特殊活动的时候，把布娃娃带回家。帮助他们在班级书中记录这次出访。

教学目标
• 激发孩子们用文字和图片记录事件。

教学资源
1）两个布娃娃或线织的娃娃：一男一女； 2）纸、铅笔、剪刀和胶水； 3）一些糖纸和绳子。

教学准备
• 制作一本书：
— 把糖纸对半剪开。
— 在纸张的左边打一些洞。
— 用绳子把纸张系起来。
— 把娃娃的照片贴在封面上，写下名字"和塔拉与托比特殊的外出日"（使用你指定的名字）。
• 孩子们应该很熟悉并且知道娃娃的名字。如果孩子们知道自己家中有特殊的活动，例如：生日、去奶奶家、一个节日或是家庭聚会，如复活节、排灯节或是开斋节，可以把你们学习的节日和特殊的场合联系起来。给孩子父母发一个通知，这样他们能够理解这个活动。

怎么做
• 这天的课上，有一个孩子已经带一个娃娃回家过了，大家围坐成圆形。这个孩子站在你的身边，抱着娃娃。他将告诉其他孩子托比或塔拉经历的事情，去过的地方，或是一起吃过的一顿饭。
• 鼓励小朋友们问问题，这样抱着娃娃的孩子可以说出更多的信息。问题可以涉及娃娃的"感受"："塔拉对……感觉很兴奋吗？""托比再次看到……很开心吗？"
• 之后的时间，你和这个孩子一对一交流。帮助这个孩子组织 1—2 句话来描述娃娃的经历和此次访问的"感受"。替孩子记录或是根据他们的个人能力尽力帮助他们把想法写下来。
• 孩子们现在可以把他们写的话贴在班级书的书页上，并配上图。
• 定时和全班一起读读这本书。

小贴士　如果他们有任何照片、票根、邀请函和节目单等，都可以贴在书页上。

跨领域链接

认识与理解世界：交流。

约翰·帕拉特
《周五发生的趣事》

· 和孩子们一起阅读这本书，然后帮助他们补充这个故事内容。

教学目标
- 鼓励孩子们写的时候用故事中的语言。

教学资源

1）约翰·帕拉特的《周五发生的趣事》（海雀图文出版社 1984 年出版），或是另一本没有文字只有图片的书； 2）纸、铅笔、可循环使用黏胶材料。

教学准备
- 一起读这本书。

怎么做
- 和一组孩子一起玩这个游戏，观察书中孩子们探险的图片。
- 问问孩子们在故事的不同部分发生了什么。
- 鼓励孩子们根据图片所示描绘孩子们的活动。
- 帮助孩子们用故事中的语言来总结他们的句子。例如，一个孩子说："他们浑身是泥。"

  大人可以回答："是的，我们也可以说'他们跳进了泥潭，然后浑身是泥'。"
- 听听孩子们的想法，然后给故事的每一部分选择一句话。从书的开头到结尾，让每个孩子都可以说出一句话。
- 给孩子们一张纸让他们写下他们的句子。
- 帮助孩子们写下来他们的句子。
- 用可循环使用黏胶把写的句子粘在图片上。
- 读这本书，鼓励每一个孩子看着他们写的话。

词汇

任何适合你指定的书中的单词。

根据孩子的情况，选择合适的方式，帮他们记录，在他们写的时候提供帮助或是鼓励孩子们独立写句子。

跨领域链接

认识与理解世界：时间。

我自己的笔记本

- 提供一种简单的方式，让孩子们用旧的问候卡来制作自己的笔记本。

教学目标

- 为孩子们记录信息和想法提供一些证据。

教学资源

1）A4 纸；2）没有内附纸的旧的问候卡；3）容器——一个篮子或是一个吸引人的盒子。

教学准备

- 你需要剪去如"生日快乐"这样的词汇来减小卡片的尺寸。
- 在卡内有书写信息的地方贴上一张纸。
- 把打开的问候卡放在 4 张 A4 纸的上方。
- 把纸张和卡片的边对齐。

怎么做

- 告诉孩子们，你们将要制作一些笔记本。

  告诉他们如何打开卡片，然后将其放在纸张上面。

  帮助他们用长款订书机把这些纸订起来。

- 然后每个孩子在封面或是封面的背面写下他们自己的名字。你应当在笔记本开始页用小字加上日期。把这些笔记本放在特定的篮子里或盒子里。

- 和孩子们聊聊一些使用笔记本的方法。告诉他们这个本子可用来写他们自己想写的东西，不是你要求他们写的作业本。他们可以说说任何他们想写的内容。

  例如：

  — 写今天做过的事情；

  — 列一个清单；

  — 当他们想玩上学或侦探游戏的时候；

  — 想写一些字的任何时候。

- 当笔记本制作完成时，在书的最后一页写上完成的日期。

- 如果孩子们很快完成了一本，可以留下一些可用的材料让他们再做一本。

词汇

装订、订书机、私人的、笔记本。

 小贴士
用这个活动来检查孩子们迅速写字的能力。他们写字的速度怎样？他们拼读和书写的能力提高了吗？这是一个监测他们的这些能力的有用的方法。

跨领域链接

身体的发展：运用工具与材料。

米克·英克潘《小企鹅》

• 帮助孩子们模仿这本很棒的书，制作他们自己的企鹅形状的书。

教学目标

• 给孩子们一个机会用写的方式复述一本熟悉的书。

教学资源

1）米克·英克潘的《小企鹅》（霍德儿童书籍出版社 1994 年出版）； 2）1 张 A4 大小的白色卡纸和两张 A4 白纸。

教学准备

• 把两张 A4 纸对折放在对折的 A4 的卡纸内，并装订成书。

• 把书剪出简单的企鹅的样子。

• 和孩子们一起阅读《小企鹅》这本书。

怎么做

• 给孩子们看企鹅形状的书，讨论如何装饰成《小企鹅》这本书的样子，例如：把它的背和头涂成黑色。

• 帮助孩子们给封面和封底的企鹅头、背和嘴上色，创造出自己的企鹅。

• 告诉他们讲一个《小企鹅》的故事。

• 看着书中的图片，问问孩子们发生了什么事。一起整合一句话，例如："因为北极熊很可恶，所有的企鹅都游走了。"

• 帮助孩子们在他们书的第一页上写下这句话。根据孩子们的情况选择一个恰当的方法：他们可以抄写你写的句子，尝试自己写或是贴上打印的纸条。

• 现在看着第二张图片，问问大家企鹅为什么不开心。

• 一直继续下去，直到你们在书的 8 页上用 8 句话总结这个故事。

词汇

游泳（过去式）、遇见、漂浮、发现、航行、翻转、飞行、认出、骤升。

小贴士　　将蓝色背景纸盖在展板上，然后加上白色卡条纸做底线。这样孩子们在展示企鹅书的时候，好像它们站在冰山上一样。

跨领域链接

认识与理解世界：地点。

斯特拉·布莱克斯通
《我的奶奶去了集市》

· 和孩子们玩游戏尽力去记住奶奶买的东西。然后他们可以制作自己的书记录物品。

教学目标

· 给孩子们提供材料和激励物来制作他们自己的书。

教学资源

1）斯特拉·布莱克斯通的《我的奶奶去了集市》（贝尔福特出版社 2006 年出版）； 2）普通 A4 纸和 A4 卡纸； 3）地球仪或地图。

教学准备

· 把两张 A4 纸放在对折的 A4 的卡纸内，装订成一本个人书。

· 和孩子们一起阅读《我的奶奶去了集市》这本书。

· 打印出这本书的标题，按照你做好的书的大小打印出若干份。

怎么做

· 阅读这本书几次后，在地图上找一找书中提到的国家。

  问问孩子们关于每个地方知道多少。

  可能他们来自那个国家，去过那里或在书中或电视上看过相关的内容。

  讨论奶奶去过的不同国家后买的各种各样的东西。

· 和孩子们玩一个游戏：

  － 打开这本书的任意一页。

  － 告诉孩子们这个国家的名字。

  － 问问奶奶买了什么。

· 让孩子们依次问问题。

· 玩一个传统的记忆游戏：

  － 围坐成一圈。

  － 以一句话开始游戏："我的奶奶去了集市，然后买了一个鼓。"

  － 下一个孩子说："我的奶奶去了集市，然后买了一个鼓和一个……"

－ 下一个孩子重复这些短语，加上两个物品，再加上他们的想法。

－ 只要孩子们能记住清单上的物品，一直可以玩下去。

（在传统的游戏中，孩子们可以任意选择物品，但要根据书本内容来玩游戏，则要提到书中的物品。）

• 当孩子们喜欢玩这个游戏后，给他们看已准备好的书。帮助他们把标题贴在封面上。他们可以读出来吗？

• 让他们画出他们记住的书中的物品。总共 8 个物品。他们可以记住所有的物品吗？

• 如果可能，孩子们可以给图片写上标签或是你可以帮他们写。

• 如果他们完成了他们的书，鼓励他们在封面上写名字。

• 把书放在一边，供孩子和家长们阅读。

词汇

日本、澳大利亚、中国、墨西哥、瑞士、非洲、俄罗斯、秘鲁。

小贴士　　　　通过延伸学习，可以在书中展示不同国家的语言、服装和习俗。

跨领域链接

认识与理解世界：交流。

附录 1

参考文献

英国教育部官方文献

DfEs （2006） *Primary National Strategy. Primary Framework for Literacy and Mathematics*. Ref: 02011-2206

DfEs （2007） *Letters and Sounds: Principles and Practice of High Quality Phonics*. Ref: 00282-2007.

DfEs （2008） *Practice Guidance for the Early Years Foundation Stage. Non-statutory Guidance*. Ref: 00266-2008.

音乐

Soothing music e. g. Dvorak's *New World Symphony*

Strong, quick music e. g. Rimsky-Korsakov: *Flight of the Bumble Bee*

'How many people live in your house?' in *Tinder-box: 66 Songs for Children* （1983）, London: A&C Black.

参考图书

Ahlberg, A. （1980）. *Mrs Wobble the Waitress*, London: Puffin Books.

Alakija, P. （2007）. *Catch That Goat! : A Market Day in Nigeria*, Bath: Barefoot Books.

Andreae, G. and Sharratt, N. （2002）. *Pants*, London: Picture Corgi.

Blackstone, S. （2006）. *My Granny Went to Market*, Bath: Barefoot Books.

Burningham, J. （1979）. *Mr Gumpy's Motorcar*, London: Picture Puffins.

Burningham, J. （1979）. *Mr Gumpy's Outing*, London: Picture Puffins.

Butterwick, N. （2008）. *My Grandma is Wonderful*, London: Walker Books.

Butterworth, N. and Inkpen, M. （2006）. *Jasper's Beanstalk*, London: Hodder Children's Books.

Carle, E. （2002）. *The Very Hungry Caterpillar*, London: Puffin Books.

Carle, E. （2009）. *The Tiny Seed*, London: Simon & Schuster Children's.

Collins, M. （2001）. *Circle Time for the Very Young*, London: Paul Chapman Publishing.

Exley, H. （2006）. *Me and My Grandma*, Watford: Exley Publications.

French, V. and Bartlett, A. （1995）. *Oliver's Vegetables*, London: Hodder Children's.

Garcia, E. （2009）. *Toot Toot Beep Beep*, St Albans: Boxer Books.

Hedderwick, M. （2010）. *Katie Morag and the Two Grandmothers*, London: Red Fox Books.

Holub, J. （2000）. *Light the Candles: A Hannukah Lift-the-flap Book*, London: Picture

Puffins.

Hughes, S. (1985). *Alfie Gives a Hand*, London: Collins Picture Lions.

Hutchins, P. (1993). *The Surprise Party*, London: Red Fox Books.

Hutchins, P. (2001). *Rosie's Walk*, London: Red Fox Books.

Inkpen, M. (1994). *Penguin Small*, London: Hodder Children's Book.

Mayo, M. (2003). *Emergency!*, London: Orchard Books.

Prater, J. (1984). *On Friday Something Funny Happened*, London: Picture Puffins.

Roennfeldt, R. (1980). *Tiddalick: The Frog Who Caused a Flood*, London: Picture Puffins.

Rosen, M. (1993). *We're Going on a Bear Hunt*, London: Walker Books.

Shoshan, B. (2005). *That's When I'm Happy*, London: Little Bee.

Zucker, J. (2002). *Eight Candles to Light: A Chanukah Story*, London: Frances Lincoln.

Zucker, J. (2005). *Lighting a Lamp: A Divali Story*, London: Frances Lincoln.

Zucker, J. (2005). *Lanterns and Firecrackers: A Chinese New Year Story*, London: Frances Lincoln.

附加

你自己选择的传统故事。

围绕某个主题，如微小动物、鸭、食物等，有关的非虚构类书。

诗歌和童谣

'Fingers Like to Wiggle, Waggle' in Matterson, E. (compiler) (1991). *This Little Puffin*, London: Penguin.

'Shop, shop, shopping' by Georgie Adams in Waters, F. (1999). *Time for a Rhyme*, London: Orion Children's Books.

'Ten Dancing Dinosaurs' in Waters, F. (1999). *Time for a Rhyme*, London: Orion Childen's Books.

'Garden Rhyme' by Phil Rampton in Toczek, N. and Cookson, P. (2007). *Read Me Out Loud: A Poem to Rap, Chant, Whisper or Shout for Every Day of the Year*, London: Macmillan Children's Books.

'What is White?' by Mary O'Neil in Rumble, A. (1989). *Is a Caterpillar Ticklish?*, London: Puffin Books.

Number rhymes and action songs from:

Matterson，E.（compiler）（1991）. *This Little Puffin*，London： Penguin.

Good Morning Mrs Hen

附加

你自己选择的童谣。

附录 2

活动索引*

---

* 此部分按英国早教大纲（EYFS）中的教育目标及领域对本书中的活动进行归类整理，且此处中文译文按中文阅读习惯梳理了汇总表格。

领域	子领域	活动名称	页码
创造力的发展	想象力与想象性游戏	小餐馆（1）	43
		大灰狼！	46
		挖掘机跳舞吗？	57
		取三件物品	78
		今天谁在小木屋里？	168
交流、语言与读写	故事架构	很久以前（2）	69
		故事示意图	178
		杰克和杰尔	197
	故事场景	故事场所	109
		乔的太空旅行	289
	故事人物	很久以前（1）	68
		谁说的？	115
		我是谁？	119
		猜猜这个故事	174
	角色扮演	艾玛·加克莱《突突嘀嘀》（1）	49
		高登的修理厂（1）	162
		灰姑娘忙碌的一天	235
	阅读大量的简单词汇	关键词游戏	146
		沙子里的字母	255

致谢

向所有赋予我们和孩子们灵感的作者、诗人和艺术家致谢！

向以下允许我们使用其出版物的版权方致谢：

本书中引言第 2 页的摘录来自于英国皇冠出版社 2008 年版《早期基础阶段实践导引》（学校与家庭儿童部）第 41 页以及英国皇冠出版社 2006 版《小学读写与数学概论》（国家小学教育战略）第 20 页；本书正文中第 94 页和第 206 页的引言来自于皇冠出版社 2008 版《早期基础阶段实践导引》（学校与家庭儿童部）第 42 页。

部分材料无法追溯其版权所有，我们向所有本书引用的材料所有方致谢。

Introduction

Games, Ideas and Activities for Early Years Literacy will provide you with a wealth of resources to enhance your delivery of the Communication, Language and Literacy (CLL) area of learning in the Early Years Foundation Stage (EYFS).

Combining aspects from different areas of learning is recognised as good early years practice. Making connections helps children to make sense of their world and their learning and offers opportunities to reinforce their skills. So, although we have organised these literacy activities into three discrete areas, there will obviously be elements of all aspects of literacy in any activity. Whenever children are writing, for example, they also need to read what they have written, and whenever one child is speaking someone else will be listening. The interdependence of literacy skills will always exist. We have chosen one area of literacy to have greater weight for each activity, but you may decide to modify the activity and focus on a different aspect of literacy.

The three parts of this book are in line with the main elements of the CLL area of learning: talking, reading and writing. Each of these is then sub-divided into three sections, as follows:

Talking

Includes: *Language for Communication* and *Language for Thinking*.

- **Sharing ideas:** encouraging children to contribute to conversations and discussions as they listen to others, take turns and respect other people's ideas.
- **Saying what I mean:** helping children to become more precise in their language, in the way they express their thoughts and ideas, and by developing their working vocabulary.
- **Remember, reflect, retell:** helping children to remember details and sequence events, as they listen well, think about what they have heard, and recall key elements.

Reading

Covers: *Reading*.

250+activities for *Linking Sounds and Letters* can be found in our other book in the Classroom Gems series – *Early Years Phonics*.

- **World of books:** introducing children to how books work, and ideas to help you use your book area in imaginative ways to create a stimulating and welcoming environment.
- **Finding out:** introducing children to the print that is all around them in posters and signs, and in non-fiction such as instructions or recipes, as well as learning to recognise some common words.
- **Enjoying stories and rhymes:** helping children to recognise the elements of a good story by sharing published literature in activities based on well-known stories and rhymes.

Writing

Includes *Writing* and *Handwriting*.

- **Finger play:** fun ways to practise fine motor skills ready for handwriting, as well as opportunities to use the basic letter shapes.
- **Writing it down:** activities across all areas of the curriculum which help children learn about the importance of recording information.
- **Making a book:** writing down your ideas – factual or creative – in ordered ways to make books in all shapes and sizes to share.

'*Literacy should be at the heart of curriculum planning*'

Primary National Strategy, 2006, p. 20.

The activities have all been designed to fit in with things that happen every day in an Early Years setting so that they can easily be included in your curriculum plans. There are ideas for each area of the curriculum, including using your role-play area, exploring the world, creating art and display and learning how to make friends. There is a strong emphasis on practical participation and many activities take the children outside, in line with the recommendations of the Early Years Foundation Stage. There are ideas for creating interesting scenarios for talking and many of the activities provide opportunities for assessment.

In each section there are suggestions for using stories, poems or rhymes as an inspiration for children's own reading, writing and talking. Reading stories aloud to children is of course a valuable experience in itself, not only sharing the pleasure of reading but also modelling the rhythms and structure of language and widening children's vocabulary.

Each activity stands alone so you can do as many or as few as you wish. Although we suggest other curriculum areas that might link to the activity, the ideas are flexible and can often be adapted to fit into other themes in your planning. The activities can easily be pitched to different levels of ability and you will find that many are suitable for small groups and therefore ideal for a support assistant to use with those children who need extra practice or opportunities to extend themselves.

The page layout has clear headings and is user-friendly.

Title: where there are a number of activities on one theme or based on the same book we have numbered these （1） so that you can combine the activities if you wish.

A 'paper-clipped' note*: underneath the title of each activity we briefly introduce and explain the activity to help you find the one that suits your needs.

Aim: the aim of the activity comes directly from the CLL section of the EYFS. It is based on any of the four categories （Developing matters, Look, listen, note, Effective practice, or Planning and resources） and can therefore be easily used in your planning if required.

Resources: any resources that are needed are listed.

Preparation: if there is anything you need to do beforehand, this is indicated.

What to do: the activity is explained in step-by-step instructions and includes ideas and examples to aid the busy practitioner.

Vocabulary: new or unfamiliar vocabulary developed through the activity is clearly listed.

Tip: A handy tip offers additional helpful advice to ensure the smooth running of the activity or to suggest how an activity might be extended or adapted.

Cross-curricular: this alerts the practitioner to where the activity fits in with another of the six areas of learning in the EYFS, thus making maximum use of your preparation.

Children's learning and competence in communicating, speaking and listening, being read to and beginning to read and write must be supported and extended. They must be provided with opportunity and encouragement to use their skills in a range of situations and for a range of purposes, and be supported in developing the confidence and disposition to do so.

Practice Guidance for the Early Years Foundation Stage, May 2008, p. 41.

Young children learn as they play and it's important that they enjoy what they are doing and see a purpose in their learning. In this book you will find lots of fun activities based on play that will help to develop your children's communication and literacy skills.

---

* 此处本书按中文版版式排版，如序言第 2 页所提，中文版版式设计为一个蓝色底纹框加左上角"心形"标志。

About the authors

Gill Coulson and Lynn Cousins have worked extensively in primary schools, mainly teaching in the Early Years and Key Stage One. Gill was a deputy head, and Lynn was head of an infant school with Beacon status.

They have both continued to study throughout their teaching careers; Gill gained an M. Phil. degree, researching the teaching of reading, and Lynn gained an MA (Ed.) in early years education.

Since leaving the school environment, Lynn has been an editor of educational publications and is a freelance writer on education. She has a number of published books and was involved in compiling *The International Primary Curriculum* with Fieldwork Education.

Throughout her career, Gill has maintained a strong interest in children's literature, using it as an inspiration in the classroom, helping children learn to read and compose their own writing. She is currently teaching focused writing groups in a number of Milton Keynes schools.

Gill and Lynn have written *Early Years Phonics* in the Classroom Gems series, and Lynn has written *Shaping Children's Behaviour in the Early Years* for the Essential Guides series.

Acknowledgements

Authors' acknowledgements

With thanks to the authors, poets and artists who have inspired us and many children.

Publisher's acknowledgements

We are grateful to the following for permission to reproduce copyright material:

Extract on page xii from *Practice Guidance for the Early Years Foundation Stage*, May 2008, p. 41 (Department for Children, Schools and Families), © Crown copyright 2008; Epigraph on page 2 from *Primary Framework for Literacy and Mathematics*, p. 17 (Primary National Strategy 2006), © Crown copyright 2006; Epigraphs on pages 108 and 230 from *Practice Guidance for the Early Years Foundation Stage*, May 2008, p. 42 (Department for Children, Schools and Families), © Crown copyright 2008. Crown Copyright material is reproduced with permission under the terms of the Click-Use License.

In some instances we have been unable to trace the owners of copyright material, and we would appreciate any information that would enable us to do so.

Part 1
Talking

Given the significance of speaking and listening for children's learning and overall language development, it is important to ... identify places in the timetable where children can revisit, apply and extend the speaking and listening skills which they have been explicitly taught.
Primary Framework for Literacy and Mathematics, 2006, p.17.

As children develop speaking and listening skills they build the foundations for literacy, for making sense of visual and verbal signs and ultimately for reading and writing.
Practice Guidance for the Early Years Foundation Stage, May 2008, p.41.

Chapter 1

Sharing ideas

Introducing circle time

Encourage the children to come up with ideas for making Circle Time successful.

Aim

- To help children demonstrate appropriate conventions in a group.

Resources

- A small object such as a shiny, smooth shell or stone, small enough to fit in a child's hand.

Preparation

- Sit together quietly.

What to do

- Explain to the children that you are going to spend some time sharing some ideas together. Everyone should be able to see and hear everyone else. Ask them what they think would be a good way to sit so that everyone can do this. Let children offer their own suggestions.
- When a circle is suggested ask the children to move quietly so that everyone is sitting that way. Can everyone see everyone else? Tell them that when we sit like this we call it 'circle time'.
- Explain that when they are in circle time there have to be some rules so that everyone gets a chance to speak, and to make sure that everyone listens carefully. Encourage the children to suggest some rules.
- As they make their suggestions repeat them in positive ways, e. g. if the child says, 'We mustn't shout', you say 'We must do what then?' 'We must speak quietly – but clearly, so that everyone can hear.'
- Gather together a few rules about speaking one at a time, listening to each other, being polite about other people and so on.
- Have your small object ready. Show this to the children, and tell them that this would be a way to help them to remember about speaking one at a time. The person who is holding this is the only person who can speak. They must be ready

to pass it on when they have had their turn.

- Practise using this small object. You start, saying something like, 'My name is . . .' . Then hand it to the next child in the circle. When it gets back to you say a new starter sentence.

- You are now ready to engage the children in other circle time activities.

Try: **www. circle-time. co. uk** for more ideas.

Collins, M. (2001) *Circle Time for the Very Young*, London: Paul Chapman Publishing.

Vocabulary

listen, take turns, speak clearly, polite

Tip

Some useful starter sentences could be:

I like it when . . . . . .

I am sad when . . . . .

My favourite food is . . . .

My friend . . . . is special because . . . .

Cross-curricular link

PSED: Dispositions and Attitudes.

Garden centre (1)

 Plan and make some model plants to sell in your garden centre.

Aim

- To ask children to think about how they will accomplish a task, talking through the sequence of stages.

Resources

- A selection of seedlings/plants at various stages of growth
- Small pots filled with plasticene or dough（soil）
- Green straws, green paper（stems and leaves）
- Coloured paper（flower heads）
- Edible seeds（flower seeds）

Preparation

- Plant and care for seeds over a number of weeks so that the children are aware of the stages of growth.

What to do

- Talk about the pattern of growth of the plants the children have grown. Can they remember the order of the stages, e. g.
  - pot of soil with the seeds hidden inside it
  - a small shoot showing through the soil
  - a seedling with leaves
  - a plant with a bud
  - a plant with a flower
  - a plant with seeds forming
- Explain to the children that they are going to make some models of plants to sell in their shop. Talk about which stage of growth each child would like to make. Will it be a seedling or will it have a bud?
- Show the children all the resources that you have collected together. Identify the resources and ask what each one might be used for.
- Can they tell you what they might use to make their own set of plants? Can they

tell you what they will do first?

- Let the children make their own versions of the plants. As they work, ask questions about what they are doing, why they are doing it and what they will do next.

Vocabulary

first, next, later, afterwards, last

Tip   If possible, provide some real plants at different stages of growth to remind the children of what happens.

Cross-curricular link

KUW: Exploration and Investigation.

Follow-the-leader

Children organise their own parade, deciding on costumes and instruments, and planning everyone's position.

Aim

- To help children talk about and plan their roles.

Resources

- Dressing-up clothes, including hats, beads, scarves
- Musical instruments, e. g. shakers and tambourines

Preparation

- Practise playing follow-the-leader – without dressing up.
- Make sure all the children know what to do, encouraging them to look at the person leading and copy what they do. Include sound effects as well as different movements.
- Children can take it in turns to be the leader for a short time.

What to do

- Place boxes of clothes, accessories and instruments outside so that children can get dressed up and choose an instrument.
- Decide who will be the leader of your parade, and then the order of those who will follow.
  - Look at how everyone is dressed. Do you want all your princesses together?
  - Children can decide whether to use instruments or not and whether they sing, or whether it will be a very quiet parade.
  - Should the instruments lead the parade?
- Take your parade all over the grounds.
- Leave the resources out, ready for children to use later.

Vocabulary

first, in front, behind, next to

Tip   You may need to restrict the space that can be used by the parade so that other children can play safely with other equipment.

Cross-curricular link

PD: Movement and Space.

At the doctor's

Thinking about the conversations that would be appropriate in a doctor's surgery.

Aim

• To encourage children to take turns, listen to others and use appropriate conventional expressions.

Resources

Role-play area set up as a doctor's surgery

What to do

• Talk with a small group of children about the parts they will play in this session – patient, receptionist, nurse and doctor. Help the children dress up in the appropriate clothes for their part.

• Explain that the patient has hurt their leg and needs to see the doctor. Ask them to think about:

  – how the patient hurt their leg

  – what the doctor will need to ask the patient

  – what the receptionist might say to the patient

  – how the nurse will help the doctor

  Give the children time to plan what they will say and how they will say it.

• The children act out the scenario of a patient coming to the doctor's surgery with an injured leg, e. g.

  – The receptionist greets the patient and asks them to take a seat, then tells the doctor the patient has arrived.

  – The nurse helps the patient walk to the doctor, who asks how the leg was hurt.

  – The patient explains and the doctor examines the leg, asking questions to find out where the pain is.

  – The doctor asks the nurse to pass items needed to treat the injury, then tells the patient when they need to see the doctor again.

  – Before the patient leaves, the receptionist makes a new appointment.

Vocabulary

please, thank you, Can I. ...? How did you. ...? , Where ...?

Tip   The first time the children do this activity, it may be appropriate for the adult to take one of the parts to model the type of conversation.

Cross-curricular link

CD: Developing Imagination and Imaginative Play.

Emergency! by Margaret Mayo (1)

Enjoy a book that has lots of exciting and interesting descriptive words.

Aim

• To extend children's vocabulary.

Resources

• A copy of Mayo, M. (2003) *Emergency!*, London: Orchard Books

• A selection of emergency vehicles as featured in the book

Preparation

• Read and enjoy the book with the children

What to do

• Sit in a circle with the emergency vehicles in the centre. As you read each page of the book, choose a child to point to the vehicle mentioned on that page. Then everyone can repeat the line 'Help is coming – it's on the way!' as the child returns to their place in the circle.

• When you have finished the book and all the vehicles have been identified, tell the children that this time you will only read the bit that describes the emergency and they must try to remember which vehicle came to help, e.g. '*Emergency! Traffic build – up on the motorway – who can help?*'

• Choose a child who knows the answer to pick up the vehicle while you read the description of the vehicle moving, e.g.

  '*Vroom! Police motorbike*

  zipping, revving, cars directing'

• The child can then repeat the phrase 'Help is coming – it's on the way!' before they return to their place in the circle.

• Finally, tell the children that this time you are going to describe what the vehicle is doing and they have to guess which vehicle it is. Read the section of text that describes the sound and movement of the emergency vehicle, e. g.

'*zoom on their way, swoop, swoop, swooping and water scooping*'

Can anyone guess which vehicle it is?

- The child who identifies the vehicle correctly can move the vehicle around the inner circle while you reread the relevant page.
- Leave the toy vehicles out with the play-mat so the children can act out some of these emergency situations in their free play.

Vocabulary

police car, breakdown truck, ambulance, helicopter, snow plough, lifeboat, inflatable boat, police motorbike, fire-fighting plane, fire engine, crane

Tip The children might enjoy acting out some of these emergency situations outside during imaginative play. You could call out the emergency and the children pretend to drive or fly the vehicles that come to the rescue

Cross-curricular link

PSED: Sense of Community.

Wedding (1)

Organise a wedding for your teddies, encouraging children to explain their choices.

Aim

• To help children to expand on what they say.

Resources

• Photos from a wedding

• A selection of teddies and dolls

• Dolls' clothes and other items, e. g. camera, flowers, veil, book

What to do

• Have any of the children been to a wedding? Encourage them to talk about their experiences.

• Look at the photographs and identify the bride, etc. Talk about other people who are involved, e. g. the registrar (or other official), photographer.

• Share experiences until everyone has a simple understanding of what happens.

• Let the children choose which teddies will be married and which will play other parts. Ask them to explain their choices.

• Show them the selection of clothing available. Ask the children to choose what each teddy should wear, encouraging them to negotiate. Let them get the toys ready for the wedding.

• Clear a space where the wedding can be held and act it out.

Vocabulary

bride, groom, bridesmaid, guest, registrar, photographer, dress, jacket, tie, veil, flowers, camera

Tip   Be sensitive to different cultural experiences.

Cross-curricular link

PSED: Sense of Community.

Collect and sort

 Children have fun matching objects to their possible descriptions.

Aim

- To extend the children's vocabulary by grouping and naming.

Resources

- Large paper plates
- Access to small objects around the room
- Hoops
- Paper for labels

Preparation

- Make a selection of labels, each one with a single descriptive word on it, e. g. shiny, smooth, hard.
- Give each child a paper plate and ask them to collect ten small objects from around the room. They should all fit on the paper plate.

What to do

- When the children have ten objects each, they should sit in a circle with the plate on the floor in front of them.
- Place a hoop in the middle of your circle. Reach into your pile of labels and pick one at random. You may want to ask individual children to reach into a container full of your labels and pick one.
- Place the label in the hoop and tell the children that you are looking for objects that are . . . . . , e. g. shiny.
- Go round the circle asking each child in turn, 'Do you have something shiny to go in the hoop? '
- Each child in turn looks at his own selection of objects and chooses one – or not.
- As the game progresses children may start to wish they had saved their red squashy toy for 'squashy' as they had several red objects they could have chosen for 'red' . But no one knows what the labels will say!

- If you play this again on another day, will children choose a wider selection of materials?

Vocabulary

Any descriptive words, such as: shiny, smooth, hard, soft, round, red (etc.), long, thin, fat, squashy, solid, heavy

Tip   Add to your labels if you play this again so that the children can't anticipate the criteria.

Cross-curricular link

PSRN: Calculating.

Bert's day

Make up a story about a character, using everyone's ideas about what should happen throughout his day.

Aim

- To encourage children to make up their own stories.

Resources

- Play-mat
- Model buildings
- Toy van

Preparation

- Lay out your play-mat with a selection of buildings, e.g. garage, shop, farm, houses.
- Take it outside on a fine day.

What to do

- Choose a name for your main character, e.g. Bert. Explain to the children that they are going to help you tell the story of Bert's day.
- Choose a different child who will be Bert driving his van at each stage of the story.
- Tell the children that Bert is off in his van to go to the garage to get some petrol. A child will 'drive' the van along the roads on the play-mat.
- While he is there he sees some bunches of flowers for sale. He buys some for his mum.
- He drives his van to his mum's house. Decide which house is his mum's and which of the roads he will drive along. When he gets there he gives his mum the flowers. She loves them.
- She asks Bert to take a jar of the jam she has been making to Old Tom . . . . . .
- The story continues in this way. Every time Bert delivers something he is asked to go somewhere else with another delivery.
- How will the story end?

Vocabulary

Any repetitive phrase that you can include in the story

Tip   This story structure lends itself to a drama activity as you can create parts for as many children as are in your group.

Cross-curricular link

CD: Developing Imagination and Imaginative Play.

Invisible ink

Sharing ideas on why things happen as the children discover the magic of wax-resist.

Aim

- To encourage children to listen attentively and respond with relevant comments.

Resources

- White paper
- White wax crayons
- Thin, watery paint

Preparation

- Ensure the children have had plenty of experience making marks with crayons.

What to do

- Gather a small group of children around the art table or work outside if it's fine. Tell the children you are going to write a secret message.
- Colour some bold letter shapes with the white crayon on a piece of white paper. Ask the children:
    'Why can't they see the message clearly?'
    'Why isn't white a good colour to use?'
- Explain that it's invisible. Then look disappointed – 'Oh dear, but how will anyone see the message?' Ask if anyone has any suggestions of what to do.
- Show them the paint. Tell them you have an idea of how to see the invisible message.
- Lightly paint over the paper and see how the marks show through the paint.
- Can the children explain why it has happened? Listen to their ideas.
- Let the children have a go at writing an invisible message then painting over it.

Vocabulary

white, invisible, shiny, smooth, resist

Tip The marks need to be quite bold and thick, and the paint needs to be thin enough if this activity is going to work.

Cross-curricular link

KUW: Exploration and Investigation.

Mixing paint (1)

Encourage the children to predict what they think will happen when they mix colours together.

Aim

- To provide an opportunity for children to present ideas to others.

Resources

- Red, yellow and blue paints
- Paper, brushes and water
- Mixing trays

Preparation

- Plenty of previous opportunities for free painting.

What to do

- Working with a small group of children, talk about the three primary colours.
  - Can they name them?
  - Which do they like best and why?
- Tell the children that they are going to use these to make some new colours.
- Ask them to choose two colours each, e. g. blue and yellow.
- Can they guess what colour they'll make if they mix these two together?
- Let them experiment with mixing two colours together to make a new colour, e. g.
  - red and blue to make purple
  - blue and yellow to make green
  - red and yellow to make orange
- Talk about the new colours they have made, and how they made them. What colours did they start with, and what have they made?
- Now ask them to explain how they made their new colour to another child from the class.

Vocabulary

red, blue, yellow, green, orange, purple, mix

Tip Encourage the children to paint blobs of the colours they use and the colour they make – these can be used to create a display that records their findings.

Cross-curricular link

CD: Exploring Media and Materials.

Mixing paint (2)

A chance for children to describe what happens when they experiment with colours.

Aim

To provide the children with meaningful speaking and listening activities.

Resources

- Red, blue, black and white paints
- Mixing trays, brushes and paper

Preparation

- You will need to do the painting the day before the sorting activity.

What to do

- Working with a small group of children, tell them that they are going to change the blue and red colours.
- Let each child choose a colour and put some of it on their mixing tray. They then paint a blob of this colour on their paper.
- Now let them add a small amount of black to the colour in their mixing try and paint another blob. Encourage them to compare the darker shade to the original colour and describe what has happened.
- Ask them to predict what will happen when more black is added. Let the children add more black and produce darker shades of their chosen colour.
- Working with another group, repeat the activity, but this time ask the children what they think will happen if they add white to their chosen colour.
- Encourage them to paint blobs by adding white and recording the lighter shades.
- Set the shades of colour aside to dry overnight.
- Next day: cut out the blobs of colour so you can make several sets of six shades. Provide time for the children who painted them to explain how they were made.
- Now give out a set of six shades to a pair of children. Ask them to put the colours in order from light to dark. Encourage them to talk and negotiate as they arrange the colours in order.

Vocabulary

red, blue, black, white, mix, dark, darker, light, lighter, paler, shade

Tip Set up a display to remind the children what they have experienced using the blobs of colour, enlarged vocabulary and photographs taken as the children work.

Cross-curricular link

CD: Exploring Media and Materials.

Mini-beasts (1)

Set up a role-play area that helps children to imagine life from someone else's perspective.

Aim

To encourage children to imagine and recreate roles.

Resources

• Oversized T-shirts in a variety of plain colours

Preparation

• Set up a role-play area as a garden:

  – Make oversized paper leaves, grass and flowers from paper. Fix these to a wall display board at ground level. It should resemble a giant garden. Do this as a separate activity with the children.

• Put the T-shirts in a crate or basket nearby.

What to do

• Gather the children together near the 'garden' they have made. All sit on the floor so that the 'grass' etc is taller than them.

• Talk about the height of the 'grass' etc. compared to their height.

  'This is what a garden must look like to a spider or a beetle'.

• Ask the children to imagine being an insect in the garden. Can they think of anything else that might be in a garden and that would look big to a spider, but not to us, e.g.

  – a foot

  – a ball

  – a bird

• Encourage the children to play in the garden they have made wearing one of the T-shirts to look like the mini-beast that they want to be. You could try black for a beetle, red for a ladybird, etc.

Vocabulary

huge, tiny

Tip
Write out some nursery rhymes about mini-beasts. Put them near your 'garden' and read them together. Try:

Little Miss Muffet

Incy Wincy Spider

Ladybird, Ladybird, Fly Away Home

Cross-curricular link

CD: Developing Imagination and Imaginative Play.

Rhyming instructions

Have fun with rhymes as the children change for PE.

Aim

• To encourage children to enjoy using rhyming words.

Resources

• PE kits

• Adult helpers

Preparation

• Make up a simple rhyme to fit your circumstances（see example below）．

What to do

• Let the children collect their bags that contain their PE clothes， ready to get changed for PE.

• Tell the children you have made up a special little rhyme to remind them what to do. Ask them to listen out for the rhyming words as you say it.

  Can anyone guess the ending?

    Put your bag on the table

    Put your clothes on the chair

    Put your shoes on the floor

    And put your socks in there!

• Keep repeating the rhyme as they get ready for PE. Encourage the children to join in. Will anyone remember it next time?

• Can the children help make up rhymes for other routines， e. g. ， juice time/lunch time/getting ready for going home?

Vocabulary

Pairs of rhyming words： chair – there， last – fast， ready – steady， stop – hop.

Tip   More ideas for working with rhythm and rhyme can be found in *Games*，

Ideas and Activities for *Early Years Phonics* in the Classroom Gems series.

Cross-curricular link

PSED: Self-care.

Should we paint today?

Children create different weather conditions and talk about how they affect their painting.

Aim

• To help children to link cause and effect to explain their choices.

Resources

• Paint, paper and easels
• Straws, watering can, newspaper
• Aprons and waterproof covering

Preparation

• Set up four painting easels outside on a fine day with no wind. This is a messy activity so position it away from walls, other activities or the door into the setting.

What to do

• Explain to the children that they are going to think about painting outdoors. Sometimes we can do this, sometimes we can't.

• One reason for this might be the weather. Why? Listen to the children's ideas and talk about them.

> 'What difference would it make if it was breezy, or very windy? '
> 'What if it was showery or there was a heavy rainstorm? '

• Tell the children that they are going to make these four different kinds of weather today so that they can find out what would happen to their paintings in these different conditions. Encourage the children to suggest some ideas for creating weather effects, eg:

Activity 1: A breezy day

Paint your picture. While it is wet,

– blow onto it

– blow through a straw onto it

Activity 2: A very windy day

Paint your picture. While it is wet,

– flap a newspaper near it

– take it off the easel and wave it around

Activity 3: A showery day

Paint your picture. While it is wet,

– splash water onto it with your fingers

– use a pipette to drip water all over it

Activity 4: A wet day

– wet the paper before you paint your picture

– use a watering can to soak the paper after you have painted your picture.

• Have two children at each of the four activities. Start by asking the children to discuss what they think will happen with 'their' weather.

• Observe them as they carry out the activity. When they have finished, ask them:

'What happened?'

'Why?'

'Were you right?'

'Would this be a good painting day?'

Vocabulary

reason, effect, decision

Tip   Children can work in pairs at different activities and then come together as a group to report their findings.

Cross-curricular link

KUW: Exploration and Investigation.

What a lot of nonsense!

Make up some silly words as you adapt a well-known rhyme.

Aim

• To encourage children to experiment with words and sounds.

Resources

A copy of 'Fingers Like to Wiggle, Waggle' in Matterson, E. (compiler) (1991), *This Little Puffin*, London: Penguin.

Preparation

• Enjoy singing this finger rhyme with the children.

What to do

• Ask the children to show you how to wiggle their fingers as they join in the rhyme.

• Tell them the next time you say the rhyme you are going to try something new.

• Start to tap your fingers together as you begin the rhyme.

• Ask the children to suggest words for this movement, e. g.

   tippy tappy

Sing the first verse.

• Tell the children they can say any silly words they like as they move their fingers.

• Ask for ideas, e. g.

   bingy bongy

   dimby dumby

   Enjoy the frivolity as their words get sillier and sillier!

• Choose a few favourites that work well. Then tell the children which ones to use for each of the four verses. Encourage them to keep moving their fingers as they say their silly words.

Vocabulary

Any two-syllable nonsense words that begin with the same initial sound

Tip   You might want to use this activity to focus on alliteration by choosing two words that start with the same sound, or on rhythm by demonstrating the two syllables in *wiggle* and *waggle* by clapping.

Cross-curricular link

CD: Creating Music and Dance.

Asking questions

Plan a set of questions that the children could ask a visitor.

Aim

• To help the children to form questions appropriate for a visitor.

Resources

• Question words prepared on card or interactive whiteboard, e. g. what, when, where, how, who.

Preparation

• Arrange a visitor who will come to talk to the children about their job, e. g. librarian, nurse or policeman.

What to do

• Tell the children that you are going to have a visitor and who it is.
  Ask them what they know about this person's work.

• Tell the children that you want to get some questions ready to ask the visitor.
  – What would they like to find out?

• Show the children the question words. Read each word in turn.

• Model how to create a question with one of the words, for your visitor, e. g.
  'What part of your job do you enjoy best? '
  'Where do you go to work? '
  'Who do you work with? '

• Try to form questions like these which are open-ended and allow the visitor to talk rather than just answer yes or no.

• Help the children think of more questions to ask, e. g.
  'When did you decide to be a nurse? '
  'How do you arrest people? '

• Write down their ideas and let them practise asking them.

Vocabulary

what, when, where, how, who

Tip   Keep a copy of the children's questions to prompt them when the visitor is there.

Cross-curricular link

PSED: Sense of Community.

Problem-solving (1)

 How will the children cooperate with each other as they try to sort themselves out in height order?

Aim

• To encourage children to work with others to devise a plan.

Preparation

• This will follow on from some work on comparing sizes.

What to do

• Explain to the children that you want them to stand in a line with the tallest child at one end, and the smallest child at the other end.

• To do this they will need to find out who is the tallest in the whole group, who is the second tallest and so on. They should work together to sort out the answer.

• Let them try for a little while. Observe them to see how they are working it out.

  – Is any one child organising the group?

  – Are they allowing everyone else to contribute ideas?

• Stop the group and gather them all together.

  – Ask them to tell you how they are trying to work this out.

  – Give everyone time to add their own ideas or comment on suggestions put forward by others.

• Ask the children to complete the activity. Remind children to ask, e. g.

  'May I . . . ? '

  'Should we . . . ? '

  'What do you think about . . . ? '

Vocabulary

taller, shorter

 Tip If your group is quite small or struggling with the activity, suggest they compare any two children and then take the taller one each time and compare that child with another. Continue until you have the tallest person. Repeat for each position in turn.

Cross-curricular link

PSRN: Shape, Space and Measures.

Problem-solving (2)

A chance for children to cooperate and negotiate as they build a shelter from the sun.

Aim

- To work with other children to negotiate plans and activities.

Resources

- Large piece of fabric
- String

Preparation

- Look around your outside area.
- Where would you fix a shelter?
- Are there any trees, railings, etc. which may be useful?
- If not, leave some chairs, boxes, lengths of wood, etc. outside.

What to do

- Explain to the children that they have been shipwrecked. Decide how far your 'island' extends within your grounds. They have to stay on this 'island' until a boat comes to pick them up, so they need to build a shelter to keep the hot sun off them.
- Provide a small group of children with a piece of fabric and the string. This is all that was washed up from their ship!
- Explain that they have to work together to find a place to build their shelter, and a method for doing it. Provide help with tying knots in the string etc. , but encourage the children to come up with their own solution to the problem.
- Take note of the group dynamics:
    - Who takes the lead?
    - Who is content to leave it to others?
    - Who works hard in the team?

Vocabulary

shelter, protect, safe

Tip   Make these on hot days and use them as real shelters.

Cross-curricular link

PSED: Self-care.

Problem-solving (3)

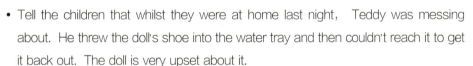

Working together, the children help Teddy find a way to retrieve the doll's shoe from the water tray.

Aim

• To encourage children to interact with others, creating and testing plans.

Resources

• Water tray
• Teddy
• Doll
• Doll's shoe

Preparation

• Before the children arrive, put the doll's shoe in the centre of the water tray.

What to do

• Tell the children that whilst they were at home last night, Teddy was messing about. He threw the doll's shoe into the water tray and then couldn't reach it to get it back out. The doll is very upset about it.

• Ask them if they can work out a way for Teddy to get the shoe out. Make sure that they understand that Teddy has to do this – they can't simply reach in and get it for him.

• Spend time talking about their ideas. They may decide on, e.g.
  – Something that is long that Teddy can reach with and hook the shoe out (perhaps a fishing net, or a stick with something tied to the end of it).
  – Something that will float on the water and will carry Teddy across to get the shoe out with his paws (a boat, a piece of wood or anything else that they can find to float).

• Encourage children to think through their ideas, talking about 'if' and 'could', before they actually test their idea.

• At the end of the session each group of children in turn can explain their plan to the others. Did it work?

Vocabulary

Useful questions to encourage discussion: What would happen if .....? Is it possible that ....? Could we .....? Is it safe to ......?

Tip   This is a good opportunity to reinforce water safety rules.

Cross-curricular link

KUW: Exploration and Investigation.

Chapter 2

Saying what I mean

Café (1)

Discuss what will be needed to set up a café. Encourage the children to think carefully about the equipment and organisation as an adult records their ideas.

Aim

- To provide activities where children use talk to anticipate what they will be doing.

Resources

- Large piece of paper and pens for adult to scribe ideas.

Preparation

Encourage children to share their experiences of going to cafes. Some questions to ask them are:

- What do you like to eat and drink?
- Who do you go with?
- Do you know the café's name or where it is?
- Have you been to a café for a special occasion?
- Have you sat outside at a café?

What to do

- Tell the children you are going to create a café. Ask them to think what will be needed.

  Draw pictures or write simple words to record the children's suggestions, e. g. , plates, cutlery, cups, tables and chairs.

- To guide their planning ask them to think about:
  - How will the customers pay?
  - How will they know what they can choose?
  - How do they place an order?

  The children might decide they need to have a food counter and pay at a till, or they might want waiters and waitresses.

- It will be quite easy to change the café from one style to another to give more variety after a few days. During the summer months you could try setting up the café outside or try creating an ice cream van!

Vocabulary

cake, sandwich, burger, coke, juice, fruit, ice cream, menu, till, customer, waiter/ress

Tip   Try changing your café to offer different types of food, e. g. Indian, Chinese or Caribbean.

Cross-curricular link

CD: Developing Imagination and Imaginative Play.

Hunt the book

 Use walkie-talkies to locate books in the library.

Aim
- To encourage children to use talk to organise and clarify thinking.

Resources
- Simple walkie-talkie device
- Access to a library or book collection outside of the classroom or working area

Preparation
- Check the books available so that you know what is there at the time of this activity.

What to do
- Explain to the children that two of them are going to go to the library and choose a book. They will need to remember what it looks like and where it is, then they return to the classroom.
- Two other children now go to the library with the walkie-talkie.
- The two children in the classroom guide the two in the library to find the same book.
- Think about:
  - Is it on the top shelf?
  - Is it a big book?
  - What is the picture on the cover?
  - What colour is it?
- The two in the classroom keep giving clues until the others think they have found it. They return, with the book, to find out whether they have located the right book.
- Now swap roles.

Tip If you have two copies of any book, use one in each area for less able or younger children.

Cross-curricular link
KUW: ICT.

Wolf!

 The children listen carefully to instructions as they play a musical Red Riding Hood game.

Aim

• To help children to listen and respond with relevant actions.

Resources

• Music to dance to

Preparation

• You will need a large space to play in.

• Set up your music.

What to do

• Choose a few children to be trees, to make the forest. If you have extra adults, they could play this role. The 'trees' should spread their arms out like branches.

• Everyone else dances round the trees to the music.

• When the music stops, call out an instruction. The children can choose how they act out the instruction. Try:

  - Pick some flowers for Grandma

  - Skip down the path

  - Check the cakes in your basket

  - Your hood has come off

  - Eat one of the cakes

• But sometimes you will call out WOLF! ! Then everyone must quickly hide behind a tree. The last person to hide is 'out' and becomes another tree, until there is only one person left dancing.

 Tip Watch for children who can think of an action quickly. Is there anyone who struggles with this?

Cross-curricular link

CD: Developing Imagination and Imaginative Play.

I do, you do

 Children work in pairs to make identical models. One child explains and the other follows the instructions.

Aim

- To provide an opportunity for children to explain instructions clearly, using a range of positional language.

Resources

- Interlocking cubes or coloured bricks
- Something to create a screen across the middle of the table

Preparation

- Two children each have ten cubes or bricks. They should each have an identical mix of colours.
- Seat the children so that they can't see what the other one is doing. They could be back to back, or you could create some sort of screen between them.

What to do

- Child One makes a simple model using any number of their cubes. This could even be a simple line of cubes.
- Child Two has to make an identical model by following instructions.
- Child One gives instructions one at a time, and Child Two signals when they are ready to hear the next instruction.
- When Child Two has finished, the children show each other their models. Are they the same?

Vocabulary

next, after that, on top of, underneath, in between, together

Tip You may need to demonstrate first, letting both children follow your instructions.

Cross-curricular link

PSRN: Shape, Space and Measures.

Shine a light

 Children use a torch and describe exactly what they can see.

Aim

To provide an opportunity for children to use meaningful speaking and listening.

Resources

- One or two small torches
- A dark corner, cupboard or box
- A selection of small toys

Preparation

- Set up your dark area and hide a few toys in there.
- Show the children how to turn the torches on and off.

What to do

- Tell the children that some toys are hidden away in the dark cupboard/box. Explain that everyone will take turns to use the torch to see the toys.
- When they are shining the torch they must choose one toy to describe to the others, e.g.

    'I can see something that is round and smooth and small.'

    Can the other children guess what it is?
- If they guess it correctly, the toy is brought out of the cupboard.

    Then another child has their turn.

Vocabulary

big, small, soft, hard, shiny, fluffy, round, square, long, thin...

Tip Younger children may need to see the toys and talk about them before they are hidden.

Cross-curricular link

KUW: ICT.

Toot Toot Beep Beep by Emma Garcia (1)

Help the children to sort the vocabulary in the book into two sets of 'fast' or 'slow' words.

Aim

• To increase the range of children's vocabulary.

Resources

• A copy of Garcia, E. (2009) *Toot Toot Beep Beep*, St Albans: Boxer Books

• Pieces of paper

• Cars

• Two setting circles labeled 'fast' and 'slow'

Preparation

• Remind the children of the story by reading it again.

What to do

• Sit in a circle with the labelled setting circles in the middle.

• Look at the first vehicle in the book. How does it move away?
  'It zooms'.

• Choose a child to take one of the cars and show what 'zoom' would look like.

• Ask the children whether 'zoom' means fast or slow? Once everyone has agreed, write the word 'zoom' on a piece of paper and place it in the correct setting circle.

• Continue through the book, finding the word, testing it out and deciding whether it is going to join 'zoom' as a 'fast' word or it will go into the other circle of 'slow' words.

• When you have a full set of words, read through all the 'fast' words and then all the 'slow' words together.

• Everyone can now take a car. You will read one of the words at a time and they will demonstrate with their car each time – will it be fast or slow?

• Finish with all the cars parking quietly in the car park.

Vocabulary

zoom, speed, trundle, rush, glide, roll, hurtle

 Tip   Use this as part of your garage role-play activities.

Cross-curricular link

CLL: Role play.

Telephone your order

 Talking on a telephone is a fun way to use adjectives as the children identify or describe a fruit or vegetable.

Aim

• To provide an opportunity for children to participate in meaningful speaking and listening activities.

Resources

• Two toy telephones or out-of-use adult ones
• A selection of fruit and vegetables familiar to the children

Preparation

• Ensure that most children can name the items and describe some of their properties.

What to do

• Sit in a circle with a selection of fruit and vegetables in the centre.
• Explain that you are the customer ringing the greengrocer's shop, but you don't know the names of all the things in the shop. A child will be the shopkeeper who answers the phone and tries to help.

> Adult: Do you have any vegetables that are hard and long and coloured orange?
>
> Shopkeeper: Yes, we do – they are carrots. How many do you want?
>
> Adult: I would like two large ones please.
>
> Shopkeeper: OK, I'll save two large carrots for you.
>
> Adult: Thank you very much. Goodbye.

• Let another child take the role of shopkeeper and answer your next call.
• When the children are confident about the game encourage them to play both roles-the customer and the shopkeeper.

Vocabulary

round, long, soft, hard, smooth, big, small, yellow, green, red, orange, purple. . .

Tip You could play a similar game with zoo or farm animals pretending the customer is setting up a new zoo or farm.

Cross-curricular link

KUW: ICT.

Put it on

 A lively activity helping children to give clear and precise instructions about getting dressed.

Aim

• To encourage children to use talk to organise and sequence events.

Resources

• A large jumper

• If possible， have another adult to be your model

What to do

• Place the jumper on the floor or on a nearby table.

• The children have to tell the adult how to put the jumper on.
  Explain to the children that the adult will do exactly as they suggest.

• Ask the children：'What should she do first？'
  Children's suggestions may be to 'put your head through the hole'
  The adult should do this-don't pick it up， just try to do it where the jumper is!
  Play it up - make it a comic act.

• Have great fun together as the children try to think of all the stages they have missed out.

• Some children may like to come out and have a go at putting the jumper on.
  Will the others remember all the necessary stages of instructions?

Vocabulary

through， under， inside， outside， over， pull

Tip   This could be done on another occasion with shoes that fasten or a coat that needs to be fastened up for a wintry day.

Cross-curricular link

PSED： Self-care.

Is it you?

 Children identify someone in the group by responding to your clues.

Aim

• To provide an opportunity for children to use a broad range of adjectives correctly.

Resources

• A set of names of the children in the group, written on individual pieces of paper

What to do

• The game starts with everyone standing up.

• Pick a name at random from those you've written out. Don't let anyone else know who it is.

• Tell the children that they have to work out who it is, e. g.

  'The person I'm thinking of has long hair'

  'So, all those without long hair sit down.'

  'The person I'm thinking of has black shoes'

  'So, all those without black shoes sit down.'

• Continue until there is only one person left standing. Check the name on the piece of paper. Have you found the right child?

• That child then comes to the front and starts the game again by choosing another name.

Vocabulary

long, short, colour words, tall, curly, straight

Tip You may have to help the children work out whether to sit or stay standing until they become more familiar with the game.

Cross-curricular link

PSED: Sense of Community.

Mini-beasts (2)

 Children think of words to describe how mini-beasts move before pretending to be one.

Aim

- To extend the children's vocabulary.

Resources

- Drum
- Tambourine or shaker

What to do

- Explain to the children that they are going to pretend to be some of the mini-beasts that live in the garden. Ask everybody to try to move like a butterfly. Then encourage the children to try being a spider. Continue with any other mini-beasts, e. g. a caterpillar, a bee or a snail.
- Sit together and ask them to suggest some words to describe how the different creatures move. Take one mini-beast at a time and collect some words, e. g.

  caterpillars – crawl, creep

  butterflies – float, fly, flap

  spiders – scurry, scamper

  bees – buzz, hover

  beetles – scuttle

  Be ready to add some words so that children can increase their word knowledge.
- Now everyone stands in a space ready to play a game.
- Tell the children that they are to be intrepid explorers, hunting for creatures in the garden. *Move quietly, don't alert them!*
- You beat the drum as the children move stealthily around the space in time to the beat.
- You stop beating the drum, and begin to shake the tambourine or shakers. At the same time call out one of the movements you all thought of:

  – Float like a butterfly

- Scamper like a spider
- Hover like a bee, etc

The children have to follow the instruction, before you start beating the drum again.

Vocabulary

float, fly, flap, scamper, scurry, buzz, hover, scuttle, crawl, creep

 Tip   Play this outside if you can.

Cross-curricular link

PD: Movement and Space.

Do the digger dance

The children follow your instructions to work in pairs as driver and crane.

Aim

• To encourage children to use talk to give and follow instructions.

Preparation

• Look at cranes in real life if you can.

• Watch a video clip of cranes in action.

What to do

• Ask the children to find a space of their own big enough for them to stretch their arms out in all directions without touching anything, or anyone else.

• Children can practise moving like a crane, e. g.

'Stretch out your arms and then clasp your hands together to look like the arm of a digger or crane.'

'Keep your feet still, and move you 'crane' as far as you can.'

'Now practise shuffling your feet round as you move your 'crane' – but don't move away from your space.'

• Once they can act the part of the crane, give the children verbal instructions as if you were the driver:

Move your crane up high.

Turn your crane towards the door.

Bend your crane down to the ground.

Wait while someone fastens the big crate onto your hook.

Now slowly lift your crane. Don't drop the crate.

Turn towards . . . etc.

• Children can now work in pairs taking it in turn to be the crane or the driver, giving and following instructions.

Vocabulary

up, down, round, towards left, right

Tip　　Children could wear a 'hard hat' when they are the driver.

Cross-curricular link

CD: Developing Imagination and Imaginative Play.

What's inside?

 Children can investigate and photograph fruit to create a lift-the-flap book or display.

Aim

- To encourage children to use talk to organise and clarify their thinking.

Resources

- Fruit
- Sharp knife
- Camera
- Folded pieces of card and glue

Preparation

- Take some photographs of the fruit you have collected, one photograph for each piece of fruit.

What to do

- Encourage the children to look at the fruit and handle it carefully. Ask them to look, touch and smell as they investigate.
- Try to expand their vocabulary as they compare and describe the fruit, e. g.
  - Which is the heaviest/shiniest/hardest?
  - Has anyone eaten any of these fruits?
  - Can the children explain how it tastes?
- Tell the children you are going to cut the fruit in half. Ask them what they expect to find when the fruit is cut open, e. g. colour, juice or size of stone. Make sure everyone has a chance to explain their ideas.
- When the children are ready, cut the pieces of fruit in half. Let the children describe what they see, smell and feel.
  - Is it what you expected?
- Help the children take photographs of the inside of the fruit. When these are printed out, match them up with the photographs of the outside of the fruit. Stick the photograph of the outside of the fruit on the front of a folded piece of card, and the

photograph of the inside of the fruit can be stuck inside the fold.

- The folded cards can either be displayed on the wall to create an interactive display or stuck into a book to create a lift-the-flap book that the children will enjoy reading afterwards.

Vocabulary

hard, soft, smooth, furry, heavy, light, juice, flesh, skin, stone

Tip If you label the fruit this will help with the children's understanding of how print works.

Cross-curricular link

KUW: Exploration and Investigation.

How are you feeling?

Extend the children's vocabulary and understanding by reading the expression in different faces.

Aim

• To introduce new words into children's vocabulary.

Resources

• Pictures of people with various expressions

• Mirrors

What to do

• Explain that you are going to think about people's faces. Ask them what we see when we look at someone's face and listen to the children's answers.

• Explain that what we are feeling shows on our faces and this is called our expression.

• Illustrate by making a happy face and a sad face. Then encourage the children to use these expressions too.

• Show the children one of your pictures and encourage the children to explain how that person might be feeling, e.g.

  – The person might be looking shocked.

  – Can the children make any suggestions about why this person might the shocked?

  – Have they ever felt shocked?

  – Ask them to show you a shocked expression.

  – Suggest that it helps to think about something that makes you feel that way.

  Repeat the procedure with a different expression.

• Lay all the pictures out on the floor and hand out the mirrors.

• Let each child choose a picture and use the mirror to recreate that expression. Take it in turns to show each other their different expressions and talk about how the person in the picture is feeling and why.

Vocabulary

impatient, irritated, shocked, surprised, proud, smug, joyful, tired, worried, lonely, puzzled, angry, pleased, delighted, frightened

Tip   To extend this activity you could try linking two similar expressions and exploring the differences with the children, e. g. shocked and surprised.

Cross-curricular link

PSED: Self-confidence and Self-esteem.

Emergency! by Margaret Mayo (2)

Children describe the various emergencies and who will come and help.

Aim

• To use stories from books to focus children's attention on predictions and explanations.

Resources

• A copy of Mayo, M. (2003) *Emergency!*, London: Orchard Books

Preparation

• Read and enjoy the book with the children.

What to do

• Use the illustrations in the book to ask the children to describe each emergency.

  – Can they explain what has happened?

  – Can they suggest which emergency service will be needed?

  – Can they predict how the emergency service will help?

• The children might also talk about who has phoned for the emergency service, e.g.

  – Was it the man in the sinking boat or the lady on the beach with the umbrella?

• Use a toy telephone to let the children take turns to dial 999 and ask for the service required in the different scenarios shown in the book.

• Use the pictures of the emergency vehicles on the first and last pages of the book.

  – Can the children name each vehicle?

  – Do they know who drives each type of vehicle?

  – Can they remember which emergency each vehicle attended?

Vocabulary

police car, breakdown truck, ambulance, helicopter, snow plough, lifeboat, inflatable boat, police motorbike, fire-fighting plane, fire engine, crane

Tip   Be aware that this may be a sensitive topic if children have been involved in emergency situations.

Cross-curricular link

PSED: Sense of Community.

Chapter 3

Remember, reflect, retell

After the big parade

 Work with the children to create a display about a parade that they have seen.

Aim

- To remind the children of a parade by creating a display about it.

Resources

- Souvenirs and photographs of the parade
- Any video clips of a parade in your area
- Back your display board with paper or fabric and add a large label

Preparation

- Many festivals and ceremonies include a parade or procession. You may have a parade as part of your local school or village traditions. Perhaps you have even taken part.

What to do

- Show the video, share out the souvenirs and encourage the children to comment on them.
- Pose the following questions and give time for the children to think about their answers and join in the discussion.
  - What did you see?
  - What did you hear?
  - How did it make you feel?
- Allow time for the children to make paintings or collages of the performers in the parade.
  Cut out the paintings of people in the parade and fix them to the display board, pointing out that people are one behind the other in a parade. Work from left to right, to reinforce the convention of writing.
- Add any other items you have collected to your display.

Vocabulary

first, in front, behind, next to

Tip   Compare one parade with another if children have seen different ones.

Cross-curricular link

PSED: Sense of Community.

Once upon a time (1)

Children make some fairy-story puppets to retell their favourite stories.

Aim

- To use puppets to encourage children to retell stories.

Resources

- Wooden spoons
- Scraps of fabric and elastic bands
- Felt-tip pens and wool

Preparation

- Read the fairy tale that you want to focus on and identify the characters.
- Make your puppets of these characters:

  Use felt-pen to draw a face onto the bowl of the spoon.

  Add some wool 'hair' .

  Use elastic bands to hold some fabric 'clothes' in place over the handle.

What to do

- Read or tell the children the chosen fairy tale again. As you read, the children can act out the story with their puppets.
- Repeat the story. This time the children can add the words/speech of their character, as you pause in the telling of the story.
  - Can they make appropriate voices?
  - What would Grandma sound like?
  - What voice would the wolf use when he was pretending to be Grandma?
  - What voice did Goldilocks use when she was frightened at the end of the story?
- Children can now try to retell the whole story with their puppets.

Tip   If different groups of children focus on different stories you can soon collect a range of puppets to leave out for later use. Label some boxes, one for each set of characters.

Cross-curricular link

CLL: Story characters.

Once upon a time (2)

Let's tell a story together.

Aim

- To encourage children to use intonation and story language.

Resources

- A picture book of the story you want to retell （optional – see Tip）

Preparation

- Plenty of opportunities for listening to stories.

What to do

- Sit in a circle together and choose a favourite story that all the children know, e. g. *The Three Little Pigs*. Ask them if they can remember the story.
- Tell them you are going to retell the story together. Ask who would like to start. Prompt them to begin with 'Once upon a time . . . '
- When the first child has said a sentence let the next child carry on. Continue around the circle until the end of the story. If a child omits something, be ready to gently prompt them, e. g. 'Oh, don't forget to tell us what he built his house with.' If a child uses incorrect grammar, try to help them rephrase their words, e. g. 'I think you could say: So they both **ran** to the third little pig's house.' If a child struggles to recall the next event in the story, ask if anyone else can help.
- Encourage the children to use repeated phrases from the story, e. g. '*So he huffed and he puffed*'.
- The last child can be prompted to end with '*. . . and they lived happily ever after*'.

Vocabulary

once upon a time, *lived happily ever after*, and repeated phrases from the story of your choice

Tip   If the children find this game too difficult at first,   use a picture-book version of your story to prompt them.

Cross-curricular link

CLL: Story structure.

Swirling and whirling around

Talking about the magical effects the children can create with oil, washing-up liquid and food colouring.

Aim

• To prompt children's thinking and discussion through involvement in their play.

Resources

• One-litre plastic bottles – one between two children
• Cold water
• Vegetable oil
• Washing-up liquid
• Food colourings
• Pipettes

Preparation

• Make sure the children know how to use pipettes. Have some available for water play in the days before you want to do this activity.

What to do

• Half-fill a bottle with cold water. Drop some food colouring in – one or two drops only. Watch and talk about what you see.
• **EITHER:** Add some washing-up liquid – one or two drops. Watch and talk.
• **OR** Add some cooking oil – one or two drops. Watch and talk.
• Children can experiment with what they add, and the order in which they add things to the water. Be ready with your questions so that you can support their thinking.

Vocabulary

Useful questions include:

What are you doing?

What will you do next?

What do you think will happen?

What did you notice?

Is this the same as when you added . . . first?

Do you know why this happened?

What happens if you add more than one colour?

 Tip Demonstrate one variation only so that the children are free to use their own ideas for experimenting with the materials.

Cross-curricular link

KUW: Exploration and Investigation.

Birthday (1)

Helping children think about a story and what happens， before acting it out for themselves.

Aim

• To encourage children to respond to and retell stories.

Resources

• Hughes S.（1985）*Alfie Gives a Hand*, London： Collins Picture Lions.

Preparation

• Read the story to the children.

• Discuss with the children:

  – Why Alfie takes his comfort blanket to the party.

  – How Bernard behaves at the party.

• Keep asking the children:

  – What happens next in the story?

  – How does she/he feel?

What to do

• Let the children choose who will be Alfie， Bernard， Min and others at the party. The adult can be Bernard's mother.

• Act out the birthday party.

  – Alfie arrives with his blanket and gives his present to Bernard.

  – All the children play with bubbles， then Bernard pops Min's bubble and she cries.

  – They sit down to tea and sing to Bernard.

  – Bernard frightens Min.

  – Alfie is holding Bernard's hand but Min won't join the circle.

  – Alfie puts down his blanket so he can hold Min's hand too.

  – Everyone plays Ring-a-ring-o'-roses.

• Change roles and try acting out the party scene again.

Vocabulary

worried, sad, shocked, frightened, kind, happy

Tip How does Alfie give a hand? Do the children understand this also means to help?

Cross-curricular link

PSED: Self-confidence and Self-esteem.

Birthday (2)

 Start with a well-known story and have fun suggesting different outcomes.

Aim

To encourage children to predict possible endings to stories and events.

Resources

Hughes, S. (1985) *Alfie Gives a Hand*, London: Collins Picture Lions.

Preparation

- Read the story to the children and discuss Alfie, Min and Bernard's feelings and behaviour.

What to do

- Ask the children what might change if something different happened.
  - What if . . . Alfie had been too worried to go to the party?
  - What if . . . Min had not been scared of Bernard?
  - What if . . . Bernard had been sent to his room to calm down?

  How would the birthday party have turned out then?
- Choose one of the ideas to try. Let the children choose who will be Alfie, Bernard, Min and others at the party. The adult can be Bernard's mother.
- Act out the different birthday party and afterwards compare the outcome with the original story.

Vocabulary

worried, sad, shocked, frightened, kind, happy, sorry, mean, friendly, angry

Tip This would make a good follow-on activity from Birthday (1), p. 84.

Cross-curricular link

PSED: Self-confidence and Self-esteem.

Roses are red

Model how to change the words of a traditional rhyme to send positive messages to each other.

Aim

• To help children make up their own rhyme.

Resources

• Make an enlarged copy of the traditional rhyme

   Roses are red

   Violets are blue

   Sugar is sweet

   And so are you

Preparation

• Teach the children the traditional rhyme.

• If possible, show them roses and violets.

What to do

• Sit in a class circle, and read the traditional rhyme to the children. Let the children follow the words on the enlarged copy.

• Tell the children you are going to change one line of the rhyme to make a new one. Explain that you are going to use names from children in the class, and that you are going to use the rhyme to say kind things to each other.

• Demonstrate by choosing one child's name to include in the third line of the rhyme. Include another child by pointing at them as you say the last line, e. g.

   Roses are red

   Violets are blue

   James is happy

   And so are you

• Encourage the children to repeat the rhyme with you so that everyone points to any other child when they say the last line.

• Think of other kind things to say about each other. Use these ideas in the rhyme and let everyone repeat them.

404

Vocabulary

happy, friendly, helpful, kind, cheerful, smart, clever

Tip With more able children you could write down their ideas for them to select and use in their own rhymes.

Cross-curricular link

PSED: Making Relationships.

Take three

 Children make up a story together based on three random objects they select.

Aim

• To help children use language to imagine roles and experiences.

Resources

• Small world toys, e.g. farm or zoo animals, vehicles, dolls' house furniture and people.
• Box or basket.

Preparation

• Collect together about ten objects and place them in an attractive box or basket.

What to do

• Sit in a circle with a small group of children.
• Choose one child to close their eyes and reach into the basket.
  Ask them to choose one object and then open their eyes and tell everyone what it is.
  Repeat this with two other children.
  Place your three objects in the middle of your circle.
• Another child can then choose the setting for your story. It could be e.g.
    the seaside
    the cupboard under the stairs
    a strange planet
• Encourage imaginative ideas.
• Explain to the children that you are all going to help to make up a story involving the three chosen objects and the special place you have decided on.
• Remind the children of familiar story openings, e.g.
    One day . . .
    Once upon a time . . .
    In a land far away . . .

- Now take it in turns to make up a story, adding to each other's ideas as you go along. When you reach the end, remind the children of familiar endings, e. g.

  And they all lived happily ever after.

  And that was the end of their exciting day.

Tip　　Try sitting in your role-play area, and using that as the setting for the story.

Cross-curricular link

CD: Developing Imagination and Imaginative Play.

A Bigger Splash
by David Hockney

Who jumped in?   Children look carefully at a painting,   describing what they see and think about it.

Aim

• To give children an opportunity to speak clearly,   showing awareness of the listener.

Resources

• A copy of *A Bigger Splash* by David Hockney.

Preparation

• Tell the children they are going to take turns talking about a picture.

• Explain that there are no right or wrong answers.

• Remind them to listen carefully to what others say.

What to do

• Show a group of children the picture,   and ask everyone to tell you something they can see in the picture. The children might mention：
  - swimming pool
  - blue sky
  - seats round the pool
  - modern house
  - diving board
  - And the splash!

• Now ask the children to think about the picture. Prompt them with questions such as：

    'How would it feel to be there? '
    'What's the weather like? '
    'What would the water feel like? '
    'How was the splash made? '
    'Who made the splash? '

'Where are the people? '

'Who lives there? '

'Where do they think this place is? '

- Encourage the children to develop their ideas by asking:

'Why? '

'What makes you think that? '

Vocabulary

splash, spray, dive, diving board, swimming, water, deep, pool, blue, hot, sun, holiday

Tip The children can go on to share their experiences about holidays or swimming.

Cross-curricular link

KUW: Place.

All Aboard by Zoe Kakolyris

 Children play 'I spy' using a busy picture.

Aim

• To provide a stimulating focus for children's discussion.

Resources

• A copy of *All Aboard* by Zoe Kakolyris. See **www. zoes-world. co. uk** for details.

What to do

• Ask the children to look carefully at the picture, choose someone special and work out what they are doing. Start the game by saying, 'I spy a girl doing a handstand, can you see her too?'

• Everyone takes a turn to describe what the person they've chosen is doing. The rest of the group should look carefully and try to find the person.

• Now encourage them to speculate:

 – Where is the train going?

 – Where have all the children come from?

 – Can you see any adults? Why not?

 – Can you see any animals?

 – Where is the train driver?

• It may be appropriate to extend the game further:

Describe your favourite person in the painting by their appearance, e. g.

 – Boy or girl?

 – Hair?

 – What are they wearing?

 – How old are they?

• Can you think of a name for them?

Vocabulary

jumping, eating, dancing, singing, sitting, walking, talking, laughing, climbing, lying

 Tip   The children can go on to make a shared picture. Everyone draws a person on a large sheet of paper. *What will your person be doing?*

Cross-curricular link

CD: Being Creative.

Create a character

 The children have fun dressing up in a uniform as you photograph them behind a picture frame.

Aim

• To encourage children to use their own experience of the world.

Resources

• Dressing-up clothes

• An old picture frame

• Camera

• A selection of non-fiction books about people and their jobs

• Access to an Internet provider suitable for Early Years children, e. g. www. espresso. co. uk

• Writing program on a computer, or paper and pens

Preparation

• Read non-fiction books about real people.

What to do

• Working with a small group of children, look together at some of the non-fiction books about people. Use the Internet to find out more about people's work. Do the children know any nurses, doctors, police or firefighters? Encourage them to share their experiences.

• Let the children dress up as someone new. Take it in turns to pose behind the old picture frame. Photograph the children as if they were pictures in the frame. The encourage them to talk about their character.

  – Who are they?

  – What is their job?

  – Where do they live?

  – How old are they?

• Help them write a sentence about their character, e. g.

    My name is Saskia and I am a firefighter.

You might want them to do this on the computer or you to act as a scribe. Remember to help them re-read their writing afterwards.

- Create a class book by collecting together several photographs and sentences. The children will enjoy reading it again and again.

Vocabulary

job, work, uniform

Tip Try to challenge stereotypes when selecting books and information about people and the jobs they do.

Cross-curricular link

PSED: Sense of Community.

Traditional tales

 Fun in the role-play area starting from a traditional tale.

Aim

- To provide an opportunity for children to enact stories as the basis for further imaginative play.

Resources

- A copy of any of the traditional tales
- Dressing-up clothes
- Role-play items to match your chosen story

Preparation

- Make some simple adaptations to your role-play area, e. g.
  - Put out three bowls and chairs of different sizes
  - Create a bridge across a strip of blue paper

What to do

- Retell a traditional story to the children, encouraging them to join in with repeated phrases, e. g.

  '*I'll huff and I'll puff and I'll blow your house down.*'
- Take a small group of children into the prepared role-play area. Ask them who they think might live here.
- Encourage them to use the events of the story in their play. Try taking on a role yourself, e. g.

  '*I'm going to sit by this bridge and see who tries to cross it.*'

  Pick up the wolf mask and invite the children to be the three pigs while you try to blow their house down.
- Remember to use stories that are relevant to your children; perhaps you might use a scenario from the story of Rama and Sita at Diwali time.

Vocabulary

Language from the different stories

Tip Include opportunities for reading and writing during these story-based activities, e. g. leave a note on the table from Mummy asking Red Riding Hood to take the basket of fruit to Grandma.

Cross-curricular link

CLL: Story events.

The Surprise Party
by Pat Hutchins

 Play Chinese Whispers with literary phrases from a well-known story.

Aim

• To encourage children to play with language.

Resources

• Hutchins, P. (1993) *The Surprise Party*, London: Red Fox Books.

Preparation

• Read the story to the children to help them appreciate how the message changes.

• Discuss the meaning of some unfamiliar vocabulary, e.g. hoeing the parsley or raiding the poultry.

• Look at how the words I'M HAVING A PARTY are written.

   Is Rabbit still whispering his message?

What to do

• Explain to the children that when you whisper it is not always easy to hear clearly. Tell them you're going to play a whispering game where messages are often mixed up and that's part of the fun!

• When everyone is sitting in a circle, the adult whispers one of the phrases from the book to the child on their left, e.g.

   '*Rabbit is hoeing the parsley tomorrow*'

• That child then whispers the message to the next child, and so on round the circle.

• When the message gets back to the adult she repeats it aloud for everyone to hear.

• Now tell the children what the original message was.

   – Has it changed?

Vocabulary

Phrases from the book.

Tip You'll have more fun if you use a complicated phrase which is more likely to be changed than an easily recognisable message like 'I'm having a party tomorrow'.

Cross-curricular link

PSED: Making Relationships.

What's going to happen?

To provide an opportunity for the children to think about stories and speculate about what happens next.

Aim

• To help children to draw conclusions and speculate about the plot of a story.

Resources

• Burningham, J. (1979) *Mr Gumpy's Motorcar*, London: Picture Puffins.
• Burningham, J. (1979) *Mr Gumpy's Outing*, London: Picture Puffins.

Preparation

• Read the stories yourself before discussing them with the children.

What to do

• Read the story of Mr Gumpy's outing in the boat.
  Show the children the picture of everyone in the boat when they were going along happily.
  Ask children to guess what they think will happen next.
• If they suggest the boat will sink, ask them why that might happen, then continue to the end of the story.
• Count up how many people and animals were in the boat before it tipped.
• Look at each picture in turn.
  – Can they remember what Mr Gumpy said to the children and each animal?
  – Why do they think everyone wanted to go in the boat?
  – Would they like to have been there?
• Now show the children the second book about Mr Gumpy.
  Read the first two pages then ask the children what they think might happen next.
  When they guess that the children and animals will want to join him, carry on with the story.
• Stop reading when they are driving along happily.
  Ask the children what they think might happen.
  They may use ideas from the previous book or they may make other suggestions.

- Read on to the next pages until the rain starts, then ask for the children's ideas:
  - Do they notice that the car has no roof?
  - Does anyone think about what will happen to the track across the field in the rain?
- When the wheels began to spin and Mr Gumpy needs someone to push:
  - Who do the children think will help and why?
- Read on until they get the car going and the sun comes out.
- Tell the children that the ending is not going to be exactly the same as the first story.
  - How do they think the story will end?
- Read to the end.
  - Were you right? Did it end as you thought it would?

Tip This activity can easily be adapted to other books that have one character appearing in both stories.

Cross-curricular link
CLL: Story events.

Nursery rhyme competition

 A team game to show how many nursery rhymes your children know.

Aim

- To encourage children to recall and enjoy familiar nursery rhymes.

What to do

- Divide the children into three groups, each with an adult.

  Explain that you are going to have a competition to find out who knows the most nursery rhymes.

  Give each group a number. Group One has to be ready with a nursery rhyme.

- Start by encouraging everyone to count to 10 keeping a steady beat. As soon as '10' has been said Group One has to say their nursery rhyme together.

- As soon as they stop they start the count, 1, 2, 3 . . . . .

  When they reach '10', Group Two should immediately say their chosen rhyme.

- Children then start the count to 10 again, which is the signal for Group Three to say their first rhyme.

- Continue in this way, round and round the groups until:

  - One group repeats a rhyme that has already been said, or

  - One group can't think of another rhyme

  That group is now 'out'.

- The competition continues between the other two groups until a winner is declared. Everyone can still join in with the counting and the arbitration!

 Tip   Encourage the children to use any number rhymes and other favourite rhymes that they know.

Cross-curricular link

PSED: Dispositions and Attitudes.

Part 2

Reading

Plan an environment that is rich in signs, symbols, notices, numbers, words, rhymes, books ... allow plenty of time for children to browse and share these resources with adults and other children.
Practice Guidance for the Early Years Foundation Stage, May 2008, p. 42

Chapter 4

World of books

Candles (1)

Explore the magic of candlelight as you read books about festivals of light.

Aim

- To encourage children to add to their first-hand experience of the world through books.

Resources

- Books about festivals with a focus on light, e. g.

    Zucker, J. (2002), *Eight Candles to Light: A Chanukah Story*, London: Frances Lincoln

    Zucker, J. (2005), *Lighting a Lamp: A Divali Story*, London: Frances Lincoln

    Zucker, J. (2005), *Lanterns and Firecrackers: A Chinese New Year Story*, London: Frances Lincoln

    Holub, J. (2000) *Light the Candles: A Hannukah Lift-the-flap Book*, London: Picture Puffins

Preparation

- Set up a display within your book area.
- Use a dark fabric to cover a table or drape from a noticeboard.
- Against this, display some candles, candlesticks, lanterns and lamps that represent those used in the different festivals.

What to do

- Plan your reading session for when it is getting dark.
  Switch off the main lights and light a lamp or a candle in your reading area.
  Read one of the books each day.
- Ask the children what they remember about the previous day's story. Encourage the children to compare the different ways that lights are used in these festivals.
  - What do they notice that is the same?
  - When do they light candles at home?
- There are many festivals that feature candles and light when you could introduce this activity – Divali, Hannukah, Christmas, birthdays.

Vocabulary

light, lamp, lantern, candle

Tip If you want to light a candle, only do so when the children are all seated quietly with you. Stand your candle in a metal biscuit tin that has been filled with sand, and place it on a firm surface out of the children's reach. Have your fire blanket close by you. Pass the matches to another adult to put away as soon as you have used them.

Cross-curricular link

KUW: Communities.

Candles (2)

The children read a rhyme together then adapt it to their own names.

Aim

- To encourage children to begin to 'read' by themselves.

Resources

- Book containing the nursery rhyme *Jack Be Nimble*
- A large version of the rhyme

Preparation

- Say the rhyme together so that the children become familiar with it, and maybe learn to say it themselves.

What to do

- Say the rhyme together and add some actions.

    Jack be nimble – dance around on tiptoes

    Jack be quick – stand on the spot and jog as fast as you can

    Jack jump over the candlestick – jump up high

- Sit together and look at your large version of the rhyme.

    Draw the children's attention to the layout of a poem on the page.

    Did they notice that each line is short?

- Say the rhyme together, with you pointing to the words.

    Sometimes, you keep quiet and let the children supply the next word.

    Individual children might like to come out and read it out loud to the group.

- Now form a circle.

    Hold hands and sing and act it again, but with a different name each time, e. g.

    All be nimble

    All be quick

    'Freddie' jump over the candlestick

    Listen for your name. Only that child jumps into the centre of the circle of children.

Vocabulary

nimble, quick

 Tip Make an old-fashioned candlestick from cardboard tubes and a paper plate and use this in the centre of the circle for children to jump over.

Cross-curricular link

PD: Movement and Space.

Candles (3)

 The children make a book about your festivals of light.

Aim

• To create a class book that the children can read.

Resources

• Camera
• Printer
• Photograph album

Preparation

• Take photographs of the children with any candles, lamps, lanterns, etc. that they have used during a festival shared in their home.

  – You could borrow the light from the family and take the photograph in your setting.

  – You could borrow a photograph from home.

What to do

• Help the children to place one photograph on each page of the album.
• Encourage the children to create a short sentence about their own picture and help them to write it, or write it for them.

  Cut out the sentence and fix it in the album next to the photograph.

• Decide together on a suitable title and make a front cover and add the book to your candle display.

  Read the book together.

  Individual children could read their own page to the group.

• When you have changed your display, keep it in your book-box so that the children have access to it, and can read it whenever they choose.

Vocabulary

children's names, festival names

Tip   If you use an album with a sticky plastic sheet over each page, it makes it easy for the children to mount their own work.

Cross-curricular link

PSED: Sense of Community.

All the little ducks

 Work with the children to set up a springtime display featuring ducks.

Aim

• To enable the children to experience a range of books on one topic.

Resources

• Books about ducks
• Display board and surface area
• Yellow fabric or paper
• Pictures and models of ducks

Preparation

• Cover the display board with appropriate paper. Yellow is an obvious choice. Display some pictures of ducks and the words of 'Five Little Ducks' (See 'Five Little Ducks' activity on page 629 in Chapter 9: Making a Book)
• Find four or five books about ducks. You could even put some yellow cushions in your book area to continue the yellow theme.

What to do

• Show the children your chosen books about ducks. Stand them on the shelf, or on a table in your book area. Make sure that the children can reach them.
• Over the week, read all of these books to the children. Encourage the children to read/look at the books themselves.
• Children can add other duck books to the collection – ones from your book area or ones from home.
• Children can add their own drawings and paintings of ducks to the wall display, bring in toy ducks or make models of ducks to stand on the shelf with the books.

 Tip Include some non-fiction books as well as stories and rhymes.

Cross-curricular link

KUW: Exploration and Investigation.

How to...

Help the children to create some recipe books by taking photographs as you cook.

Aim

- To help children learn that information can be retrieved from books.

Resources

- Digital camera
- Sticky labels

Preparation

- Decide what you are going to cook, and collect ingredients and utensils.
- Share some recipe books with the children so that they start to recognise their use.

What to do

- At each stage of your cooking process choose one child to take a photograph.

  Aim to have:
    - The ingredients
    - Children putting aprons on
    - Each stage of cooking
    - Washing up/tidying away
    - The finished food

- Help the children to print out the photos.

  Lay them out so that everyone can see them.

  Are they in the right order?

- Ask the children to sort the photographs into the correct sequence. Explain why this is important.

  'What would happen if you cooked this in the wrong order?'

- Now, punch holes in them and tie them together.

  Help the children to form a simple sentence for each picture.

  Scribe it onto a sticky label, then each child can stick one onto the relevant photograph.

What's missing? A title, or cover.

Children can make this and add it to their book of instructions.

Tip   Do this each time you cook to build up a recipe section in your children's book corners. Perhaps they could borrow a recipe and take it home to try making it again.

Cross-curricular link

KUW: ICT.

Holidays (1)

Make a collection of postcards from holiday destinations, sort these into sets with the children and create a display.

Aim
• To create an environment for your children that is rich in print using labels and books.

Resources
• A collection of postcards

Preparation
• Talk to the children about holidays and day trips out.
  Ask where they have been.
• Encourage them to bring in postcards of places they have visited.
  Put up a notice for the parents and allow a few days to collect all contributions.

What to do
• When you have a good collection of postcards spread them out on the floor.
  Let a small group of children explore the images on the cards.
  Use this as another opportunity for talking and sharing experiences.
• Then using sorting rings or large sheets of paper sort the postcards into three or four sets. Ideas could include: seaside, hotel, theme park or village.
  Encourage the children to make decisions about sorting, and be accepting of their ideas.
• Ask the children for suggestions for a label for each set. What should it be?
  Let the children watch as you write out some appropriate labels for their sets.
• Display the postcards in their sets.
  Now get the children to find books that link to their sets and add these to your display. Try to include both fiction and non-fiction books.
• Encourage other children to come and look at the display.
  Explain that the postcards have been sorted into sets.
  – Can they read the labels or work out what they might say?

Vocabulary

seaside, mountain, lake, town, village, hotel, pool, theme park

Tip   Read some of these books during story time.

Cross-curricular links

PSRN: Calculating.

My tune

 Children compose and read their own music.

Aim

• To provide an opportunity for children to practise tracking symbols from left to right.

Resources

• Strips of paper
• Sticky circles
• Instruments

Preparation

• Fold each strip of paper into four sections to make a line.

What to do

• Give each child a strip of paper and three sticky circles. Explain to the children:

'You can stick one of your circles into one of the sections of your paper. Choose any section you like. '

'Now stick another circle in another section, and the third circle in a different section. '

'You should have three sections with circles, and one empty section. '

• Explain to the children:

'When you see a circle you will play your instrument. '

'When the section is empty you will rest. '

Demonstrate with an instrument so everyone understands.

• Using a percussion instrument the children will now play their own piece of music. Starting at the left and moving along to the right of the strip of paper, the child will play one beat for each circle, and rest for the space.

• You count a strong, 1-2-3-4 rhythm to help them keep time.
Several children can all play their own tunes at the same time, as you count.

- Once they are familiar with this process let the children:
  - swap strips with a friend, or
  - turn their strip round and play the new tune.

Variations for more able children

- Place the strips one under the other and play a longer tune. An adult can point to each strip in turn to keep children together.
- Make some strips that have eight sections and six circles.

Tip   If you want to use chime bars, let the children choose from C, G, D, A, E. These form the pentatonic scale and will always harmonise.

Cross-curricular link

CD: Creating Music and Dance.

Story places

 Using picture books that fit in with your theme to help your children think about settings for stories.

Aim

- To help children begin to be aware that stories have settings.

Resources

- Several story books on your chosen theme, e.g. setting: in the garden.

  Use, e.g. Butterworth, N. and Inkpen, M. (2006) *Jasper's Beanstalk*, London: Hodder Children's Books;

  Carle, E. (2002) *The Very Hungry Caterpillar*, London: Puffin Books;

  Carle, E. (2009) *The Tiny Seed*, London: Simon & Schuster Children's;

  French, V. and Bartlett, A. (1995) *Oliver's Vegetables*, London: Hodder Children's Books.

What to do

- Show the children the chosen story books and remind the children of the stories.
- Take one of the books and ask the children where the story happens. Repeat this for the other books.

    'Who notices anything?'

    'All of these books take place in . . .'
- Explain that this is called the 'setting'. It is where the story happens. Think about what you might find in this setting, e.g. in the garden you may find flowers, beetles, swings or a sandpit.
- What about other settings? What do you think you might find if the story was set in . . .

    . . . the forest: wolf, trees, birds

    . . . the sea: mermaids, shells, fish

    . . . a house: mummy, bed, television
- Can the children think of any books with these settings?

    Children may be able to look through your book box to find something they remember that has one of these settings.

Read some of these books each day.

Leave them out together so that children can look at them whenever they want to.

Vocabulary

setting

Tip Your starting point could be any theme/setting which fits with your current work.

Cross-curricular link

CLL: Story setting.

My grandma

 Make a collection of books for the children to think about their own grandma.

Aim

- To encourage children to add their own experience of the world.

Resources

- A copy of *Little Red Riding Hood*.
- Other stories that feature grandmas, e. g.

  Hedderwick, M. (2010) *Katie Morag and the Two Grandmothers*, London: Red Fox Books;

  Butterwick, N. (2008) *My Grandma is Wonderful*, London: Walker Books;

  Exley, H. (2006) *Me and My Grandma*, Watford: Exley Publications.

Preparation

- Ask the children to collect books that have a grandma in them.

What to do

- Ask the children to retell the story of Little Red Riding Hood.

  Show them a picture of the grandma in your copy of the story.

- Let the children look at the pictures in other books and find pictures of grandmas.

  Ask the children if they've got a grandma (be sensitive to alternative names).

  Collect names they call their grandma, e. g. Nana, Granny ...

- What's special about their grandma?

  – What is she like?

  – What does she do for them?

  – Does she come to visit them?

  – Does she look like a grandma in the story books?

    What do they like doing with their grandma?

    Can they walk from their house to grandma's house like Red Riding Hood does?

- Do the children understand the relationship between them and their grandma, e. g.

- Is she Daddy's mum or Mummy's mum?

- Can they tell you if they are a granddaughter or a grandson?

Perhaps you could show photographs of you as a child with your grandma.

- Type out and display all the alternative names for 'Grandma' (see Tip).
Display them with the story books you have collected.

- If the children are keen to explore this further, maybe you could make a book collection about grandads too.

Vocabulary

Grandma, Granny, Nana, Nannie

Tip
Display the names used for 'Grandma' in the languages spoken by families in your setting to raise awareness of different languages and scripts, e. g.

Mamie (French), Abuela (Spanish), Oma (German), Babcia (Polish)

Cross-curricular link

KUW: Time.

Books at home

Everyone reads the books they have taken home and votes for their favourite.

Aim

- To emphasise the importance of parents reading with children.

Resources

- A collection of books, e. g. books about bears.
- A3 sheets of paper showing the title of each book, one book per sheet.
- Stickers in three colours.

Preparation

- Select a set of seven or eight books linked by a theme.
- Display a notice informing parents about the special books on loan this week.
- Make an attractive display with the books for children to choose from.
- Put the A3 sheets in an accessible position for children to record which book they have borrowed.

What to do

- Collect a group of children together to look at the books. Let them handle the books and talk about those they know and those they'd like to read.
- Tell them they can take one of these books home for their parents to read with them. Explain that you are going to find out which books most people enjoy best.
- Help the children choose a book each for taking home and write their name under the book's title on the A3 sheet.
- Next day, encourage parents and children to select a sticker to indicate their opinion of the book they have read, e. g.

  green: excellent – really enjoyed

  yellow: good – worth reading

  red: OK – not my favourite

- Then introduce the books to another group of children. Repeat the activity until everyone has taken at least one book home.

- Encourage the children to count up the coloured stickers collected for each book. Which one is the class favourite?

Vocabulary

excellent, really enjoyed, worth reading, recommend, favourite, interesting

Tip   Try to provide dual-language books to match the language spoken in the home, and be sensitive to the fact that not all families are literate – you can always do this activity with helpers in the setting if that is more appropriate.

Cross-curricular link

PSED: Self-confidence and Self-esteem.

Who said that?

 Using traditional stories to introduce your children to speech bubbles.

Aim

• To create a display that encourages children to learn about print and talk about stories.

Resources

• A selection of familiar story books, e.g. traditional tales.
• Large speech bubbles cut from A3 pieces of paper.

Preparation

• Write in the speech bubbles some repeated phrases used by characters, e.g.

   What big eyes you've got, Grandma

   Who's been eating my porridge?

   Little pig, little pig, let me come in

   Someone's been eating my porridge and it's all gone!

• Display these in your book area with the selection of books close by. Use the words 'Who said that?' as a title for your display.

What to do

• Collect together a small group of children. Ask them if they know what speech bubbles are. Some children may recognise them from cartoon stories or comics.

• Explain that speech bubbles show you the words people say. Tell them that these speech bubbles are from stories they know. Point to the title words as you ask – 'I wonder if anyone will know who said that?'

• Now read one of the speech bubbles together.

   'Can anyone think who said that?'

   Read the other speech bubbles together and establish the character and story.

• Encourage the children to find the characters in the story books provided. Help them display these with the speech bubbles.

• Can anyone think of a different example of speech from one of the stories? If possible, extend your display with your children's suggestions.

Vocabulary

speech bubble, talk, words, say, said, character

Tip

Pointing at the words as you read the displayed words will help the children recall the words and encourage them to join in.

Cross-curricular link

CLL: Story characters.

We're going to the zoo

Help the children to choose and photocopy their own version of a story.

Aim

• To help the children develop an understanding of the structure of stories.

Resources

• Prepared pages of a story （see Preparation） .

• Access to a photocopier.

Preparation

• On individual sheets of A4 paper write:

an opening sentence， e. g. *One fine day we all went to the zoo.*

a closing sentence， e. g. *And we all went home for tea.*

and several pages with the name of an animal， possibly a picture and a number， e. g. *two elephants*

For older children， have a choice of opening and closing sentences.

• Put each sheet into a plastic wallet and store in a ringbinder.

What to do

• Explain to the children that they are going to make their own story.

'What's a good way to start a story? '

Listen to their suggestions.

• With the children， photocopy today's beginning and give them each their own copy. Help the children to read it.

• Now look at the collection of animal pages.

'Who can read what they say? '

Encourage all of the children to have a go.

• They need to choose three of the animal pages and photocopy them.

Add these to their opening sentence to begin to make a book.

• Now talk about the fact that stories have to end.

'Who can think of some endings? '

Photocopy and hand out today's ending. Read it together.

- Fix all your pages together to make your own book.

- On another day, repeat this process to make a different story, e. g. *We're going on a picnic and we'll take ...* and gradually build up your resource file of story ideas.

Tip Keep the pages in the plastic covering when the children are photocopying to protect the master copies.

Cross-curricular link

KUW: ICT.

Who am I?

 Photograph the children dressed up as story-book characters and make an appropriate speech bubble to display alongside.

Aim

• To encourage children to retell narratives and discuss characters.

Resources

• A selection of familiar stories e. g. traditional tales.

• Dressing-up clothes.

• Camera.

• Paper for speech bubbles or writing program on a computer.

Preparation

• Introduce the children to speech bubbles using the activity 'Who said that?', p. 132

• Make sure the children are familiar with the stories in your selection.

What to do

• Work with a small group of children.

Ask them to choose a favourite story from the selection.

Encourage the children to retell one of their favourite stories.

Can they tell you the main events of the story in sequence?

• Let them dress up as one of the characters and talk about their chosen character.

Take a photograph of the child dressed up.

• Now tell each child they must think of something that their character says in the story.

Help them choose a well-known or repeated phrase.

Either let the children help you type the words onto the computer, then print the character's words and cut them into a speech bubble.

Or let the children watch you write their words onto a paper speech bubble.

• Display the speech bubble next to the child's photograph.

Can the other children guess which story-book character they are?

• Use the words 'Who am I?' as a title for your display.

Vocabulary

dialogue from your chosen stories

Tip   Choose stories that are suitable for your class and reflect their cultural diversity.

Cross-curricular link

CLL: Story characters.

Outdoor reading

 Take your book corner outside on a fine day.

Aim

- To create an attractive book area where children and adults can enjoy books together.

Resources

- Cushions
- Blankets
- Books
- Movable book trolley, unit, shelf or boxes

What to do

- Tell the children that it's such a fine day that you think it would be fun to make a book corner outside.
- Take a small group of children outside to talk about the best area to use. Encourage the children to justify their ideas and listen to each other's suggestions.

  'Do we want it to in the sun? Why not? '

  'What about sitting on the path? Would it be comfortable? '

  'Do we want to be near the bikes or the doorway? Would it be safe? '

  'What about under the tree or canopy? Is it a quiet place? '

- When you have chosen the best place, help the children plan what they need and, if possible, involve the children in moving things outside. Let the children put the items in place to make it a comfortable, safe place to read. Do they want any special rules about how to use the books outside?
- Then let them sit down and enjoy the books.

Vocabulary

cushion, blanket, trolley, box, unit, shelf, book

Tip　　　Make time for the group who have set up the book area to tell the other children about it.

Cross-curricular link

PSED: Behaviour and Self-control.

Bookmarks (1)

Make a bookmark to help your children keep their place as they read.

Aim

- To create a resource to help children with their reading.

Resources

- Glitter
- Laminating sheets and laminator

What to do

- Help the children to sprinkle glitter onto a sheet of laminating film. Fold over the top sheet and laminate according to your own equipment.
- Cut this into strips which can be used as bookmarks. Keep them in an attractive pot near your books for anyone to use.
- Sit with a group of children. Make sure that each child has a book and a bookmark.
- Practise using the bookmark to point to the words you are reading. Use this time to reinforce reading from left to right, and moving from the top to the bottom of the page.

Tip   Because these bookmarks are almost transparent they don't hinder the children who are able to 'read ahead'. They can still see the next word or spot that the sentence continues onto the next line.

Cross-curricular link

KUW: Designing and Making.

Bookmarks (2)

 Children make their own special lolly stick bookmark.

Aim

• To create a personal marker and encourage children to read.

Resources

• Lolly sticks

• Variation 1： Felt-tip pens；Variation 2： Scraps of felt and wool， and old gloves

What to do

• Choose which idea to use with your children today.

Variation 1 – for children who can write their own names：

• Help the children to write their name along the length of the lolly stick using the felt-tip pens. Practise on a piece of scrap paper， if necessary.

• Leave a little space at the end of their name， where they can add a small drawing， e. g. a flower， flag or car.

Variation 2 – involves making a finger puppet：

• Cut the fingers from the gloves and give one to each child. These should be 2 – 3 cm long.

• Help the children to stick features onto their finger puppet， e. g.

    – black spots onto a red finger to make a ladybird.

    – two large eyes on a green finger to make a frog.

    – nose， eyes and mouth with some wool hair， to make a face.

• Push the lolly stick inside the finger puppet and glue in place.

 Tip   Children can use their lolly stick bookmarks to identify the book they have chosen to take home today.

Cross-curricular link

KUW： Designing and Making.

Chapter 5

Finding out

Garden centre (2)

Using labels to identify the parts of a sunflower and help children read.

Aim

• To help children understand the concept of a word.

Resources

• Carle, E. (2009) *The Tiny Seed*, London: Simon & Schuster Children's

• A pot of sunflowers

• Yellow and green tissue paper, PVA glue, edible seeds (e.g. pumpkin seeds)

• Some large, and some small, labels cut from card

Preparation

• Read and enjoy the story of *The Tiny Seed* by Eric Carle. Look carefully and think how Eric Carle might have created the pictures in it.

• Allow time for the children to look carefully at the sunflowers. Can they identify the different parts of the plants?

What to do

• Work as a group to create a huge sunflower collage for your wall.
Ask the children to identify each part of the flower in turn. Write the word clearly on a label and stick it next to the flower part with removable adhesive.

• Read the labels together. Look at the initial letter for each one as you do so.

• Remove the labels, mix them up and hand them out to the children.
Ask each one in turn to read their label and tell you where it goes. Stick them back up. Repeat until everyone has had a turn. Start with your more able children to give the others a chance to learn or remember what the labels say.

• Leave out some sets of small labels using the same words so that children can choose to make small collage flowers and stick on labels. These could be used in your Garden Centre role play or as a 'catalogue' of different flowers that the customers could buy.

Vocabulary

stem,   leaf,   bud,   flower,   seeds

Tip   The arrangement of seeds in a sunflower is quite complicated.   Point it out to
the children but don't expect them to be able to repeat it in their own work.

Cross-curricular link

KUW: Exploration and Investigation.

What's in your name?

Have fun with this letter recognition game as the children respond to the letters in their names by stepping towards the leader.

Aim

• To help the children remember the letters in their name.

Resources

• A set of plastic letters in a bag – as long as you have all the ones in this group of children's names you may not want to use all 26 letters of the alphabet.

• Scrap paper for writing their names.

Preparation

• Check that everyone knows the letters in their own name.

• The children can write them out to take with them when they play the game in case they need to check.

What to do

• Choose someone to be the leader. This adult or child stands at the front with the bag of letters. The other children line up facing the leader, about six or seven strides away.

• The leader reaches into a bag and picks out a letter at random. Do they know the letter's name? If not, be ready to help.

• The leader then calls out the letter's name and holds it up for everyone to see. If any child has that letter in their name they take one stride forward towards the leader.

   'If you have two of this letter, you take two strides.'

• The leader continues picking and calling out letter names. The first child to reach the leader takes over as leader. Everyone else returns to the base line.

Tip   An adult needs to monitor the game for accuracy and to help those who are still learning how to spell their own name.

Cross-curricular link

PSED: Making Relationships.

Breakfast time

Using cereal boxes to help children recognise words and symbols.

Aim

• To encourage the children to recall words or symbols that they see frequently.

Resources

• Cereal packets
• Pictures of cereal plants or containers of seeds: use oats, rice, wheat and corn
• Hoops and labels

Preparation

• Set out hoops with one picture or container of grain and the appropriate label in each.

What to do

• Spend some time looking at the cereal packets. Can the children identify the different cereals by their packaging and labelling? Talk about, e. g.
  – which one you like best
  – which one you had today
  – which one you've never tasted
• Show the children the pictures of cereal plants or the containers of seeds from the plants. Explain to them that the cereals in the packets are made from the seeds/grains of these plants.
• Look at and identify one of the plants, e. g. rice.
  Can the children suggest which cereals might be made from rice? The clue is usually in the name. Help the children to spot this. Find the boxes that are made from rice and place them in the 'rice' hoop.
• Repeat for the other cereals.

Vocabulary

oats, wheat, rice, corn

Tip   You could make a display with your boxes, or use them in your shop.

Cross-curricular link
PSRN: Calculating.

Carnival head-dresses

 Children make their own hat to wear during a carnival parade.

Aim

• To help children carry out an activity by reading the instructions.

Resources

• Card or strong paper long enough to fit a child's head

• Collage material, including long lengths of ribbon, flowers, sequins and glitter

• Sticky tape and glue

Preparation

• Write out three instructions at a level to match the children's abilities.

• Use a diagram, or a diagram with labels, or short, clear, simple sentences.

    1. Choose a band.

    2. Decorate the band.

    3. Fix the ends together.

What to do

• Read the instructions to the children or ask them to tell you what they say.

  Can they work out the correct order for the instructions?

  Fix the instruction sheets in order, where the children can see them as they work.

• Check that the children understand the instructions.

  They can now make their own hat using these simple instructions.

  Keep asking the children which instruction they are working on.

• When they are finished ask the children to check that they have completed all of the instructions.

Vocabulary

instruction

 Tip Make sure that the children decorate their bands with items that will flow and float in the air as they dance in the parade.

Cross-curricular link

KUW: Designing and Making.

Where are we?

 Go for a walk with the children and photograph all the familiar signs you see in the street.

Aim

• To provide an opportunity for children to recognise words on signs and symbols.

Resources

• Digital camera and printer

Preparation

• You are going to be taking the children out of the setting, so prepare well in advance, keeping to the rules of your setting for doing this.

• Look around the local area so that you can plan the best route for spotting signs and symbols.

What to do

• Go for a walk with the children in the streets around your setting.

• Take photographs of any signs that let you know where you are. Try:

 – Street names

 – Directions to town, the theatre, etc.

 – The board with your own setting's name on it

 – Similar boards for schools or churches

 – Names of shops, factories, garages, businesses

Look out for familiar logos, e. g.

 – Bus stop

 – Road signs showing children crossing

 – Takeaway restaurants

• On returning, the children can work with an adult to print out their photographs.

• Can the children read or recognise any of the signs? Provide clues – the first letter if that is helpful. (It is helpful for 'Main Street'. It isn't helpful for 'Shoreditch'.) The children may recognise logos for fast food outlets, car dealerships and petrol stations etc.

Vocabulary

direction, sign, logo

Tip You could create a display by cutting up an old street map to make mounts for your photographs or as a trim to go round the edge of your display board.

Cross-curricular link

KUW: Place.

Birthday (3)

Teddy's having a birthday party and he sends invitations to everyone. Help the children to read their invitation from Teddy.

Aim

• To provide some simple texts which children can decode.

Resources

• Party invitations and envelopes

Preparation

• Select a party invitation either printed from a computer program or some simple, bought paper invitations.

• Fill out an invitation for every child from Teddy.

• Put the invitations in a named envelope for each child.

What to do

• Show the children the envelopes that have been left in the classroom. Let them collect the envelope addressed to them if they recognise their name. Less able children might be able to select their name from a group of three or four.

• Working in small groups, encourage the children to open their envelopes and find out what's inside. Who can recognise that it's an invitation to a birthday party?

• Encourage the children to try to read who it is from.

  'It's Teddy's birthday and he's having a party. '

• Then try to work out the day and the time of the party.

  'How old will Teddy be? '

• Make the party for the following day so the children can read their invitations with their parents at home too.

Vocabulary

envelope, name, party, Teddy, Monday/Tuesday/Wednesday/Thursday/Friday, one/two/three o'clock

Tip   For older children you could help them to find Teddy's birthday on a calendar. Do they know when their birthday is?

Cross-curricular link

PSRN: Numbers as Labels and for Counting.

Catch That Goat!
by Polly Alakija (1)

Look at the illustrations in this super book. Then help the children to create their own market stall.

Aim

• To encourage children to use illustrations to find out information from a book.

Resources

• Alakija, P.（2007）*Catch That Goat!: A Market Day in Nigeria*, Bath: Barefoot Books

• Paper and paint

• Tables and role-play resources

Preparation

• Read and enjoy the story.

What to do

• Spend time looking at the illustrations to work out what the different market traders are selling. Use the shop signs, nothing both the words and the images. Look at the goods on display for additional clues.

• Now make your own market.

  – Arrange the tables in a line.

  – Use class or nursery resources such as model fruit and vegetables, packets from the shop, plates, etc. from the house, dressing-up clothes and musical instruments to fill your market stalls.

• Children can work in pairs to paint a sign for their stall. They could try forming the word or use a symbol. Help the children to tape their sign across the front of their table/stall.

• Your market is now ready for role-play use.

Vocabulary

market, stall, market trader

Tip   If you have a street market nearby,   visit it before you start this activity.

Cross-curricular link

KUW: Communities.

New for old

 Replace the old labels in your room and remind the children of the routines involved as they make new ones.

Aim

- To create an environment for the children that is rich in print.

Resources

- Digital camera
- Printer
- Laminator

What to do

- Ask the children to have a look at the different labels that are up in the room. Do they notice that they are torn, damaged, grubby, etc.? Explain to them that it is time to change these labels for some new ones.
- Tell the children that you are going to use photographs and words to give information, or to act as reminders about how to behave or use the resources. Discuss the possibilities.

  Be ready with some ideas to help the children, e.g.

  Photograph: someone's hands in a basin with the tap running and soap all over their hands

  Words: 'Wash your hands'

  Where will it go?

  Photograph: someone sweeping the floor near the sand tray

  Words: 'Clear away when you have finished'

  Where will it go?

  Photograph: child wearing an apron

  Words: 'You need to wear an apron'

  Where will it go?

- Now, take the photographs with the children. Let them do as much as possible of this.

- Write out the words and let the children copy them on the computer. Laminate and then put up your new labels.

Vocabulary
label, information

Tip
This is a good activity for the beginning of any term as it is a chance to reinforce your setting's routines.

Cross-curricular link
PSED: Behaviour and Self-control.

Bags of words

 A lively game for helping children to build sentences.

Aim

• To provide an opportunity for children to read a range of words and simple sentences.

Resources

• Six carrier bags in different colours, labelled 1 – 6

• A large die

• Strips of card numbered 1 – 6

• A selection of simple sentences linked to your theme, using five words each, e. g.

 – I can play the drum/triangle/guitar

 – I like to eat pizza/chips/cakes

 – I can see the bat/ball/cat/house

 – I am in the car/house/room/bed

Note that the final word in each sentence should be different each time.

Preparation

• Cut each sentence into five separate words and a full stop. Put the first word of each sentence into the bag numbered 1, the second words into the bag numbered 2 and so on. Put all the full stops in bag 6.

• Hook the bags up all around the grounds of your setting.

What to do

• Everyone sits in a circle outside. Give each child a strip of paper numbered 1 – 6 on which to place their sentence pieces as they collect them.

• The first child rolls the large die in the centre of the circle and reads the number. They have to run to find the bag that has that number on it and collect a word – or a full stop.

• If a child already has that number they pass.

Make this fun, e.g.

The child has to stand up and stamp that number of times on the floor before handing the die on to their neighbour.

- Continue until everyone has a sentence. Now read them to each other.

Vocabulary

- Any words that you are focusing on in your reading or writing

Tip   Use words you want the children to recognise in their reading. Laminate them if you want to reuse the activity.

Cross-curricular link

PSRN: Numbers as Labels and for Counting.

Mini-beasts (3)

Write out the children's questions on bookmarks to encourage them to hunt for information in simple non-fiction books.

Aim

- To reinforce and apply children's reading ability whilst retrieving information from non-fiction texts.

Resources

- Non-fiction books about mini-beasts
- Strips of card

Preparation

- At the start of the new topic ask the children what they would like to find out about mini-beasts. Form their ideas into simple questions.
- Write each question along the length of the strip of card, e. g.
  - Are all ladybirds red and black?
  - How many legs has a spider got?
- Now place one card, like a bookmark, in a non-fiction book at the page that you know contains the answer.

What to do

- Place a crate of non-fiction books, with their bookmark questions, outside.
- Children work in pairs to choose a book. Help them to read the question and then hunt for the answer on the page indicated.
- Encourage children to scan the page for key words, e. g. *spider*, *legs*.
- Help them to read the relevant sentence, recognising familiar words. Now, talk about the meaning.
- Leave paper and pencils and crayons available so that children can record their information whilst you help another two children with reading their question.

Vocabulary

how? what? where? when? why?

Tip Write the title and page number on the back of the bookmark so that you can replace them quickly when someone has helpfully tidied them all away for you!

Cross-curricular link

KUW: Exploration and Investigation.

Treasure hunt clues

This game makes reading exciting as the children follow the clues to find the treasure.

Aim

• To help children rapidly decode words.

Resources

• Simple clues written on pieces of card using vocabulary that your children are learning to recognise – no more than six clues, e. g.

  – Look behind the door

  – Look under the car mat

  – Look near the sand toys

  – Look in the book box

• Treasure – fruit snack for the day/a lost toy/a new toy/a new book for story time.

Preparation

• Put the cards in place behind the named items and hide the final treasure.

• Remember to keep the first clue to start the game.

• Include outdoor clues if the weather is fine.

What to do

• Working with a group of children, tell the children what treasure they are going to hung, e. g.

  To find today's snack

• Explain the game so the children understand how to follow the clues. Read the first clue together, e. g.

  Look behind the door

  Let the children start the hunt.

  When they discover the correct door, they will find the second clue card.

• Let the children retrieve the next clue from its hiding place.

  – Who can read the clue?

• This will lead them to the next object hiding a clue card.

- Continue until all the clues have been found and read.
- When the treasure is found, share it with the rest of the class.

Vocabulary

look, behind, on top of, under

Tip   When the children are familiar with the treasure hunt game you can introduce more challenging clues that involve guessing, e. g.

Look behind something tall and red.

Cross-curricular link

PSRN: Shape, Space and Measures.

Key word bingo

Chalk some words in grids on your playground and create a fun way to practise key words outdoors.

Aim

• To develop children's grapheme correspondence so that they can rapidly decode words.

Resources

• Chalk

• Set of key words （see vocabulary list opposite）

• A fine day!

Preparation

• Draw two grids on a hard surface outside – each with six sections.

• Write one of the key words in each section of the two grids.

• Make sure you have these twelve key words in your set of key word cards.

What to do

• Divide the children into two teams of six and let them stand near their grid. Explain the game of bingo to the children if they haven't played it before.

• Show everyone a key word card.
  – Who can read it?
  – Is that word on your grid?

If it's there, one of the children stands on that word on their grid.

• Then show the next word.
  – Who can read it?
  – Is it on your grid?

• Continue until all of one team are standing on all six words on their grid. They are the winners!

• Swap the teams around and play again with a different grid. Can anyone read all the words on their new grid?

Vocabulary

twelve high-frequency words taken from Letters and Sounds: Appendix 1, e.g. the, and, a, to, said, in, he, I, of, it, was, you

Tip   Have some extra key words in your set that are not on the grids to add further interest.

Cross-curricular link

CLL: Reading a range of simple words.

Guess who! (1)

 Children will enjoy reading their names as they play this game.

Aim

• To help children understand what a word is by using names.

Resources

• Name labels

Preparation

• Make sure everyone knows the names of all the children in the class.

What to do

• Sit in a circle with all the name labels in the centre.

• Ask the children what the words are.

  – Do they recognise them as names?

  – Can they spot their own name?

• The children take turns to find their own name and take it back to their place in the circle. When everyone has their name label, hold them up so they can be seen.

• Choose a child to put their name back in the centre. Let that child choose the next one to put their name label back. Continue around the circle until everyone has returned their label.

• Now let the first child pick up someone else's name.

  – Can they read the word?

  – What sound does the word begin with?

  – Does that sound match the first letter written?

• When the child has read the name they can give it to the owner of the name label. Now take turns until everyone has retrieved and read someone else's label. Save the name labels to play with again another day.

Vocabulary

children's names

Tip   Use this activity to apply children's developing phonic knowledge.

Cross-curricular link

PSED: Sense of Community.

Guess who! (2)

Take photographs of pairs of children facing away from the camera. Can the children recognise one another from their back view?

Aim

• To help children understand what a word is by using names.

Resources

• Name labels
• Camera

Preparation

• Make sure everyone knows the names of all the children in the class.

What to do

• Work with a small group for this activity. Have name labels for that group.
• Begin by discussing having your photograph taken.

    What do you usually do?

    Well, today you're NOT going to look at the camera and smile, you're going to turn your back!

• Let two children stand together showing their backs to the rest of the group.

    Do you think you still know who it is?

    How can you tell who is who?

Encourage the children to talk about height and the clothes they are wearing. Consider hair colour and length as well. Find the name labels for these children, and then repeat the activity with different pairs of children.

• Ask the children to choose a partner who looks different from them. Now take photographs of each pair with their backs turned. If possible, let the children watch as the photographs are printed.
• Display the photographs so they are accessible to the children. Put reusable adhesive on the back of the name labels and leave them near by.
• Encourage the children to match the names to the photographs. Let other children in the group try naming the photographs.

Vocabulary
children's names

Tip Next day, put the labels next to the wrong photographs and let the children sort them out.

Cross-curricular link
PSED: Sense of Community.

Key word tunnels

 Take a group of children outside for a ball game that includes reading practice.

Aim

• To provide an opportunity for children to read some familiar words.

Resources

• A set of enlarged cards of the key words you are working on
• Container
• Ball

Preparation

• Put the key word cards in the container so that they can't be read.
• Take it outside with you.

What to do

• Choose three children to make the tunnels. They should stand in a line facing the other children with their legs wide apart, but with the sides of their feet touching the feet of the child next to them. They form three 'tunnels' with their open legs.

• Each of these three children picks a card from the container as you hand it to them. They should hold their cards so that the other children **can't** read them yet.
• The remaining children form a line. The first child comes forward and rolls a ball through one of the 'tunnels'.
  – Which one will it go through?

- If it goes through a tunnel, that child holds up their key word card.
  - Can the child who rolled the ball read it?
- If they can, they swap places with the child making that tunnel.
- Before getting into place as a 'tunnel', they should pick another key word card from the container.
- A helpful child can retrieve the ball while the original card is replaced in the container, amongst the other cards. The child who made the tunnel goes to the end of the line of those children waiting to roll the ball.

Vocabulary

Any key words such as I, on, the, and, here, is

Tip Putting the cards back into play means that there is a chance to reinforce learning and support any children who find this task difficult.

Cross-curricular link

PD: Movement and Space.

Key words of the week

The children cut and stick key words from newspaper headlines that you have selected.

Aim

• To help children recognise some key words.

Resources

• A4 paper
• Scissors，glue
• Headlines and titles from newspapers，magazines and leaflets
• Set of key words

Preparation

• Cut out headlines or other bold，clear print from the newspapers etc. Check that they contain the key words you want to practise and that the content is suitable for young children.
• Set out scissors，glue，paper and key words.

What to do

• Show the children one of the key words and read it together.
• Share out some of the magazine cuttings.
• Ask the children if they can find this same key word there.
• The children can now cut out the word and stick it onto one of the sheets of paper. You should end up with a set of papers，each with one key word on it in various fonts，sizes，and colours，arranged all over the paper.
• When everyone has stuck on their word，read the paper together.
• Everyone reads their own word when the adult points to it. Of course，they are all the same!
• Repeat this activity for the other key words.

    You may decide to focus on one word with one group of children，**or** you may decide to write one key word onto each sheet of paper，and leave all the papers out. The children will then hunt for words to cut out and stick onto the correct piece of paper.

Vocabulary

Any key words that you want to focus on, e.g. the, and, is, on, here

Tip

For older children, give each child one piece of paper, for them to collect the complete set of the key words.

Cross-curricular link

PD: Using Equipment and Materials.

Key word race

 An energetic running and reading game. Each team has eight key words to read in order to win the game.

Aim

- To develop children's grapheme correspondence so that they can decode words.

Resources

- Set of key words （see vocabulary list opposite）

Preparation

- Enlarge and photocopy the key words onto A4 pieces of card.
- Laminate them to make them more durable if you want to reuse them.
- You will need eight key words for each team （they can be the same eight for each team）.

What to do

- Set out the eight key words to make the outline of a square about a metre wide.

Put the children into teams and ask them to line up opposite the square, some distance away.

- The first child runs to the key word square and picks up a word they can read. The child says the word loudly and checks with their team （or an adult） that it's correct.

They then place the word in the centre of the square before running to the back of his team line.

- The next child runs to the key word square and picks up a card to read. If they read the word wrongly the adult can tell the child what the word says, but the child must then replace the word in its original position in the square before running back to their team.
- Continue until all the words have been read correctly and placed in the centre. The first team to read all their words wins the race.

Vocabulary

High-frequency words: see 'Letters and Sounds' in the Appendix.

Tip   Choose key words that are becoming familiar to the children.

Cross-curricular link

PD: Movement and Space.

Holidays (2)

Children stick pictures on plates, then use sentence starters to write a holiday diary.

Aim

- To provide an opportunity for children to write simple sentences.

Resources

- Seven paper plates
- Pictures of holiday destinations and houses
- Card for sentences

Preparation

- Prepare some sentence starters: e. g.

  On Monday she went to

  Make one for each day of the week, except Sunday.

  Write: *On Sunday she went home again.*

- Cut out some pictures of tourist destinations. These could be, e. g. a park, the seaside, a forest, a mountain.

- Cut out some pictures of the outsides of houses.

What to do

- Work with a small group of children, and explain that they are going to write a holiday diary for 'Auntie Flo' – or make up your own funny name.

- Let the children choose one house picture and stick it onto a paper plate. This is Auntie Flo's house.

- Look at the destination pictures together and identify them. Each child chooses one place for Auntie Flo to visit on her holiday. They stick their chosen pictures onto the other paper plates. The plates can now be arranged in a line, finishing with the house.

- Now, show the children the sentence starters. Read them, identifying the days of the week.

  – Can everyone say the days of the week in the right order?

- Place the starter sentences below the paper plates. The first one has the words *On Monday she went to . . . .* The second on has the words *On Tuesday she went to . . . ,* and so on until the last one, which will be *On Sunday she went home again.*
- Help the children to write the names for the places she will visit. Place these at the end of the appropriate sentence starter.
  - Can you read her diary?
- Swap the plates around and match the sentences to make a different holiday diary.

Vocabulary

days of the week, diary

Tip   Make a collection of books that feature the days of the week in your book corner.

Cross-curricular link

KUW: Time.

Word wall

Use this activity at the start of any new theme or topic. The children make pictures which you label together to create a word bank.

Aim

• To encourage children to use phonic knowledge to read simple words.

Resources

• Available display board and backing paper
• Art materials
• Paper and pens for labels

Preparation

• Cover your display board with a neutral backing paper.

What to do

• Explain to the children about your new theme, e. g. *along our street*.
  What do they think they will be finding out about?
  Make a note of their ideas, e. g. car, bus, market, shop, pelican crossing, traffic lights, people.
• Children can create their own pictures of their ideas with paint, collages or cut-outs from magazines. Let the children help to mount these and attach them to the display.
• Gather the children together near the display board. Point to one of the pictures, and ask the children to tell you what it is.
• Write the word on a large piece of paper. As you write, encourage the children to suggest:
  – what sound it starts with
  – how you will write that down
  – what sound is in the middle
  – what sound comes at the end
  Read the word together when you have finished, and then do the same for each picture in turn.

- When all the words are written, choose a child to come and pick one of the labels and show it to the group.
  - Who can read it?
  - Who can point to the picture it matches?

  Fix the word in place, and continue until your word wall is complete.
- The children can now use it when they are writing topic-related work.

Vocabulary

Any words linked to your theme

Tip If possible, dedicate one of your display boards for this as a regular starting activity. Attach the pictures and words in a way that allows you to remove them easily so that you can change it regularly.

Cross-curricular link

CD: Being Creative.

Gordon's garage (1)

 Create a frieze with the children for your role-play garage.

Aim

• To include print in your role-play area for children to read.

Resources

• Pictures of vehicles
• Roll of paper
• Marker pen, glue and scissors

Preparation

• Talk with the children about different kinds of road vehicles: cars, vans, bikes, trucks, etc

    Can they name any specific makes of car?

• Encourage the children to create some pictures of individual vehicles, about A4 size.

• Cut a length of paper from the roll, long enough to form a frieze which you can fix round the inside walls of the role-play area. Lay it along several tables pushed together.

What to do

• Remind the children that they are helping to set up a new role-play area: Gordon's Garage. Tell them,

    'Gordon fixes vehicles in his garage. Which ones might he fix?'

• Let the children show you their pictures, telling everyone what it is, perhaps even the make or model of car.

• Starting at the left-hand side of the paper write, in big bold letters, *Gordon can fix ...'*

    – Encourage the children to identify the letters you are writing.

    – Can they guess what the words might say?

    – Read it together when it is done.

• Now choose one of the pictures. The child who made it glues it down onto the frieze, after the words. Underneath write its name/model/make – as the child wishes. Now read the words, *'Gordon can fix a Mini'*, for example.

- Add the second picture, and its name, and then read it all again.

  'Gordon can fix a Mini, a bus'

  Continue in this way until you have used all of the pictures.
- Fix your frieze in place around Gordon's Garage.

Vocabulary

car, bike, motorbike, coach, bus, van, lorry, etc.

Tip Car magazines are a good source of pictures for cutting out if you don't want to spend time making them.

Cross-curricular link

CLL: Role play.

Chapter 6

Enjoying stories and rhymes

Café (2)

 Let the children share the experience of wobbling like Mrs Wobble.

Aim

• To encourage children to compare the feelings of characters with their own experiences.

Resources

• Ahlberg A. （1980） *Mrs Wobble the Waitress*, London: Puffin Books

• Tray

• Unbreakable plates, cups or pans

Preparation

• Share the story with the children up to the part when Mrs Wobble loses her job and all the family are upset.

   – Do the children understand why Mrs Wobble is crying?

   – How do they feel if they see someone crying?

   – Have they ever dropped anything?

   – What was it?

   – What happened?

   – How did they feel?

What to do

• Tell the children that they are going to be waiters/waitresses. Who thinks they can carry a tray of pots?

• Collect together some unbreakable plates, cups or pans. Count them and pile them up on a small tray.

• Let the children take it in turns to walk across the room balancing the pile. Give everyone a clap if they manage to do it.

• If they drop them, everyone shouts 'Mrs Wobble wobbled! '

Vocabulary

The character names, as well as balance, careful, wobble, drop, tip, fall, how many

501

Tip　To extend the game: let the children estimate how many items they think they'll be able to balance, then encourage them to keep a tally of how many items they carried without wobbling.

Cross-curricular link

PSRN: Numbers as Labels and for Counting.

Who's in the cottage today?

 Children will love this fun way to introduce a story.

Aim

- To provide props to encourage the children to identify the characters in a story.

Resources

- Card for cottage picture (see *Preparation* for details)
- Small pictures of story book characters

Preparation

- Fold a large piece of card so that it will stand up – like a birthday card. On the front, draw and colour a traditional fairy-tale cottage.

- Cut the door on three sides so that it will fold open – like an Advent calendar door.

- Choose one of the character pictures, and fix it in place inside the card so that you can see it when you open the door. Close the door to hide it from view. Fix it so that it can be easily changed for a different character.

- The children might be involved in making the cottage using collage materials, but make the characters yourself so that you don't give the answers away!

What to do

- When the children are sitting ready for their story, show them the cottage. Ask them who might live in a cottage like this one. Encourage as many responses as you can, e.g.
  - Goldilocks
  - one of the Three Bears
  - one of the Three Little Pigs
  - the wolf dressed up as Grandma
  - Grandma herself
  - Red Riding Hood
  - the witch in *Hansel and Gretel*

  Why do they think this person might live here? Is there a clue anywhere?

- Now choose a child to come out and open the door to reveal today's character.
  - Did anyone get it right?
  - Can you remind everyone of what happened to that character?
  - Who usually lives in the cottage in this character's story?
- Now tell or read the story to the children.

Tip You might want to extend the idea by having a window that opens, and put another picture clue behind it, to discuss before you open the door.

Cross-curricular link

CD: Developing Imagination and Imaginative Play.

Toot Toot Beep Beep
by Emma Garcia (2)

The children identify the sound words and repeat them at the appropriate places in the story.

Aim

• To help children to match, recognise and read some simple words.

Resources

• A copy of Garcia, E. (2009) *Toot Toot, Beep Beep*, St Albans: Boxer Books
• Pieces of card

Preparation

• Copy one of the sound-effect phrases, e.g. '*vroom vroom*', onto each card. Make as many copies as you need so that the children can have one each.

What to do

• Introduce the book to the children and then spend some time looking at the first double-spread page. Encourage the children to identify each vehicle by colour and type.

• Look at the second picture of the busy flyover. Which of the vehicles can they see this time?

• As you continue through the book, you read the printed words, and then encourage the children to make the sound-effect noises as you point to the large printed version of the words.

• When you have read and enjoyed the whole story, turn to any page and point to the large print version of the sound effect.

  'Who can remember what this says? '
  'What is the first letter/first sound? '

Repeat for a few of the other pages.

• Give everyone a card with one sound on it. Ask the children to read them and try to remember what it says. Check that everyone can read their card.

- Now read the story again – without showing the children the pages. At the appropriate places the children should make the sound effect that is written on their card.
- Finish with the page about all the cars being quiet in the car park!

Vocabulary

All the sound effect words in the book

Tip

To create a display of colour words:

- Print on some paper by pressing it into paint that has been spread around with the fingers on a washable surface.
- When dry, cut out shapes to make the vehicles from the story or others of your own design.
- Add your colour names labels.

Cross-curricular link

KUW: Place.

Toot Toot Beep Beep
by Emma Garcia (3)

Write some simple sentences using the ideas in this book and help the children create their own sentences from these ideas.

Aim

- To encourage the children to compose some simple sentences.

Resources

- A copy of Garcia, E.（2009）*Toot Toot Beep Beep*，St Albans：Boxer Books
- Seven strips of card

Preparation

- You will be using the following seven sentences， adapted from the text of the book:

    The red jeep zooms off.

    The black car speeds off.

    The blue van trundles off.

    The yellow taxi rushes off.

    The pink limousine glides off.

    The green camper van rolls off.

    The purple car hurtles off.

  Write five of the sentences onto the strips of card， leaving two strips blank.

- Enjoy the story together before going through the book again， encouraging the children to say some of the words when you pause. Try missing out the colour words and the movement word， e.g.

    '*Honk honk goes the ...... city taxi， and off he ...* '

  If necessary， say the first sound of each word to help the children remember.

What to do

- With the children watching， write a sentence on one of the blank strips of card， e.g.

    The yellow taxi rushes off.

Ask the children if anyone can read this. Let several children have a turn at reading it.

- Now cut the card into three parts,

  The/yellow taxi/rushes off.

  Muddle the pieces up, hand them to three children and ask them if they can put the pieces back together in the correct order. Ask the other children to read and check when they have done this.
- Repeat this process with another sentence.
- Now, read the other sentences with the children.
- Cut all of the strips into three parts, and place the pieces into piles:

  One pile of 'The'

  One pile of vehicle colours and names

  One pile of movements.
- Explain to the children that they should take one card from each pile and use all three pieces to form a sentence.
- Challenge the children to see how many different sentences they can make from these broken sentences.
- Those who are able might choose to copy and illustrate their sentences later.

Vocabulary

sentence, colour words, movement words

Tip   To make an easier version, remove the colour words.

To make a harder version, add the second descriptive word for each vehicle that you will find in the book.

Cross-curricular link

KUW: Place.

Guess the story

 Provide the children with objects and see if they can recognise the story they come from.

Aim

• To encourage the children to recall details from familiar stories.

Resources

• A basket or attractive container

• A selection of story books

• Illustrations of characters and a few objects, e. g.

  – For Cinderella: a party shoe, a mouse, a magic wand

  – For Red Riding Hood: some flowers, a basket, shawl or old-fashioned spectacles

  – For the Three Little Pigs: some straw, a brick, some apples

  – For Goldilocks and the Three Bears: three bowls in different sizes, a broken chair (from the dolls' house), a packet of porridge oats

Preparation

• Choose three books – one that you will read, and any other two.

• Place the objects for the story you will read in your basket, and have your picture of one of the characters ready.

What to do

• When everyone is sitting ready for a story, show the children the basket and identify what is in it.

  – Does this remind the children of any stories that they know?

  – What part do these objects play?

  – Who owns them?

  If they need a further clue, show them the character's picture.

• Once the children have identified the story, show them the three books.

  – Can they recognise the right one from the cover?

  – Ask the children what clues they can spot on the cover.

• Now read and enjoy your story.

Vocabulary

cover, title, illustration

Variation Make your clue objects more obscure, e.g. salt and sugar for the Three Bears.

Cross-curricular link

CLL: Story characters.

"Shop, Shop, Shopping" by Georgie Adams

Help the children write their own version of this poem.

Aim

• To provide an opportunity for children to experiment with words and texts.

Resources

• 'Shop, Shop, Shopping' by Georgie Adams can be found in Waters, F. (1999) *Time for a Rhyme*, London: Orion Children's Books.

Preparation

• Read and enjoy the rhyme with the children.

• Can they spot the rhyming words?

• Read it again and see if anyone anticipates the rhymes.

What to do

• Repeat the beginning of the rhyme, then ask the children to help you make a new list of what to buy.

'What do you buy when you go shopping?'

• When you have a few suggestions, write them down and try to think of words that rhyme.

• Next, choose a rhyming pair and add an adjective to each item, e.g.

– a red skirt

– a school shirt

Continue with two or three more rhyming pairs.

• Finish your poem with the ending of the original poem.

Vocabulary

pairs of rhyming words, e.g.

spoon – balloon

pie – tie

skirt – shirt

fish – dish

peg – egg

jug – mug

map – cap

chocs – box

van – pan

pig – wig

Tip   Next time, try playing this as a remembering game: say the first word and see if the children can provide the rhyme.

Cross-curricular link

KUW: Communities.

Story map

Help a small group of children work together to make a picture of a story.

Aim

- To encourage children to talk about the sequence of events in a story.

Resources

- A large sheet of paper
- Pens and crayons

Preparation

- Read a story of your choice to the children.

What to do

- Arrange a small group of children around the large sheet of paper. Tell them you want to make a big picture of the story.
- Ask who can remember what happens at the beginning of the story. Encourage two children to draw the opening part of the story.
- Then ask what happens next. Encourage the next two children to draw the second part of the story. Continue until the main events in the story have been recorded.
- Now ask the children to retell the story pointing to the pictures they have drawn. As they do this, use a bold felt-tip pen to draw arrows from each picture to the next to indicate the order of events.
- Ask the children if their story map is finished.
  - Can it be improved in any way?
  - How could we show what story it is about?
  - What about adding a title?
  - Does the story map clearly show the order of events?
  - Would it help to add numbers next to the pictures?
- The children may decide they want to add more detail or colour to their pictures.

Vocabulary

beginning, next, ending, order, title, map

Tip   An adult could draw the pictures as very young children retell the events of the story in sequence.

Cross-curricular link

CLL: Story structure.

"Ten Dancing Dinosaurs" by John Foster

Change what happened to the dinosaurs and help the children create a new poem using this classic framework.

Aim

• To provide an opportunity for children to experiment with words and texts.

Resources

• "Ten Dancing Dinosaurs" can be found in Waters, F. (1999) *Time for a Rhyme*, London: Orion Children's Books.

Preparation

• Read and enjoy the rhyme or choose another one which follows this pattern, e.g. 'Five Little Pussy Cats', found in Matterson, E. (compiler) (1991), *This Little Puffin*, London: Penguin

What to do

• Encourage the children to spot the rhyming words as they listen to the poem.
• Notice that the word at the end of line one rhymes with the number word, e.g. 'line' – 'nine'.
• Write out the first line of the poem.
• Now suggest to the children that you change what happened to one of the dinosaurs.
• Ask for another idea, e.g.
    One slipped and bumped her head.
• Write the new words but finish the line with the original wording.
• Continue with new ideas about what happened to each dinosaur throughout the poem.

Vocabulary

Lots of interesting vocabulary to discuss in this poem, e.g. 'gyrating', 'hijacked'.

Tip   It would be lovely to paint these dancing dinosaurs!

Cross-curricular link

PSRN: Calculating.

Catch That Goat !
by Polly Alakija (2)

What happens next? Look for clues in the illustrations as you enjoy this story together.

Aim

- To encourage children to suggest how the story will progress, and end.

Resources

- Alakija, P. (2007) *Catch That Goat! : A Market Day in Nigeria*, Bath: Barefoot Books.

Preparation

- Before you share this story with the children, read the information on the last few pages. This will help you to set the context for children who are not from Nigeria.

What to do

- Each picture in this story book has clues in it as to where the goat or the missing items have gone. Read it slowly, giving the children a chance to look carefully at the illustrations.
  - Who spots the clues?
  - Can they see the goat, or part of the goat?
  - Can they see the missing item?
- Make time to count the items that the market traders have left on their stalls.
- When you reach the page where Mama calls out to Ayoka, stop and ask the children.
  - Can anyone guess where the goat is?
  - Can you guess what the goat has done?
- Encourage the children to work out the ending before you turn to that page.

Tip   This might be an opportunity to look at 'speech bubbles'. Most of the spoken words are in rectangular 'speech bubbles'. Can the children work out why Mama's words at the end of the story are shown in jagged 'bubbles'?

Cross-curricular link

KUW: Communities.

Using finger puppets

Make up a story with the children based on your finger puppet characters.

Aim

- To encourage children to retell narratives in the correct sequence drawing on the language pattern of stories.

Resources

- Animal finger puppets

What to do

- Working with a small group of children, let each child choose an animal finger puppet.
- The adult takes the lead in making up a simple story, encouraging the children to move the puppets and join in or repeat the words, e. g.

  One day a baby elephant was feeling lonely, so he went out for a walk looking for new friends.

  He met a monkey.

  'Will you play with me? ' asked baby elephant.

  'Not yet, ' said monkey. 'I'm looking for nuts. '

  So baby elephant walked on until he met a hippo.

  'Will you play with me? ' asked baby elephant.

  'Not yet, ' said hippo 'I'm rolling in the mud. '

  So baby elephant walked on until he met a penguin . . .

- Continue the narrative with the other animal puppets.

  Until, finally, the last animal said yes!

  Then everyone joined in and played.

Vocabulary

animal names, questions, excuses

Tip This might provide an opportunity to talk with the children about making friends.

Cross-curricular link

PSED:　Self-confidence and Self-esteem.

Pants by Giles Andreae and Nick Sharratt

 Have fun with this appealing story as the children write about their socks!

Aim

• To help children explore and experiment with sounds, words and texts.

Resources

• Andreae, G. and Sharratt, N. (2002) *Pants*, London: Picture Corgi

Preparation

• Read and enjoy the book with the children.

• Take it in turns to recite the pages using the illustrations to help.

What to do

• Read the first few pages substituting the word 'socks' for 'pants'.

• Then ask the children to join in (when they stop laughing!)

• Use the same adjectives and phrasing but change the word 'pants' for 'socks' each time as you reread the book together.

• Now ask the children if they can think of other ways to describe socks, e.g.

  – thick socks

  – holey socks

  – smelly socks

  – Christmas socks

  – princess socks

• Try to substitute their suggestions into the rhyme.

• Tell the children you need some different pictures for this new book you've made up.

• Let the children decorate sock shapes with bold patterns. Display them on a washing line with some enlarged words describing the socks.

• More able children could type these out on the computer.

Vocabulary

Adjectives from the book

Tip   When you take down the washing line, staple the socks together and glue in some of the adjectives describing the socks, to make a book for the children to enjoy.

Cross-curricular link

CD: Being Creative.

Sing along with me

 The children record and make their own tapes.

Aim

- To reinforce children's knowledge of rhymes and poems.

Resources

- Cassette player
- Blank tapes – short tapes are more child-friendly

Preparation

- Sing and say rhymes, counting rhymes and short poems together

What to do

- Set up a space where children can come along and record their favourite rhyme.
- Decide how you want to organise these, e.g.
  - One tape for counting rhymes, one for animal rhymes, etc.
  - One tape for one group of children – perhaps an age group or a working group.
- Make sure these are clearly labelled so that the children know which tape to use. An adult can help them so that they understand that they must do their rhyme after the last one already recorded.

    'What will happen if you go over someone else's rhyme?'

- Once completed, each tape can be left out in the music area or the book area for others to enjoy and perhaps join in with.
- Colour code your tapes and leave up a 'key' so that children can be encouraged to choose for themselves.
- You may have the facility to record CDs or use the computer instead.

Tip   The children might enjoy creating their own covers for their tapes if you cut the cardboard to fit.

Cross-curricular link

KUW: ICT.

That's When I'm Happy by Beth Shoshan (1)

 Act out the events of the story using some simple props to help the children remember.

Aim

• To provide props for children to talk about the sequence of events and characters in a story.

Resources

• Two large teddies and one smaller one

• A copy of Shoshan, B. (2005) *That's When I'm Happy*: London: Little Bee

• A leaf, a star, a small book, a small bed and a small cushion

Preparation

• Read and enjoy the story.

• Ask the children why the small bear might be feeling a little bit sad.

What to do

• Show the children the bears and ask which is which.

• Can they remember two things that Daddy Bear did to cheer up the small bear?
  Show the children the leaf and the star.

• Can they remember two things that Mummy Bear did to cheer up the small bear?
  Show the children the small book and a cushion.

• Can they remember what the small bear did for himself?
  Show the children the small bed.

• Now let the children take turns to retell the story using the props.

Vocabulary

happy, cheerful, sad, sorry, cheer up, smile, remember

Tip Ask the children about the things that make them happy too.

Cross-curricular link

PSED: Self-care.

That's When I'm Happy
by Beth Shoshan (2)

 The children share the experiences described in the story to find their way back to being happy.

Aim

• To encourage children to explore and experiment with texts.

Resources

• A copy of Shoshan, B. (2005) *That's When I'm Happy*: London: Little Bee
• Leaves, sticky stars, large piece of dark coloured paper, cushions and books

Preparation

• Read and enjoy the story.
• Talk about the central theme of getting back to feeling happy when you feel a bit sad.

What to do

• Tell the children you are going to try out the ideas in the story.
  After each experience, encourage them to talk about how they are feeling.
• Go outside and kick through the leaves. Choose a special one to show everyone.
  Collect some in a bag to bring inside to make a collage.
• Sit on some cushions with a friend. Choose a favourite book from the book corner to read with a friend. Can you find a word that begins with the same letter as your name?
• Let the children stick hundreds of stars all over a big piece of black paper.
  Count to a hundred together.
• Everyone lies down on the floor and goes to sleep!
• Do they think the ideas are successful for getting back to being happy?
• Let the children vote for the best way of cheering up, and record their findings, e.g.
  – everyone has a smiley face to stick on the sheets labelled with the various activities or

- use a computer program that allows you to record information as a graph
- What other ideas would they suggest?

Vocabulary
laugh, smile, giggle, happy

Tip To do this with a large group, set out all the activities, then sets of children can move between them with a supporting adult and report back.

Cross-curricular link
PSED: Making Relationships.

Good Morning Mrs Hen

 Change the colour words in this rhyme to create your own rainbow of chicks with the children.

Aim

• To help children understand what a word is.

Resources

• A copy of *Good Morning Mrs Hen* can be downloaded from

http：//www. bigeyedowl. co. uk/show_ songs. php？ t= 1

Preparation

• Make an enlarged copy of the poem.

• Two pieces of card that can be stuck over words on the poem with reusable adhesive.

What to do

• Read and learn the poem with the children. Point to the words as you read together, encouraging them to recognise the words.

• Highlight the colour words – yellow, brown and red.

• Explain that these words are the colours of hens and chicks, but you are going to have fun pretending they are other colours.

• Tell the children that they can change two colour words.

• Ask the children who can point to the words 'yellow' and 'red'? Cover these words with small pieces of card.

• Read the poem again, pausing at the blanked-out word. Ask for suggestions of other colours and write these on your cards. Now, reread your poem, e. g.

    four of them are pink

• Repeat the activity with different colours to create lots of new rhymes.

Vocabulary

yellow, brown, red, pink, green, orange, blue, turquoise, purple, black, white

Tip   Draw and cut out ten chicks and arrange them into different groups to make ten, e. g. seven in one group and three in another, or one group of two, one of three and another of five.

Cross-curricular link

PSRN: Calculating.

Tiddalick by Robert Roennfeldt (1)

Children act out the events in this traditional story from Australia.

Aim

- To help children start to recognise how stories can be structured.

Resources

- Roennfeldt, R. (1980) *Tiddalick, the Frog Who Caused a Flood*, London: Picture Puffins

Preparation

- In this traditional tale, based on an Aboriginal Dreamtime legend, the structure is:
  - There is a problem.
  - Different strategies to solve it are tried.
  - Eventually one of them works and there is a successful outcome.
- Look at the title page to see all the animals that appear in the story. Help the children to remember their names.
- Share the story with the children.

What to do

- Think about each character in the story in turn and what they say or do:
  - Everyone can try being a small frog, and then slowly getting bigger and bigger, and then quickly shrinking back to their normal size.
  - Everyone can pretend to tell a very funny story. Choose a simple joke that the children can tell, and they can laugh as they tell it.
  - Playing leapfrog would not be appropriate – so either use two stuffed animals to do this, or everyone can do 'bunny jumps'.
  - Strut around like the lizard with tummies puffed out.
  - Everyone can dance like the eel.
- Now read the story again, with the children acting out all the parts as they occur.

- The children could now work in small groups to retell the story themselves – without you reading the book for them. The order of the animals' efforts doesn't matter as long as the eel is last.

Vocabulary

the characters' names

'Once, long ago . . .' or 'Once upon a time . . .' – useful story opener.

Tip   'Dreamtime' is an Aboriginal concept of the creation of the world and includes many stories, some of which explain how people should behave. You can find out more about this if you do an Internet search for 'Aboriginal Dreamtime'.

Tiddalick would be a useful book to link with the idea of sharing, and of the effects of being greedy.

Cross-curricular link

PSED: Making Relationships.

Tiddalick by Robert Roennfeldt (2)

 Help the children create new names for the monster.

Aim

• To encourage the children to explore and experiment with sounds， words and texts.

Resources

• A copy of Roennfeldt， R. （1981） *Tiddalick: The Frog Who Caused a Flood*, London: Picture Puffins

• A soft toy version or puppet of the character if available

What to do

• Read and enjoy the story.

• Discuss the character: how he looks and how he behaves in the story.

• Sit together in a circle. Ask the children who can remember the monster's name. Take turns saying his name in 'monstery' voices.

• *Why do you think Tiddalick was called that?* If the children suggest something to do with licking， for example， use this idea to suggest a different name such as Licklack or Biggerlick.

• When the children have stopped laughing， ask them if they can think of another name for him. Praise everyone's attempts.

• If you have a puppet or soft toy， make it nod enthusiastically at everyone's ideas.

 Tip Don't try to write the new names down!

Cross-curricular link

CD: Being Creative.

Jack and Jill

Act out the events in sequence to illustrate the beginning, middle and end of a familiar rhyme.

Aim

- To help the children to understand the elements of a story.

Preparation

- Make sure the children are all familiar with the rhyme and can repeat it from memory.

What to do

- Say the rhyme together.
- Ask the children if they can tell you what is happening at the beginning of the rhyme.

  'Jack and Jill are going up a hill'.

- Choose two children to act this out.
- Ask the children if they know what happened next.

  'Jack fell down. Then Jill fell down the hill. '

- Choose some more children to act this out.
- And how does it all end?

  'Jack gets up and goes home. '

- Another group of children act this out.
- What do they think happened to Jill?
- Now position three groups of 'actors', one set for each part – the beginning, the middle and the end. These children can mime appropriate actions at the right time, as the other children repeat the rhyme.

Vocabulary

beginning, middle, end

Tip   You could try this with other rhymes where the three elements can be easily identified, e. g.

    Pat-a-cake, pat-a-cake, baker's man

    Two little dicky-birds

    Incy Wincy Spider

Cross-curricular link

CLL: Story structure.

Bigger and bigger (1)

 Help the children to read and interpret the repeated phrases in a familiar picture book.

Aim

• To develop children's understanding of the language of stories and how print works.

Resources

• A copy of Rosen, M. (1993) *We're Going on a Bear Hunt*, London: Walker Books

• Other books that have repeated phrases where the print is gradually enlarged

What to do

• When the children have enjoyed the story a few times, look at one of the pages that describes the character's movement e. g.

　　'*Stumble trip, stumble trip, stumble trip*'

• Can the children see that the words are repeated three times? Help them count.

• Ask if they notice anything that is different as the words are repeated on the page. Show them how the words get bigger and bigger and bigger.

　– Why do you think the words are printed like that?

• Listen to the children's suggestions and try out their ideas, e. g. they may suggest the words could be said slower and slower because they were feeling tired, or quicker and quicker as they went faster.

• Try reading the words quietly the first time, then louder and louder to illustrate one idea.

• Read the book again and encourage the children to join in the repeated phrases, starting with a whisper and ending with a shout!

• Ask the children to find other books that enlarge print in this way.

• Leave out a few examples for the children to explore.

Vocabulary

small, large, larger, quiet, loud, louder

Tip   For more ideas using this wonderful book see *Games*, *Ideas and Activities for Early Years Phonics* in the Classroom Gems series.

Cross-curricular link

PSRN: Shape, Space and Measures.

Bigger and bigger (2)

 The children create their own repeated phrases and enlarge the font using a computer.

Aim

• To develop children's understanding of the language of stories and how print works.

Resources

• Books that have repeated phrases where the print is gradually enlarged

• Writing program on the computer

Preparation

• To help the children understand the convention of enlarging print, read several books that demonstrate this or use activity 'Bigger and bigger（1）', p. 543.

What to do

• When the children have enjoyed the chosen story a few times, look at one of the pages that illustrate print getting larger.

• Talk about how this makes the story more exciting, e. g. '*It helps us know the beanstalk is growing higher and higher.* '

• Think of other story situations when words might be repeated, e. g.

– A monster coming nearer and nearer

• Let the children choose a starting word and type it on the computer （see vocabulary list below）. Show them how to add -*er* to the ending of their word.

• Help them to type or copy the new word three times.

• Then show them how to change the size of the font and make it larger.

• Let the children experiment until they choose the best size.

• Print out their repeating phrases and display them for others to read.

Vocabulary

small – smaller

large – larger

quiet – quieter

loud – louder

high – higher

near – nearer

Tip   Explain that the word still needs to fit on the paper when you print it if someone is getting carried away with font enlargement!

Cross-curricular link

KUW: ICT.

Bigger and bigger (3)

 Use the children's own ideas for repeated phrases to create music that grows louder or quieter.

Aim

• To develop children's understanding of the language of stories and how print works.

Resources

• Percussion instruments
• Writing program on the computer

Preparation

• Use activity 'Bigger and bigger (2)', p.545, to introduce the idea of print being enlarged.

What to do

• Play one of the instruments. Ask the children to think of a word to describe the sound, e.g. *bang* or *crash*
• Write the word three times, once in small print, then larger and larger. Demonstrate how to play the instrument by getting louder or quieter as indicated by the size of the print on the repeated words.
• Let the children work in pairs and select an instrument.
• Now ask them to think of a word to describe the sound of their instrument.
• Help the children write their words on a computer writing program.
• Ask them to copy their word three times. Then change the size of their word so that it gets bigger and bigger.
• Print out the children's words.
• Now one child points at the repeated words in three sizes of print while their partner plays the instrument matching the volume to the size of the print.
• Let the children take it in turns to play or point.
• The children can then try playing another set of words on a different instrument.
• When they are confident with the idea that small print = quiet, an adult can conduct a group of children playing a range of instruments using the words:

play, play, play
Have fun!

Vocabulary

bang, crash, boom, ting, ring, click, shake, rattle, squeak, toot

Tip   Perhaps you could introduce the children to the musical symbol for a crescendo.

Cross-curricular link

CD: Creating Music and Dance.

Part 3
Writing

Allow children to see adults reading and writing and encourage children to experiment with writing for themselves through making marks, personal writing symbols and conventional script.

Practice Guidance for the Early Years Foundation Stage, May 2008. p. 42

Chapter 7

Finger play

Candles (4)

 The children enjoy using finger painting to create their own candle designs.

Aim

• To encourage children to make shapes of letters in their play.

Resources

• Finger paint in bright colours
• Large sheets of paper

Preparation

• Fill in a candle-shape of paint on a table.
• Cut out paper that is larger than this.

What to do

• Encourage the children to use their fingertip to make a design in the paint. Try:
  - circles
  - long and short straight lines
  - zig-zags

oooo

lili

ww

These are the basic shapes that we use to write our letters.

• Now lay the paper carefully on top of the paint.
• Press gently and then remove to reveal your candle.
• The children can now add a yellow 'flame' to their candle, using paint and a brush, or a shape cut from yellow paper.

Vocabulary

round, straight, joined

Tip Some children might like to prepare their own candle shapes on the table.

Cross-curricular link

CD: Exploring Media and Materials.

Keep those fingers moving

Try warming up the finger muscles with some simple fun exercises before the children start their handwriting.

Aim

• To encourage the children to practise manipulative skills ready for writing.

Resources

• A good supply of action rhymes

What to do

• Just as an athlete warms up his muscles before a competition, it is worth doing some finger exercises before children are expected to practise their handwriting skills. Any action rhyme that involves finger movements can be used, e.g.

Two Little Dicky Birds

Tommy Thumb

Five Little Men in a Flying Saucer

• Or create your own set of exercises. Here are two ideas to start with:

– Spread your hand out on the table, palm down.

Who can lift each finger in turn without their other fingers moving?

How fast can you do it?

How slowly can you do it?

Are you quicker than your friend?

– Can your thumb touch each of your fingers, one after the other? It must be the fingers on the same hand as the chosen thumb!

Can you do it with your other hand?

How fast can you do it?

Vocabulary

thumb, finger, wiggle, stretch, curl

Tip   Children may soon be able to do some of these independently when you ask them to warm up their fingers ready for writing.

Cross-curricular link

PD: Using Equipment and Materials.

Ribbon dance

 The children swirl their ribbons around as they dance.

Aim

• To provide opportunities for the children to use large shoulder movements.

Resources

• Long lengths of ribbon

• Recorded music

Preparation

• Record some music which is lively, but with an even tempo. Waltz music is a good range to try.

• Talk with the children about the dancers in a carnival parade and how they might be waving ribbons, and making patterns with them in the air.

What to do

• The children can spend some time dancing freely to the music, swirling their ribbons high in the air, to practise the movement.

• Once they are familiar with how to make their ribbon 'dance', ask them to follow you all over the area. Explain to them that they will be like dancers in a carnival parade.

• Ask the children to try to make their ribbons move in a circle in the air. Encourage all of them to make their ribbons go in the same direction.

• Explain that when you give them a signal, they should change the direction that their ribbon is going in, making a circle the other way. Show them the signal. You might raise one hand or the other, or blow a whistle.

• When everyone needs to sit down and have a rest, ask the children:

'Is it easier with one of your hands?'

'Which one?'

'Is it the same hand that you use when you write or draw?'

• On another occasion, try making zig-zag shapes.

Vocabulary

left, right, high, low

Tip   The leader could carry a baton, flag or flower to use as an indicator of where the parade is going, or which way to twirl your ribbon.

Cross-curricular link

KUW: Communities.

Stripy flags

 A chance for children to practise their hand control as they use a computer mouse to make flags.

Aim

• To provide an opportunity to manipulate objects with increasing control.

Resources

• Computer with mouse

• Simple art program e. g.   First Paint

Preparation

• Show the children how to click on the colours they want to use.

• Give the children opportunities to play,   making marks freely using different colours.

What to do

• Tell the children that they are going to make some flags.

• Demonstrate how to use the computer program:

  – Select the widest paintbrush symbol on the computer program.

  – Remind the children how to select the colour they want to choose.

  – Use the mouse to draw a wobbly horizontal line across the top of the screen.

  – Then select a second colour and draw a similar line under the first.

  – Continue the process by selecting and drawing lines with a third and fourth colour.

• Print out your design and show the children your flag.

• The children can now have a turn at making their own flags.

• As the children produce their flags,   fix them to a line hanging over the classroom door or across a display board.

Vocabulary

click,   press,   hold,   across,   under

Tip Encourage the children to work slowly in order to control their stripes.

Cross-curricular link

KUW: ICT.

Birthday (4)

Celebrate with an iced cake, and make it into an opportunity for the children to practise writing their letters.

Aim

- To give children practise in forming letters correctly.

Resources

- Ready-made or pre-prepared cake or cakes
- Icing sugar and water mixed
- Food colouring and cocktail sticks （with points cut off） or icing pens

Preparation

- Choose which type of cake you want to decorate with the children:
  - A ready-made cake large enough for one name
  - Ready-made small cakes
- Choose either to use icing tubes or to let the children use a clean cocktail stick dipped in food colouring to write in the icing while it is still damp.
- Let the children help you ice the cake/s with a layer of water icing.

What to do

- Show the children the cakes and explain that you are going to decorate them with letters.
- Demonstrate how to write with the icing, reminding the children of the correct letter formation.
- Help the children as they decorate the cake/s with written icing.
- If you are using small cakes, try one of these ideas:
  - The children have a cake each and write the first letter of their own name on it.
  - Each child can write one letter on their cake so that altogether they spell out 'happy birthday' or a toy's name. Can they arrange them to spell out the words?
- If you decide to use a large cake, let the children take turns writing letters on the cake to make the toy's name or 'happy birthday'.

Vocabulary

start, top, down, over, round, up, squeeze

 Tip   Practise your icing writing on greaseproof paper first.

Cross-curricular link

PSED: Sense of Community.

Musical marks (1)

 Children enjoy moving to some soothing music and then paint as they listen again.

Aim

- To encourage children to use their hands to make left-to-right movements.

Resources

- Soothing music e. g.   Dvorak's *New World Symphony*.
- Large pieces of paper,   paint and brushes.

Preparation

- Prepare the paper and paint on covered surfaces.

What to do

- Play the music to the children.
- Encourage them to move with the music in appropriate ways,   e. g.   flowing arm movements and turning slowly
- Explain to the children that you are going to play the music again,   but this time they are going to paint as they listen.
- Play the music and encourage the children to paint long,   smooth waves of colour across the paper.   Encourage them to start at the left and finish on the right.
- When the paint is dry discuss what it looks like,   e. g.

    blue paint – water/sea/sky

    green paint – grass/hills

    orange/red – sunset

Vocabulary

smooth,   long,   gently,   slow,   flowing,   rising and falling

Tip   Use these paintings as a background and let the children add details like boats,   flowers,   sheep,   etc.   to fit the theme of the background colour.

Cross-curricular link

CD: Being Creative.

Musical marks (2)

 Children have fun making quick flicking movements as they listen to fast, exciting music.

Aim

- To encourage children to use their fingers to make shapes in the air and to make marks.

Resources

- Strong quick music, e.g. Rimsky-Korsakov: *Flight of the Bumble Bee*.
- Large pieces of paper, broad felt-tip pens.

Preparation

- Prepare the paper on covered surfaces.

What to do

- Play the music to the children. Encourage them to move with the music in appropriate ways, e.g. fast, flicking movements with their fingers, arms and legs.
- Explain to the children that you are going to play the music again, as they paint. Encourage them to draw quick flicking marks on the paper. Allow them to do this freely at random on the paper using a range of bright colours.
- Or, provide a circle template in the centre of the paper that can be removed later to reveal a sunburst.
- Show the children how to start on the card circle and then make flicks off the edges of the circle onto the paper.

Vocabulary

quick, flick, spiky, short, sharp, fast, jerky

Tip   Try it again using chalk on dark paper to create a fireworks picture.

Cross-curricular link

CD: Being Creative.

Paper play

 The children create a display by tearing paper. This strengthens the fine muscles in their hands and fingers.

Aim

• To encourage the children to practise manipulative skills.

Resources

• Backing paper and glue
• Picture 1: Sugar paper in shades of green and brown
• Picture 2: Newspapers

Preparation

• Cut out a piece of paper large enough to cover one of your display boards.

What to do

Picture 1:

• Explain to the children that they are going to create a forest on the display board.

• Show them how to make some trees from the sugar paper by tearing the paper. Explain how tearing will give a jagged edge to the shapes which will look more lifelike. Children can now tear the green shades of paper into large 'cloud' shapes for the tops of the trees. They will also need to tear the brown shades into long strips to make the tree trunks.

• Help them to glue these onto the backing paper to look like a forest.

• Children can add cut-out painted figures of children on a walk, or animals that live in a wood, or Hansel, Gretel and the witch's cottage – anything that will suit your current theme of work.

Picture 2:

• Explain to the children that they are going to create a display about a busy town, using only old newspapers. Discuss what might be in a town, e.g. buildings, traffic, roads. Mark a road across the lower part of your display board with a black marker pen.

- The children tear out rectangular shapes from the sheets of newsprint in a variety of sizes.
- Help them to stick the larger shapes onto the backing paper to look like a townscape of buildings. Use smaller rectangles to represent cars, buses, etc.
- When the glue is dry, help the children to draw wheels and windows onto the newsprint shapes with black felt-tip pens.

Vocabulary

tear, torn, rip

Tip Tearing strengthens the same muscles that you need for controlling a pencil.

Cross-curricular link

PD: Using Equipment and Materials.

Letter shapes

 Turn handwriting practice into an art activity for the children.

Aim

- To encourage children to practise forming letter shapes.

Resources

- Marker pens
- *Picture 1*: Light brown, green or pink paper
- *Picture 2*: Pink or light brown paper

Preparation

- *Picture 1*: Cut the paper into roof shapes. Try to make a variety of shapes.
- *Picture 2*: Cut the paper into rectangles.
- Put a small mark in the top left-hand corner of each paper so that children know where to start.

What to do

Picture 1:

- Explain to the children that they are going to add some 'tiles' onto the roof-shaped pieces of paper. Start by making one yourself as the children watch you so that they can work out what you want them to do.
- Show the children how to make a row of 'u' shapes, joined together, along the top of the roof shape, working from left to right. Remind them that they should start where you have marked the dot.
- Now, make some more rows, one under the other. When the shape is full of letter 'u's the design should look like roof tiles.
- Now let children choose one of the roof shapes and a colourful felt-tip pen. Encourage them to take care, but to keep their pen moving across the roof.
- Children can make as many as they want. Have plenty of shapes available in case anyone needs to start again.

- When all the shapes are completed, the children can help to stick the rooftops onto the lower half of some dark backing paper. Add chimneys, stars, some snow and a Father Christmas figure to complete your winter's night scene.

Picture 2:

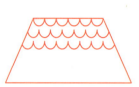 

- Explain to them that they can make a picture of a crowd of people.
- Demonstrate the process as for Picture 1, so that the children can imagine the finished image.
- Give each child a sheet of pink or light brown paper.
- Encourage them to use their pens to make circles, across the page, moving from left to right. They can make as many rows as they can fit onto their paper.
- When the paper is full the children can add eyes, mouths and a little hair to make funny faces as they create their own crowd of people.

Vocabulary

left, right, up, down, over, round

Tip   Encourage left to right movements, and moving from top to bottom of the paper.

Cross-curricular link

PD: Using Equipment and Materials.

Mini-beasts (4)

 Children use silver pens to make their own snail trail as they practise working from left to right across the page.

Aim

• To encourage children to manipulate objects with increasing control.

Resources

• Snails – if possible
• Silver marker pens
• Dark-coloured sugar paper
• Circles of paper in a contrasting colour

Preparation

• Have some garden snails for children to observe.
• Let the children watch them move across dark-coloured paper towards some tempting pieces of cucumber.   Point out their trails.

What to do

• Explain to the children that they are going to make their own snail trails.   They will use their silver marker pen to make a trail.
  – Can they think why the pens are this colour?
  – Do they remember what the real snail trail looked like?
• Remind the children to start at the left side of the paper and make a trail over to the right.   They can try to make some looped lines or curves as part of their preparation for writing.
• When they have completed their silver trail,   the children can stick a paper circle at the right-hand end of the line.
• When it is dry they can try to draw a spiral shape on the circle with brightly coloured pens.
• Add features to complete your snail,   and maybe draw a piece of cucumber for him!

Vocabulary

round, across, left, right, loop, spiral

Tip

Use your snail trail to suggest some phonics work on rhyming strings of words, e. g. 'a pale whale snail trail' .

Cross-curricular link

KUW: Exploration and Investigation.

Write outside

A selection of ideas for ways that the children can practise their writing outdoors.

Aim

- To provide the children with a variety of writing tools.

Resources

- Chalk
- Empty washing-up bottles
- Sticks, pebbles, leaves or cones

Preparation

- Collect together the outdoor writing tools you want to use today.
- Before going outside:
  - Make sure everyone is dressed appropriately – some may need aprons on.
  - Explain why natural materials are good for writing outdoors.
  - Help them understand that they can only write in the areas you show them, and with the tools you have given them.

What to do

- Explain to the children that they are going to write outside today.
- Remind the children of a word (e. g. their name) or letter shape you want them to practise.
- Before you go outside remind them to start at the left side.
  - Can everybody remember which side that is?
  Practise the writing pattern in the air.
- When you get outside, demonstrate how and where each tool may be used:
  - Chalk or squirty water bottles are for writing on hard surfaces.
  - Use blunt sticks to write in the sandpit.
  - The pebbles, cones and leaves can be placed on the grass to form letter shapes.

Vocabulary

left, right, top, down, up, round, over

Tip　This activity（as with most writing activities）should be well supervised if good writing habits are to be encouraged.

Cross-curricular link

PD: Using Equipment and Materials.

Jolly jigsaw

 Children draw a picture and then cut it up to make their own jigsaw.

Aim

- To encourage the children to use fine motor control skills.

Resources

- Large pieces of card in pale colours
- Children's broad felt-tip pens and scissors
- Pencil and ruler for the adult

Preparation

- Experience of playing with jigsaws.

What to do

- Talk to the children about the jigsaws in your setting.
  - Which is their favourite?
  - Which one is the hardest?
- Tell them they are going to make their own jigsaw.
- Ask everyone to make a colourful pattern or picture on a piece of card. Encourage them to fill all the available space and ask them to use every colour in the box! When their picture is finished remind them to write their name on it.
- Then turn the card over and let the child watch as you draw four or five interlocking lines across the reverse of the card using a pencil and ruler.

   The child now draws along the lines with a felt-tip pen before you help them cut carefully along the lines with the scissors.

- Now they can have a go at remaking the jigsaw, then share it with another child.

Vocabulary

straight, line scissors, cut

Tip   This activity can be varied to suit the ability of the children, e. g. jigsaws with only three or four pieces will be suitable for very young children.

Cross-curricular link

CD: Exploring Media and Materials.

Incy Wincy Spider

 Children make their own spider from wool and pipe cleaners before sharing the rhyme.

Aim

• To encourage the children to use fine motor skills.

Resources

• Pipe cleaners

• Wool

• Sequins

• Scissors and glue

Preparation

• Make sure everyone knows the rhyme, *Incy Wincy Spider*.

• Talk about real spiders:

  – Who has seen a spider?

  – What do they look like?

  – How do they move?

  – What size are they?

  – How many legs do they have?

What to do

• Tell the children they are going to make their own spider.

• Help each child count out four pipe cleaners to use.

• Now show them how to wrap the wool around the centre of the bundle of four pipe cleaners.   They should keep winding until the wool creates a body for the spider. Then help the children cut the wool with the scissors but remember to leave a long length of wool so the spider can dangle down.   And adult can make a knot so the wool can't unwind.

• Now let the children choose two matching sequins to create eyes for their spider.

• Help them glue the eyes onto the spider's body.

• Let the children move their spider as they recite the rhyme.

- Write out the rhyme in large print and dangle the spiders around it to create a display.

Vocabulary

numbers 1 – 4, wind, wool, scissors, cut, sequins, dangle

Tip   If you want to extend this into a writing activity – write out the instructions for making the spider on separate strips of paper and ask the children to arrange them in the correct order.

Cross-curricular link

PD: Using Equipment and Materials.

Café (3)

 A fun opportunity for writing as the children create some menus.

Aim

- To encourage children to use their ability to hear the sounds at the beginning of words.

Resources

- Printed pictures or drawings of food
- Pieces of A4 card folded in half
- Glue，felt-tip pens
- Ahlberg A. (1980) *Mrs Wobble the Waitress*, London: Puffin Books

Preparation

- After reading the story， focus on the page where Mr Wobble and the children make menus.
- Decide with the children six to eight items of food to sell in their café.
- An adult prints out multiple clip art pictures of these items （or photocopies simple drawings）.

What to do

- Show the children the folded pieces of card that will become the menus.
- Discuss the way the menu in *Mrs Wobble the Waitress* is organised with pictures and writing side by side.
- Lay out the pictures of the food， and encourage the children to identify the items.
- Let each child choose the ones for their own menu.
- Help the children glue the pictures into the menus， leaving spaces for their writing.
- Encourage them to make an attempt to write the words next to the appropriate pictures.

Vocabulary

Various food items， e. g. tea, milkshake, coke, juice, soup, burger, sandwich, fruit, ice cream

Tip Choosing words that each have a different initial letter will be helpful to children who are beginning to make use of phonic knowledge as they attempt to write words

Cross-curricular link

PD: Health and Bodily Awareness.

Chapter 8

Writing it down

Cinderella's busy day

 Start by playing a memory game with the children and then they write a list of jobs for Cinderella to do.

Aim

- To encourage the children to attempt writing in the form of a list.

Resources

- Strips of card and felt-tip pens
- Magnetic board and magnets
- Pre-prepared paper for lists

Preparation

- For the role play: print some long lengths of paper, like a shopping list notepad.
  - At the top put, 'Cinderella, today you must . . .'
  - At the bottom put, 'Signed . . .'
  - In between, list the numbers 1, 2 and 3 well spaced out.

What to do

- Sit in a circle with a small group of children to play a game.

  Explain to them that they are pretending to be the Ugly Sisters.

  Remind them how they were always spiteful to Cinderella, expecting her to do everything for them.

- You start the game by saying 'This morning I want Cinderella to . . .' and add a chore for her to do.

- Each child in turn repeats what has gone before and adds one more job to the list. You may need to limit this to four or five suggestions.

- As each chore is mentioned an adult can quickly write it down on individual strips of card. Stick these up as a list as they are given. You could use, e.g.
  - sweep the floor
  - polish the table
  - wash the dishes
  - light the fire

- feed the cat
- wash my dress
- peel the potatoes
- butter the bread
- do the shopping
- clean my shoes

Children can use the list to remind them of what has already been said.

• Now, take down the list and then play again. Children might use the same ideas but in a different order, or you might have to write out new ideas that they have thought of. Create the new list accordingly.

• Show the children the prepared paper for writing their own lists. Read it with them.

• Explain to them that when they are playing in the role-play area they can make a list of chores for Cinderella to do and fix it up on the magnetic board. The list you created during your game can be displayed nearby in case some children would like to use these ideas.

Tip
If you are the only adult with the group, write down your opening chore before you start the game, to speed up the process.

Cross-curricular link
CLL: Role play.

What's in your box?

If you are preparing boxes of fruit as gifts for the members of your community at harvest time, help the children to record the contents using this simple sentence structure.

Aim

- To help the children form simple sentences.

Resources

- Strips of paper
- Pictures of fruits with labels
- Small boxes

Preparation

- Each child will need two strips of paper, one with '*I have*' written on it, and one with '*in my box.*' Don't forget to include the full stop.
- Collect pictures of fruits. Stick them onto individual cards with the name written on the reverse. Include 'a' or 'an' or 'some' as appropriate, e.g. '*a pear*', '*an apple*', '*some grapes*'.

What to do

- Model this activity with the group of children, before expecting them to work on their own version.
- Place one of your '*I have*' cards in front of you. Now choose a picture card and place it next. After this place an '*in my box.*' strip of paper.
- Read out the sentence, including the name of the fruit, drawing children's attention to the capital letter at the beginning of the sentence and the full stop at the end.
- The children can now have a go at writing this. Give each child their own sentence opening and closing words. They can choose to draw a picture or write the name of the fruit as part of their sentence.
- Children can make as many sentences as they wish and then illustrate their work with a box of fruit, but . . .

  . . . make sure it matches the words!

Vocabulary

sentence, full stop, capital letter

Tip

Your able children might like to try inserting a colour word before the name of the fruit, e.g. '*I have a yellow banana.*' '*I have some green grapes.*'

Cross-curricular link

PSED: Sense of Community.

Dear Bear

Write a letter from a teddy bear for your children to read. Use this opportunity to develop their understanding of another country.

Aim

- To provide a reason for your children to use writing in their play.

Resources

- A new teddy bear or similar soft toy
- Paper, pens and pencils

Preparation

- The adult writes a letter as if it is from the bear and leaves it for the children to find in the classroom.
- The bear tells the children he is coming from another country to visit them.
- Try to ask a simple question in the letter e. g. Can you guess where I live?

What to do

- Once the children have found the letter, help them read what it says. Show them the paper and pens and encourage them to write a reply. Allow the children to write freely in their own way.
- Next day the bear writes back telling them something about his country and then asks them to guess what he can see from his window.
- Continue the letter exchange for as long as the children are keen, asking questions such as: What is my job? Can you guess what I wear? Then ask a final question, e. g. How will I find your school?
- Arrange a day when the new bear will visit. Discuss how to make their new friend welcome – perhaps have a little tea party when the new bear comes.

Vocabulary

This will vary depending on the country you choose, e. g.

Australia: beach, surf, sunshine, suncream, barbecue, lifeguard

Norway: mountain, high, climb, fjord, boat, fisherman, mountain rescue

Tip   Don't forget, children can draw pictures as their way of communicating.

Cross-curricular link

KUW: Communities.

Wedding (Z)

Write name labels with the children and use them to create a seating plan as if they were guests at a wedding.

Aim

- To support children in recognising and writing their own names.

Resources

- Card and pens
- Two or three small tables and chairs

Preparation

- Help the children to write their names on pieces of card.
- Show them the name cards and help the children recognise theirs.

What to do

- Tell the children that after a wedding everyone usually shares a meal together. Explain that the bride and groom plan where the guests will sit – called a seating plan – and that name cards will mark everyone's place at the table.
- Choose two of your names for the bride and groom. Let one child put these name cards in place.
- Now explain that the bride wants every girl to sit next to a boy. Help the other children to put names on the table in this way.
- Read the names with the children to check that the positioning is correct. All the children can now find their names and sit down. Talk about who is sitting next to who.
- Remove the name cards and play again with a different seating arrangement, e. g. all boys on one table and all girls on another.

Vocabulary

name, next to, who? , where?

Tip More able children can use a simple, drawn seating plan to position the name cards on the tables.

Cross-curricular link

PSED: Sense of Community.

Holidays (3)

 Help the children make a postcard by sticking a holiday picture on one side, then writing a message on the other.

Aim

• To provide an opportunity for children to do some independent writing.

Resources

• Blank postcards or pieces of card

• Holiday brochures

Preparation

• Send a postcard to school from a holiday destination you have visited.

• Read the postcard to the children.

• Explain that the photograph shows the place you were visiting.

What to do

• Ask the children if they have been on holiday.

  – Where did they go?

• Show the children the holiday brochures and talk about the different types of places, e.g. seaside, theme park.

• Let the children cut out their favourite picture.

• Show them how to stick it on one side of the card to make a postcard. Discuss who to send it to.

• Now let the children write a message on the back of the postcard. Talk about what to write, e.g. 'We went for a swim.'
  Remind them how to finish their message with their own name.

• Show the children where to write their parent or friend's name.

• Display these by hanging them from lengths of string so that both sides can be admired.

Vocabulary

seaside, hotel, pool, villa, theme park, funfair, holiday village, mountains, lakes

Tip   To keep this activity simple we don't suggest addressing the postcards, although this may be something you could include with your older children.

Cross-curricular link

KUW: Place.

On the climbing frame

Enjoy some outdoor writing fun. Help the children use split sentences to describe their positions on the climbing frame.

Aim

• To encourage children to reread their writing as they write.

Resources

• Felt-tip pens and paper
• Sentences written on strips of card

Preparation

• Write some simple sentences on strips of card describing positions on and around your climbing frame, e. g.
   - I am on/the rope
   - I am under/the slide
   - I am near/the logs
• Cut the strips into two pieces, as indicated, so the children can rearrange them to create a variety of sentences.

What to do

• Explain to the children that they are going to play on the climbing frame, but that you will stop them every now and again and ask them to tell you where they are. By doing this the children will have spoken many of the words written on your cards.
• Now, collect the children together and read the sentences you prepared. Show the children how they can swap the sentence parts to create new sentences.
• Let the children choose which sentence they would like to write, using the beginnings and ends of the sentences.
• Encourage everyone to read the sentence they have written. Now they can go and take up that position on the climbing frame.
• Allow another session of free play on the climbing equipment, then call the children together again to create a different sentence with another beginning and end from

the split sentences.

- Read their sentence and again find the position on the climbing frame.

Vocabulary

on, under, near, behind, in front, high, low, next to

Tip Create a small drawing of your climbing frame and photocopy it so the children can draw the position that they wrote about.

Cross-curricular link

PSRN: Shape, Space and Measures.

Ten Fat Sausages

 Use this familiar rhyme to inspire the children to write *Pop* or *Bang*. Then use their writing as you recite the rhyme together.

Aim

- To encourage children to write simple words.

Resources

- Ten sheets of A4 paper.

Preparation

- Cut five pieces of paper into circles and five into 'explosions' (jagged shapes).

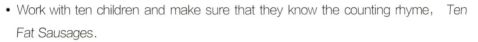

What to do

- Work with ten children and make sure that they know the counting rhyme, *Ten Fat Sausages*.

  'What do the sausages do when they are in the pan?'

  'Sometimes they go 'pop' and sometimes they go 'bang'.'

- Hand out the paper, and explain to the children that if they have a circle they write *pop* on it in big bold letters, but if they have a jagged shape like an explosion, they write *bang*.

- Explain to the children that they are all going to be sausages which explode in turn! When it is their turn, they will hold up their word and shout it out loudly before sitting down again.

- Now stand in a circle holding your papers, alternately pop and bang, and say the rhyme together.

- Don't forget to keep helping with the words of the rhyme, even after you have burst!

 Tip This is a good opportunity to let the children work out for themselves how to spell the words.

Cross-curricular link

PSRN: Calculating.

What did you make?

 Ask the children to make a label for their play dough model.

Aim

• To give the children a reason to write a simple caption.

Resources

• Dough, modelling tools

• Strips of stiff paper or card, folded so that they will stand like a place name

Preparation

• Lots of chances to use the dough in free play.

• Set up the dough table with a writing table next to it.

• Have a space ready to display the models and their labels.

What to do

• Over the day encourage children to make a model from the dough. They could choose a figure, an animal, a monster, etc. When their model is finished they should place it on the display.

• Now they go to the writing table and make a label. Show them how to make sure that they have the fold at the top so that their label will stand up.

• Decide which approach you want to take with the writing. This will depend on your children's abilities and experience:

– Encourage the children to have a go with their own spelling as they write their label, e. g.

   Tom md a modl of a scry dinosor

   (*Tom made a model of a scary dinosaur*)

– Scribe the children's words for them as they watch you write.

– Prepare some sentences that the children can copy or adapt, e. g.

   . . . . *made a* . . . .

   . . . . *'s model is a* . . . .

   Here is a . . . .

    – Talk about these with the children and read them together before they write.

• The children then stand the labels next to their models.

Vocabulary

push, pull, squeeze, made

 Tip   Try making the dough in a variety of colours by adding food colouring to the water before you mix it.

Cross-curricular link

PD: Using Equipment and Materials.

Cleaning your teeth

 Create a special word bank with children who are beginning to write independently.

Aim

• To build a resource to support the children's writing.

Resources

• Small pieces of card

• An empty set of pockets labelled with the letters of the alphabet

Preparation

• Fix the empty word pockets near the writing table and sit near it with the children.

What to do

• Talk with the children about how they look after their teeth, before asking them to write about it.

• Ask the children if they can think of any words that they might use for today's writing, e.g.

  toothbrush, dentist

• Write the word boldly on a piece of card.

  – What sound does it start with?

  Sound it out as you write, at a level that these children will understand.

• Now, show the children the word. Read it together and identify the initial letter. The child who suggested the word can come out and place it in the pocket showing that letter. The others can help if necessary.

• Continue like this until you have a good supply of words on your topic.

• Ask any child to come out, choose a word from one of the pockets and read it out loud.

  – Does everyone agree?

• The child replaces it in the correct pocket.

  – Can the child remember where it goes?

- The children can now use this resource to help them with today's writing. Remind them where they can find the other key words.
  'These are just the special words for today'.

Vocabulary

toothbrush, toothpaste, dentist, rinse, no sweets, water

Tip Remove the cards at the end of the session so that your pockets are empty, ready for next time, or for the next group of children, who will have their own ideas.

Cross-curricular link

PD: Health and Bodily Awareness.

Welcome!

 Help the children make cards for the new children joining your setting.

Aim

- To introduce children to the use of lists whilst writing with a purpose.

Resources

- A list of first names of the children about to join your setting
- Access to a computer and writing program

What to do

- Explain to the children that new children will soon be joining you, and they will be coming on a visit.
- Show them the list of names and read it to the children. Ask them to look at it carefully and notice how it is laid out.
- Tell them that you want them to design a welcome card for each person on this list.
  The children can work with you at the computer to choose and download a picture from a picture library.
- Then they can help you to create a message, e. g.

  Dear . . . We are looking forward to playing with you here on Wednesday at 10 o clock. Love from . . .

- Leave a gap for the names of the recipients and the senders, as you will be adding these later. (If you prefer not to use the names of your current children at the end of the message use the name of the group, class or setting instead.)
- Encourage the children to choose the font, colour, layout, etc. within the boundaries you will give them. Then print out the cards.
- Each child in the group can now choose one name from the list to insert in a card and write their own name at the end.
- Remind the children to tick the name they have chosen off the list so that no one is missed out. Talk about the list being a useful way to make sure of this.

- Read through the cards again with the children, checking against the list to make sure that everyone has got a card.

Tip You may need to write some of your cards in a home language other than English.

Cross-curricular link
PSED: Making Relationships.

Answer the question

 Invite the children to write their answers to your question.

Aim

• To provide an opportunity for children to write independently.

Resources

• An attractive box in which to collect answers

• Paper and pencils

Preparation

• Choose an open question to ask the children, e.g.

'What do you like doing best at school?'

• Print out or write your question in large font.

What to do

• Show the children the question, and ask them if anyone can read it. Encourage them to try, and then read the question to the children, pointing at each word as you do so.

• Explain to the children that you're interested in their answers but you haven't time to listen to everyone now.

'Please can you write your answers down and put them in the box for me to read later?'

• Show the children the box for their answers.

• Pin the question on the wall near the box.

• Remind the children to put their names on, otherwise you won't know who likes what.

• Later in the day open the box with the children and read their replies. Praise the children's attempts.

• Next time choose a different question to ask, e.g.

'Who did you play with today?'

Vocabulary

question, answer, what, who, when, where, how

Tip   This is good opportunity to assess the children's use of their phonic knowledge in their writing.

Cross-curricular link

PSED: Sense of Community.

Hoop-la

 A game for composing sentences on the go. The children jump from hoop to hoop to choose their words.

Aim

• To help children to form simple sentences.

Resources

• Five hoops

• Large pieces of card

Preparation

• Write one key word on each piece of card, e.g.

    Tom   can   see   a   dog

• Lay out the hoops in a circle.

• Place one of your cards in each hoop.

What to do

• Explain to the children that they are going to make some sentences from the words in the hoops. Spend some time reading each word.

• Demonstrate the activity yourself by reading all the words again out loud, and then talking through the process of choosing your sentence. From these five words you could make,

    Tom can see a dog

    a dog can see Tom

    can Tom see a dog

    can a dog see Tom

• Now, step into the hoop that has your first word in it, and say it out loud. Look for your second word, jump into that hoop and say it out loud. Continue through your sentence.

• Choose a child to have a go. Help the child to plan a sentence from the available words, and them jump into the hoops, saying the words out loud at the same time.

Each child in turn can now have a go.

'Which sentence will you make? '

- Encourage the other children to watch and listen carefully.

Vocabulary

sentence

Tip   Increase the choice of words for more able children or add punctuation cards and capital letters for some words.

Cross-curricular link

PD: Movement and Space.

Letters in the sand

Hide letters in the sand and watch as the children have fun making CVC words.

Aim

• To encourage children to use their knowledge of phoneme/grapheme correspondence to spell simple words.

Resources

• Three plastic washing up bowls in different colours, filled with sand
• Magnetic letters
• Individual magnetic boards

Preparation

• Place the letters in the sand in the three bowls:
• Two bowls will each have the same set of consonants, e. g.

  s, t, p, n, c, d, g, h, m, r

• One bowl will have several of each of the five vowels.
• From these you can make at least:

  can, cat, cut, dog, dig, man, mat, sit, sat, set, met, net, pan, pin, pen, pot, pit, sun, ran, run, rat, hat, hot, hen

What to do

• Sit in a circle with the children, with the bowls in the middle.
• Choose one child to come out and pick one letter from each bowl in turn. Identify the letters as they are chosen, and place them on a magnetic board. Show the children how you can arrange them to make a simple word. Read it together by segmenting and then blending the letter sounds.
• Children can now work in pairs to choose one letter from each bowl (unseen) and make another word with them on their board.
  – Can you read it?
  – Is it a real word?

- When everyone has made a word ask the children to hold up their boards so that everyone can see their word. Go round the circle reading the words together.
  - Can anyone make a different word with the same letters?

Vocabulary

consonant, vowel, sound, letter, word

Tip   Leave the bowls out near a large magnetic board. Collect as many words as you can. Read them together at the end of the session.

Cross-curricular link

CLL: Reading a Range of Simple Words.

Gordon's garage (2)

Use your old and damaged toy cars to produce a price list of repairs with the children.

Aim

• To encourage the children to use reading and writing in their role play.

Resources

• Broken or damaged toy vehicles

• Large sheet of card and pens

Preparation

• Write *Gordon's Price List* at the top of the piece of card.

• Mark the card with faint lines for guiding the writing.

What to do

• Sit round a table with a box of well-used or damaged toy vehicles.

• Let the children examine them for damage.   Talk about what is wrong with them.

• Explain to the children that they are going to decide how much Gordon will charge for repairing the vehicles.   Ask one child to describe what is wrong with the vehicle he has picked out,   e. g.

  It needs a new tyre.

• Ask the group what Gordon should charge for putting on a new tyre.   Work in pounds,   using numbers that your children can handle.   Agree on a figure,   e. g.

  £10

• Show the children the large piece of card and read the words at the top: *Gordon's Price List*.

• Use a piece of paper to work out with the children how to write down,   e. g.

  1 new tyre £10

  One child can now copy this onto the price list with a bold-coloured pen.

• Continue around the group,   describing the damage to a vehicle,   working out the price and writing it down on the price list.

Vocabulary

damage, repair, price. Vehicle parts: tyre, windscreen, headlights, etc.

Tip   This writing activity should appeal to boys.

Cross-curricular link

PSRN: Numbers as Labels and for Counting.

Who was kind today?

Write a question that invites children to notice and record positive behaviour in the setting.

Aim

• To provide an opportunity for children to read and write familiar words.

Resources

• A whiteboard and pens

Preparation

• Write the question at the top of the whiteboard, e. g.

Who was kind today?

What to do

• Show the children the board and read the question together. Explain to them that today they should be looking out for anyone that they notice being kind to someone else.

• If they see someone being kind they should write that person's name on the board, e. g.

If you see Jamie helping Sam to pick up the pencils that he knocked over – without anyone asking him to do it – then Jamie is being kind. You can write Jamie's name on the whiteboard.

• Encourage the children to suggest other kind things that they might see.

• At the end of the day, sit in a circle with the children. Look at the whiteboard and count up all the names.

• Ask who wrote a name on the board. In turn, the children can come out and tell everyone what they saw, and why they thought it was kind. Everyone can clap them for noticing.

• All the children whose names are on the list then stand up and everyone gives them a clap.

Vocabulary

kind, friendly, helpful, polite

602

Tip   Next time you use this activity, change the word at the top of the whiteboard. Try 'hard-working' or 'busy' instead.

Cross-curricular link
PSED: Making Relationships.

Lucky dip

 Play a simple game of lucky dip to give your children a fun reason to write their name.

Aim

- To support the children in recognising and writing their own names.

Resources

- Small scraps of paper and pencils
- A recycled plastic ice-cream tub or a drawstring bag to hold all the names

What to do

- Explain to the children that you are going to play lucky dip.

    'Does anyone know what the game is? '

- Explain that everyone's name – written on a piece of paper – is going into this tub or bag, then someone will close their eyes and take out one of the papers.
  They will open the paper and read the name.

    'If it's your name then you are the winner! '

- Help the children to write their names on small pieces of paper. Remind them to write their name clearly so that another person can read it. Then show them how to fold their paper and then drop it into the tub or bag.
- When everyone's name is in, give the bag or tub a good shake.

    'Does anyone know why I'm shaking the bag? '

  Do the children understand why this is a fair way to choose a name?
- Now for the exciting part . . . Ask another adult to close their eyes and put their hand into the bag and choose a paper. Unfold the paper carefully and read the name. Give them a clap!
- That child can be the first one to get their coat or snack or go to lunch. But before they go, they must close their eyes and reach into the bag and choose a paper.
  They can then unfold the paper.

    'Can you read the name? '

  Carry on for three or four names.

• Leave the bag around so that the children can carry on playing if they wish.

Vocabulary

lucky dip, name, fold, unfold, first, second, third, fourth

Tip   Remember to discard the names that have been chosen so they are not picked out again.

Cross-curricular link

PSED: Making Relationships.

Make a board game (1)

 Help the children make a simple board game starting with wrapping paper.

Aim

• To provide a purpose for children to write captions.

Resources

• A piece of colourful wrapping paper（cut to fit the size of your laminator）
• Twenty small squares of paper for the track‐15 in one colour and five in a different colour
• Pens，paper and glue

Preparation

• Lots of opportunities for the children to play board games.

What to do

• Work with a small group of children around a table.
  Explain to them that you are going to make your own board game to play.
• Lay out the wrapping paper and show them how the track will be made with the small squares.
  ‐ Do they understand why there need to be some different coloured squares?
• Help the children write one number on each square. Then stick the track onto the wrapping paper.
• Help the children write 'start' and 'finish' in the appropriate places.
• You might decide to think of a title for the game together and scribe it for them on the wrapping paper in bold print.
• Now plan with the children what captions to write next to the five differently coloured squares，e. g.
  miss a turn/go back one square/have another go/go on one square
• Help the children to write the captions carefully so that others can read them and glue them near the coloured squares. If possible，laminate the game to make it more durable.
• Play the game with counters and dice.

Vocabulary

Instructions – e. g. miss a turn/go back one square/have another go/go on one square

Tip

Adapt the activity to suit the ability of your children, e. g. for the youngest children you can have the numbers already written so the children can place them in the correct order and you can scribe their ideas for captions.

Cross-curricular link

PSRN: Numbers as Labels and for Counting.

Make a board game (2)

 Make a board game with the children using their own drawings for the board.

Aim

• To make and play a game involving the children in recognising letter sounds.

Resources

• A3 card
• Twenty small squares of paper – you will need ten in one colour and ten in another
• A set of letters on cards
• Felt pens and glue

Preparation

• Select the letter sounds you want the children to practise.

What to do

• Work with a small group of children around a table. Explain that you are going to make a board game that involves recognising letter sounds.
• Choose a title for the game, e.g. 'What sound?' and write it on the card in bold print.
• Ask them to draw pictures on the A3 piece of card. Use ideas from a story or the theme you are working on, e.g. mini-beasts.
• Show them how the track will be made with the small squares.
• Help the children arrange the squares in a pattern along the track, e.g. alternate the colours, or place two of one colour then two of the other.
• Help the children write one number on each square and then stick the track onto the decorated card. Help the children write 'start' and 'finish' in the appropriate places.
• Ask the children to choose one of the colours. Explain to the children that whenever they land on this colour they have to pick up a card. Show the children the letter cards and tell them they must say the sound for this letter. Then they return the card to the bottom of the pile.

- Tell the children if they get the letter sound wrong they stay on the same square, but if they get it right they move on to the next square.   Let everyone take a letter card in turn to check that they understand.
- Then play the game using counters and dice.
- The winner is the first to get to the finish.

Vocabulary

numbers 1 – 20,   letter sounds

Tip   You could also use this game with key word cards.

Cross-curricular link

PSED: Making Relationships.

Chapter 9

Making a book

Garden centre (3)

Introduce the children to this counting poem and add number words to their pictures to create your own version.

Aim

- To write a poem with the children.

Resources

- 'Garden Rhyme' p. 125 in Toczek, N. and Cookson, P. (2007) *Read Me Out Loud. A Poem to Rap, Chant, Whisper or Shout for Every Day of the Year,* London: Macmillan Children's Books
- The sheets of mounting paper
- Painting materials

Preparation

- Children can create some paintings of garden-related items.
- Cut them out and mount them in groups so that you have, e.g. one greenhouse, two wheelbarrows, three spades and so on up to ten.
- Use any spare pictures to create a cover, with the title *A Counting Poem*.

What to do

- Read the poem 'Garden Rhyme' to the children.
- Ask them to spot the patterns: every line starts with a number, and the numbers are in order. Practise your counting.
- Some of the lines rhyme. Can the children guess what the rhyming word will be if you pause just before it?
- Read it several times to let the children become familiar with it.
- Now bring out your paintings.
  - Can the children find a paper with just one item on it?
  - You write the label for it, e.g. *One greenhouse.*
  - Can they find the paper with two items on it?
  - You scribe again, e.g. 'Two wheelbarrows'.

  Continue in this way up to ten items on any page.

- Now you can all read your class version of the poem.
- This would be a useful format for any theme that you are focusing on.

Vocabulary

number words，rhyme

Tip   Staple the pages together inside the cover to make a counting book.

Cross-curricular link

PSRN：Numbers as Labels and for Counting.

Garden centre (4)

 Make a large concertina-style book with the children to demonstrate the lifecycle of a plant.

Aim

- To involve children in organising writing.

Resources

- Six sheets of strong A4 paper
- The set of six plant stages models made in: Garden centre（1）（see p. 8）.

Preparation

- Make the book by fixing six sheets of strong paper at the sides to form a concertina.

- Show the children the models they made of plants in varying stages of growth. As you do this, engage the children in discussions on the changes that are occurring as the plants grow.

What to do

- Encourage the children to order the six pots in their stages of growth. Stress the importance of the left to right ordering, as this will match their writing.
- Ask the children:

  'Where is the seed in the first pot?'

  'In the soil.'

  Scribe the words 'The seed is in the soil' on the first page of the concertina book.

- Ask the children how they know when the seed is starting to grow. 'It has a shoot.'

  Write 'It has a shoot' on the second page.

- Continue like this until you have:

  It is in the soil

  It has a shoot

  It has a leaf

  It has a bud

  It has a flower

  The flower has seeds.

- Show the children how you can now stick the last page to the first page and have a complete cycle of events – a lifecycle.

Vocabulary

seed, shoot, leaves, bud, soil, flowers

Tip   Leave out some small concertina-folded 'books' on the writing table for the children to make their own versions if they wish.

Cross-curricular link

KUW: Exploration and Investigation.

Big book, little book

Make some books for the Three Bears and encourage the children to match their writing to the size of the book.

Aim

• To provide an opportunity for children to use writing in their play.

Resources

• Paper, card
• Pens, pencils and crayons

Preparation

• Make some books with brightly coloured covers by stapling folded sheets of paper into a card cover. Make them in three different sizes.
• Write and draw the same information in one of each size, e.g. 'This is my bed.' 'This is my bowl.' 'This is my chair.' Match the drawing and writing to the size of the book.

What to do

• Show the children three of the books you have created. Discuss with the children:
  – What do they notice about them?
  – Can they identify them as big, medium and small?
  – Which family might own these books?
• Now look inside the books. Encourage the children to notice that they all have the same writing and pictures in them.
• Describe the writing – is it small, or bigger, or in-between-sized? Encourage as many descriptions of the size, or the comparisons between the sizes, as the children can suggest.
• Tell the children that they will find sets of books like this on the writing table, if they would like to make some more books for the bear family.
• Remind the children to match the size of their writing and drawing to the size of the book they have chosen.

Vocabulary

big, large, medium, in-between, small, little

Tip　　Prepare a 'bookcase' for the bears in your role-play cottage and encourage the children to read the books when they are playing in there.

Cross-curricular link

PSRN: Shape, Space and Measures.

My house

 The children sing a song and write a book about the number of people who live in their house.

Aim

• To help children use writing as a means of recording.

Resources

• 'How many people live in your house?' in *Tinder-box: 66 Songs for Children* (1983) London: A & C Black

• Three sheets of A4 paper and one piece of A4 card per book, enough for one book per child.

Preparation

• To make each book:

 – Lay three pieces of paper on the piece of card.

 – Fold the card and paper down the centre and staple together.

 – Then cut off the two top corners to create a roof shape.

 – Write on the last page . . . . *live in my house.*

• Make an extra book for yourself for demonstrating.

What to do

• Sing the song – *How many people live in your house?*

 Talk with the children about who lives in their house.

 Tell them they're going to make a book about how many people and animals live in their house.

• Show the children your book. Demonstrate:

 How to decorate the front and back with doors and windows.

 How each person or animal is drawn on a new page.

 When you have completed the pictures in this book about your house, count them up and complete your final sentence.

• Encourage the children to draw and write in their book. Help the children complete the final sentence by counting and then writing the number in their house.

- The children can read their books to themselves, their friends, other adults, parents and carers.

Vocabulary

mum, dad, sister, brother, baby, dog, cat, rabbit, guinea pig . . .

Tip   Remember to be sensitive about children with absent parents etc. Focusing on the number in their house and including animals can be helpful for this.

Cross-curricular link

PSRN: Numbers as Labels and for Counting.

Five Little Ducks

 Help the children make their own individual book of the rhyme.

Aim

• To encourage children's familiarity with how books work.

Resources

• A4 paper and card.

Preparation

• Make books for the children:

  – A piece of card folded in half with two pieces of paper the same size stapled inside.

  – Write *Five Little Ducks* as the title on the front of each book.

• Make sure everyone knows the rhyme.

What to do

• Give everyone a book and tell them they are going to make a book about the rhyme.
  Can they all find the front?

• Encourage the children to open the book and draw a pond on the first page.   Ask how many ducks are on the pond at the start of the poem.   Help them draw five ducks on the pond.

• Then everyone turns over to the next page and draws another pond.   Ask how many ducks came back this time.   Help the children draw four ducks on this pond.

• Continue through the book showing 5, 4, 3, 2, 1, 0 ducks.   Make the final page the same as the first when the five little ducks come swimming back.

• More able children might enjoy writing the numbers on each page.

• Write the children's names on the back cover and leave the books available for other children to read.

Vocabulary

five, four, three, two, one, none, front cover, title, author, page, turn over,

next, back cover

Tip Be careful that children don't turn over two pages at once!

Cross-curricular link
PSRN: Calculating.

Going for a walk

 After a walk with the children, make a class book based on *Rosie's Walk* by Pat Hutchins. The children can then make cardboard figures that take a walk through the book.

Aim

- To make a book about an activity the children have done.

Resources

- A3 pieces of paper
- Two A3 pieces of card for the cover
- Small pieces of card
- A copy of Hutchins, P. (2001) *Rosie's Walk*, London: Red Fox Books

Preparation

- Take the children for a walk around their local area.
- Talk about places you pass as you walk.

What to do

- When you get back, talk about your walk and read the children *Rosie's Walk*. Tell the children they are going to make a book about their walk.
- Make a list of the places in the order that you walked, using prepositions, e. g.
  - out of the gate
  - down the hill
  - across the road
  - past the shops
  - around the park
- Let the children choose which part of the walk they draw. Then an adult can scribe the appropriate descriptive phrase below their picture.
- The pages are stapled together with a front and back cover to form a book. Write *Our Walk* as the title, and encourage everyone to read it.
- Each child now draws a picture of themselves on a small piece of card. Then they can take turns to read the book and 'walk' their cardboard figure across each page.

Vocabulary

through, around, past, across, down, under

Tip   The cardboard figures can be kept in pockets made on the inside of the back cover.

Cross-curricular link

KUW: Place.

"What is White?"
by Mary O'Neil

Use this poem as an inspiration to write your own colour poem with the children.

Aim

• To write a poem with the children, scribing for them.

Resources

• Mary O'Neil's poem 'What is White?' can be found in Rumble, A. (1989) *Is a Caterpillar Ticklish?*, London: Puffin Books

Preparation

• This poem lists things that are white. There are lots of interesting words to discuss as you enjoy it together.

• If your children are very young it may be better to use only one section of the poem.

What to do

• Tell the children you are going to write a new poem about a colour. Choose a colour together for your title, e.g.

   What is red?

• Collect ideas of things that colour, e.g. traffic lights (see vocabulary list below for more ideas). Scribe the children's ideas.

• Then help them to extend them into descriptive phrases, e.g.

   Red means stop

• Develop the children's phrases, e.g.

   A glowing red light warning us of danger

• Prompt the children to use all five senses when describing and extending their ideas.

• Then, write the phrases in a list to create a simple poem, e.g.

   What is red?

   A glowing red light warning us of danger

> *Red poppies growing in a field*
> *Paper poppies to wear with a pin*
> *A huge red fire engine screeching by.*

Vocabulary

fire engine, poppies, postboxes, blushing cheeks, fire, traffic lights, danger, sunset, blood, hearts, roses, apples, lipstick, clowns' noses

Tip The children can illustrate each line of their poem to create a poetry book.

Cross-curricular link

KUW: Place.

Our day

Take photographs with the children to keep a record of your daily routine and fix these into a book to tell the story of 'Our Day'.

Aim

• To make a book about the activities the children have been doing.

Resources

• Camera

• A large scrapbook

Preparation

• Help the children take photographs of each other at significant times throughout the day, e.g. hanging up their coat as they arrive, story time, play time, lunch time.

What to do

• Look at the photographs together. Encourage the children to explain what's happening in each photograph. Decide which photograph shows the beginning of the day.

• Then put them in order showing the routines of the day. Ask:

'What comes next?'

'Do we do this before or after that?'

'What happens after that?'

'How does our day end?'

• Let the children fix the photographs into the book in the correct sequence. Read the book to them using story language and time connectives, e.g. first, later, in the end.

• Encourage them to take turns to tell the story of our day.

Vocabulary

first, then, next, after that, later, in the end

Tip   For older children the adult could scribe the story to accompany each photograph.

Cross-curricular link

PSRN: Shape, Space and Measures.

In my lunch box

 Help the children make their own simple lift-the-flap book based on lunch-box meals.

Aim

• To develop children's awareness of the way stories are structured.

Resources

• Books about food
• A lift-the-flap book
• A4 paper and card to make individual books
• Small pieces of paper and sticky tape

Preparation

• Make a lunch-box-shaped book:
  – Lay three sheets of paper between two sheets of card and staple the long lower edge so that the 'book' opens at the top like a lunch box.
• On the first page write, *In my lunch box I have . . .*

What to do

• Show the children a lift-the-flap book and examine how it works.
• Show them the lunch-box books you have prepared, and the smaller pieces of paper. Demonstrate how to stick a piece of paper on so that it can be lifted up, just like the flaps in the book.
• Read the words you have written on the first page of the lunch-box book. Encourage the children to suggest some things that might be in a lunch box. Look at your food books and a picture dictionary together for other ideas.
• The children can now draw one picture on each page of something from their lunch box. Then, help them to write the names of these foods on small pieces of paper. *Remember to put only one word on a piece of paper!*
• Help them attach these as flaps to hide their drawings.
   'Can you read your own book?'
   'Can you read your friend's book?'

Vocabulary

Any food items chosen by the children

Tip Using sticky tape that is ready cut will make the children more independent when attaching their flaps.

Cross-curricular link

PD: Health and Bodily Awareness.

Do you know your ABC?

 The children will enjoy choosing what to draw in their tiny alphabet books.

Aim

- To provide an opportunity for children to use word banks and other resources.

Resources

- Picture dictionaries
- Classroom word banks
- A4 paper

Preparation

- Cut the A4 paper in half, then fold seven of these sheets in half and staple them together to make tiny books.
- Print out the title 'Alphabet book' – one copy for each book.
- Make sure the children know an alphabet song or have some understanding of the alphabet before doing this activity.

What to do

- Work with a small group of children.

  Let the children work in pairs with a picture dictionary.

  Ask them to look for something beginning with 'a'.

  Remind the children that this is the name of the letter.

  'What can you find that begins with the letter "a"?'
- Encourage the children to negotiate between themselves so that the books aren't identical.

  'Try to choose something different from your partner.'

  e.g. apple and alligator
- Show them the tiny books you have made. Ask them to stick the title 'Alphabet Book' on the front cover, then write their name underneath the title.
- Help them write the letter 'a' on the top corner of the first page of their book. Then they can draw their chosen item on that page.

- You might choose to do six letters at a time and complete the other pages over several sessions,
- Or you may decide to help the children write all 26 letters on individual pages first so the children can complete their books independently at the writing table when they choose.

Vocabulary

The names of the letters of the alphabet

Tip

Use the opportunity to observe the children as they write their letters, and make a note of any letter formation problems.

Cross-curricular link

PSED: Making Relationships.

Joe's space journey

Encourage the children to imagine strange and wonderful things that Joe will discover on the planets that he visits.

Aim

- To enable children to create and use a word bank to write a story.

Resources

- A large sheet of black paper
- Sticky stars – gold and silver
- Paint
- Sticky labels
- Rocket-shaped books

Preparation

- Make some rocket-shaped books from paper and card.
- The children paint five or six brightly coloured planets on the black paper.
- Stick the stars all around them, and leave to dry.

What to do

- Work with a small group of children and help them to make up some names for the planets. These can be made-up words.
- Try to make words which the children will be able to spell at their own level of phonic knowledge, e. g. Zar, Bod, Lub, Niz.
- Encourage the children to write the name on a sticky label, and fix it near the chosen planet.
- Use a model space figure to be Joe and decide which planet he lives on.
  Tell the children,
    'Joe is going on a space adventure and we're going to tell his story. '
- Start from Joe's home and move him across space to another planet.
  Ask the children,
    'What will he see there? '

- Write their suggestions on sticky labels to attach near the planets, e. g.
  - blue trees
  - a dog that has green and yellow stripes

  Read the words together to remind everyone of what they say.
- Give the children a rocket-shaped book each to write their own version of Joe's journey, using the words on the picture as a word bank.

Vocabulary

Any words that the children want to use

Tip   This is an activity for those children who can already write some of the key words.

Cross-curricular link

CLL: Story Settings.

Special days out

Encourage the children to take home a doll when they have a special event at home. Help them record the visit in a class book.

Aim

• To inspire the children to record events in words and pictures.

Resources

• Two rag dolls or knitted dolls: one boy, one girl
• Paper, pencils etc., scissors and glue
• Sheets of sugar paper and some cord

Preparation

• To make the book:
  - Cut the sheets of sugar paper in half.
  - Punch holes in the left-hand side of the paper.
  - Tie the sheets together with the cord.
  - Put a photograph of your dolls on the cover of the book, and write 'Special days out with Tara and Toby' (use your chosen names!) as the title.

• The children should already be familiar with the dolls and know their names. Encourage the children to take a doll home whenever they know they will be having a special day within their family, e.g. a birthday, a visit to Gran, a festival or family gathering such as Easter, Diwali or Eid, to link in with your work on festivals and other special occasions. Send home a notice about this for parents so that they understand what it is all about.

What to do

• The day after a child has taken one of the dolls home, sit together in a circle. The child who took the doll home stands next to you, holding the doll. They tell the others about the special things that Toby or Tara did, the place they visited, or about a special meal they shared.

• Encourage the children to ask questions so that the child with the doll can expand on the basic information. Try to include questions about the doll's 'feelings'. 'Was Tara excited about . . . ?' 'Was Toby pleased to see . . . again?'

- Later in the session spend time one-to-one with the child. Help the child to form one or two sentences to describe the doll's experiences and perhaps its 'feelings' during the visit. Scribe for the child or help the child to write the ideas down, according to their individual ability.
- The child can now stick their writing onto a page in the class book, and illustrate it.
- Share the book regularly with the whole group.

Tip   If they have any photographs, tickets, invitations, programmes, etc., these could also be stuck in.

Cross-curricular link

KUW: Communities.

On Friday Something Funny Happened by John Prater

 Enjoy the book with the children, then help them write their own additions to the text.

Aim

• To encourage children to use story language when they write.

Resources

• A copy of Prater, J.（1984） *On Friday Something Funny Happened*, London: Picture Puffins, or a different book that contains pictures without text

• Paper, pencils, reusable adhesive

Preparation

• Enjoy the book together.

What to do

• Working with a small group of children, look at the pictures of the children's adventures.

• Ask the children what's happening in the different parts of the story.

• Encourage the children to describe the children's activities as shown in the pictures.

• Help the children phrase their sentences into story language. For example, a child might say, 'They're getting all muddy. '
The adult replies, 'Yes, so let's say "*They jumped in puddles and got very muddy*" . '

• Listen to the children's ideas then choose one sentence for each part of the story. Continue through the book until everyone has a sentence to contribute.

• Give the children a piece of paper to write their sentence on.

• Help the children write their sentences.

• Use reusable adhesive to stick their writing on the pictures.

• Read the book again, encouraging each child to reread the part of the story they have written.

Vocabulary

Words appropriate to your chosen book

Tip Choose whether it is more suitable to scribe for your children, offer them support with their writing, or encourage them to write the sentences independently.

Cross-curricular link

KUW: Time.

My own notebook

 A simple way for the children to make their own notebooks using old greetings cards.

Aim

- To provide evidence of how children choose to record information or ideas.

Resources

- A4 paper
- Old greetings cards， without inner pieces of paper
- Container – a basket or attractive box

Preparation

- You may need to reduce the size of the card to remove words such as 'Happy Birthday'.
- Stick a piece of paper over any written message inside the card.
- Lay the open greetings card on top of four sheets of A4 paper.
- Trim the edges to match the size of the card.

What to do

- Explain to the children that they are going to make some notebooks. Show them how to open up the card and lay the sheets of paper on. Help them to use a long-armed stapler to fix these together at the centre fold.
- The child will then write their own name on the cover or inside the cover. You should add the date in small figures at the beginning of the notebook. Keep these in the special basket or box.
- Talk to the children about some of the ways that they can use their notebook. Tell them that it is for their own writing， not for work that you have asked them to do. Can they suggest anything they might use it for? e. g.
  - to write down something they did today
  - to make a list
  - when they are playing a game such as schools or detectives
  - whenever they need to write something down

- When the notebook is complete add the finishing date at the end of the book.
- Leave materials available for children to make a new notebook if they fill this one fairly quickly.

Vocabulary

staple, stapler, personal, notebook

Tip   Use this to check the children's emergent writing. How often are they choosing to write? Is their spelling or handwriting developing? It is a useful way to monitor these skills.

Cross-curricular link

PD: Using Equipment and Materials.

Penguin Small
by Mick Inkpen

Help the children make their own penguin-shaped version of this super book.

Aim

• To provide an opportunity for children to retell a familiar story in writing.

Resources

• A copy of Inkpen, M. (1994) *Penguin Small*, London: Hodder Children's Books
• One piece of A4 white card and two sheets of A4 white paper per book

Preparation

• Fold and staple two sheets of A4 paper inside a folded A4 card to make each book.
• Cut the book into a simple penguin shape.
• Enjoy the picture book *Penguin Small* with the children.

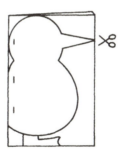

What to do

• Show the children the penguin-shaped books and talk about how to decorate the shape to make it look like *Penguin Small*, e. g. colour his back and head black.
• Help the children create their penguins by colouring his head, back and beak on the front and back cover.
• Explain that they are going to write the story of *Penguin Small*.
• Look at the first picture in the book and ask the children what's happening. Form a sentence together, e. g.

'All the penguins swam away because the polar bears were nasty. '

- Help the children write the sentence on the first page in their book. Choose a method appropriate to the children: they may copy your writing, attempt it themselves or stick a printed version on the page.
- Now look at the second picture and ask why Penguin Small is sad.
- Continue in this way until you have summarised the story into eight sentences for the eight pages in their book.

Vocabulary

Past tense verbs – swam, met, floated, found, sailed, flapped, flew, spotted, soared

Tip Cover a display board with blue backing paper, then add large pieces of white card to the base line. You can then display the penguin books as if they are standing on icebergs.

Cross-curricular link

KUW: Place.

My Granny Went to Market
by Stella Blackstone

 Play games with the children to try to remember what Granny bought. Then they can make their own book recording some of the items.

Aim

• To provide materials and stimulus for children to create their own books.

Resources

• Blackstone, S. (2006) *My Granny Went to Market*, Bath: Barefoot Books

• A4 paper and A4 card

• Globe or map

Preparation

• Make individual books by stapling two sheets of paper into a folded piece of card.

• Read and enjoy the book *My Granny Went to Market* with the children.

• Type out copies of a title for the book and print it several times to fit the books you have made.

What to do

• After enjoying the book a few times, look on the map to find the countries mentioned.

  Ask the children what they know about each place.

  Maybe they come from that country, have visited there or have seen something about it in a book or on TV.

  Talk about the various items that Granny buys as she travels to different countries.

• Play a game with the children:

  – Open the book at a random place.

  – Tell the children the name of the country.

  – Ask what Granny bought there.

- Let the children take turns asking the questions.
- Play a traditional memory game:
  - Sit in a circle
  - Start the game by saying 'My Granny went to market and she bought a drum.'
  - The next child says 'My Granny went to market and she bought a drum and a ...'.
  - The next child repeats the phrase and the two items and adds their idea.
  - Continue the game for as long as the children can remember the items in the list.

    (In the traditional game the items can be anything the children choose, but to play the game based on the book, list items mentioned in the book.)
- When the children have enjoyed playing these games a few times, show them the books you have prepared. Help them stick the title on the front of the book. Can they read it?
- Then let them draw pictures of all the items they can remember from the book. There are eight altogether. Can anyone remember them all?
- If appropriate, the children could copy labels for their pictures or you could act as a scribe.
- When they have finished their book, encourage them to write their name on the cover.

  Leave the books out for the children and their parents to enjoy.

Vocabulary

Japan, Australia, China, Mexico, Switzerland, Africa, Russia, Peru

Tip To extend this work about other countries provide books that show a range of languages, dress and customs from a variety of cultures.

Cross-curricular link

KUW: Communities.

Appendices

References

DfES references

DfES (2006) *Primary National Strategy. Primary Framework for Literacy and Mathematics*. Ref: 02011-2206

DfES (2007) *Letters and Sounds: Principles and Practice of High Quality Phonics*. Ref: 00282-2007.

DfES (2008) *Practice Guidance for the Early Years Foundation Stage. Non-statutory Guidance*. Ref: 00266-2008.

Useful websites

www. circle-time. co. uk

www. espresso. co. uk

www. zoes-world. co. uk

Artwork

A Bigger Splash by David Hockney

All Aboard by Zoe Kakolyris

Music

Soothing music e. g. Dvorak's *New World Symphony*

Strong, quick music e. g. Rimsky-Korsakov: *Flight of the Bumble Bee*

'How many people live in your house?' in *Tinder-box: 66 Songs for Children* (1983), London: A&C Black

Books

Ahlberg A. (1980) *Mrs Wobble the Waitress*, London: Puffin Books

Alakija, P. (2007) *Catch That Goat!: A Market Day in Nigeria*, Bath: Barefoot Books

Andreae, G. and Sharratt, N. (2002) *Pants*, London: Picture Corgi

Blackstone, S. (2006) *My Granny Went to Market*, Bath: Barefoot Books

Burningham, J. (1979) *Mr Gumpy's Motorcar*, London: Picture Puffins

Burningham, J. (1970) *Mr Gumpy's Outing*, London: Picture Puffins

Butterwick, N. (2008) *My Grandma is Wonderful*, London: Walker Books

Butterworth, N. and Inkpen, M. (2006) *Jasper's Beanstalk*, London: Hodder Children's Books

Carle, E. (2002) *The Very Hungry Caterpillar*, London: Puffin Books

Carle, E. (2009) *The Tiny Seed*, London: Simon & Schuster Children's

Collins, M. (2001) *Circle Time for the Very Young*, London: Paul Chapman Publishing

Exley, H. (2006) *Me and My Grandma*, Watford: Exley Publications

French, V. and Bartlett, A. (1995) *Oliver's Vegetables*, London: Hodder Children's

Garcia, E. (2009) *Toot Toot Beep Beep*, St Albans: Boxer Books

Hedderwick, M. (2010) *Katie Morag and the Two Grandmothers*, London: Red Fox Books

Holub, J. (2000) *Light the Candles: A Hannukah Lift-the-flap Book*, London: Picture Puffins

Hughes S. (1985) *Alfie Gives a Hand*, London: Collins Picture Lions

Hutchins, P. (1993) *The Surprise Party*, London: Red Fox Books

Hutchins, P. (2001) *Rosie's Walk*, London: Red Fox Books

Inkpen, M. (1994) *Penguin Small*, London: Hodder Children's Book

Mayo, M. (2003) *Emergency!* , London: Orchard Books

Prater, J. (1984) *On Friday Something Funny Happened*, London: Picture Puffins

Roennfeldt, R. (1980) *Tiddalick: The Frog Who Caused a Flood*, London: Picture Puffins

Rosen, M. (1993) *We're Going on a Bear Hunt*, London: Walker Books

Shoshan, B. (2005) *That's When I'm Happy*, London: Little Bee

Zucker, J. (2002) *Eight Candles to Light: A Chanukah Story*, London: Frances Lincoln

Zucker, J. (2005) *Lighting a Lamp: A Divali Story*, London: Frances Lincoln

Zucker, J. (2005) *Lanterns and Firecrackers: A Chinese New Year Story*, London: Frances Lincoln

Plus:

Your own choice of traditional tales

Sets of non-fiction books on a theme, e. g. mini-beasts, ducks, food

Poems and rhymes

'Fingers Like to Wiggle, Waggle' in Matterson, E. (compiler) (1991) *This Little Puffin*, London: Penguin

'Shop, Shop, shopping' by Georgie Adams in Waters, F. (1999) *Time for a Rhyme*, London: Orion Children's Books

'Ten Dancing Dinosaurs' in Waters, F. (1999) *Time for a Rhyme*, London: Orion Children's Books

'Garden Rhyme' by Phil Rampton in Toczek, N. and Cookson, P. (2007) *Read Me Out Loud: A Poem to Rap, Chant, Whisper or Shout for Every Day of the Year*, London: Macmillan Children's Books

'What is White?' by Mary O'Neil in Rumble, A. (1989) *Is a Caterpillar Ticklish?* ,

London: Puffin Books

Number rhymes and action songs from:

Matterson, E. (compiler) (1991) *This Little Puffin*, London: Penguin

Good Morning Mrs Hen can be downloaded from Internet.

Plus:

Your own choice of nursery rhymes.

Index of activities